Colombian Theatre
in the Vortex

Colombian Theatre in the Vortex

Seven Plays

Edited by Judith A. Weiss

Introductory Essay
by María Mercedes Jaramillo

Lewisburg
Bucknell University Press

© 2004 by Rosemont Publishing & Printing Corp.

All rights reserved. Authorization to photocopy items for internal or personal use, or the internal or personal use of specific clients, is granted by the copyright owner, provided that a base fee of $10.00, plus eight cents per page, per copy is paid directly to the Copyright Clearance Center, 222 Rosewood Drive, Danvers, Massachusetts 01923. [0-8387-5591-7/04 $10.00 + 8¢ pp, pc.]

Associated University Presses
2010 Eastpark Boulevard
Cranbury, NJ 08512

The paper used in this publication meets the requirements of the American National Standard for Permanence of Paper for Printed Library Materials Z39.48-1984.

Library of Congress Cataloging-in-Publication Data

Colombian theatre in the vortex : seven plays / edited by Judith A. Weiss ; introductory essay by María Mercedes Jaramillo.
    p. cm.
Includes bibliographical references.
ISBN 0-8387-5591-7 (alk. paper)
  1. Colombian drama—20th century—Translations into English.
  2. Colombian drama—20th century—History and criticism. I. Weiss, Judith A. II. Title.
PQ8175.5.E5C65 2004
862'.64099861—dc22   2004006337

PRINTED IN THE UNITED STATES OF AMERICA

Contents

Introduction: Death by History: Translating Texts from the Edge of the Vortex JUDITH A. WEISS	11
Colombian Theatre MARÍA MERCEDES JARAMILLO	20
Soldiers C. J. REYES et al.	35
Old Baldy JAIRO ANÍBAL NIÑO	58
Lucky Strike SANTIAGO GARCÍA	78
Roadhouse TEATRO LA CANDELARIA	122
Pilot Project ENRIQUE BUENAVENTURA	145
Femina Ludens NOHORA AYALA et al.	170
*The Orgy** ENRIQUE BUENAVENTURA	199
Bibliography	214

Unless noted with an *, all plays are translated by Judith Weiss.
*Translated by Gerardo Luzuriaga and Robert Rudder.

Acknowledgments

To the many artists who developed the collective creations, my thanks for having given us such searing and entertaining chronicles, and to the authors, my thanks for their permission to include their plays in this anthology.

My gratitude to the late Enrique Buenaventura, who inspired this collection: At the 1982 Latino Theatre Festival in New York, I promised to translate some of his plays, with an enthusiastic R.G. Davis as witness. I only regret that it has taken me so long to get around to it, and that *el Maestro* will not see this shared volume and greet it with his eternal humour. And to Jacqueline Vidal and Nicolás Buenaventura Vidal, who carry on his work and his spirit.

The idea for an anthology originated in the Latin American Drama course I have taught and the student productions I have directed at Mount Allison University. I thank Paul Del Motte and Decima Mitchell of the Windsor Theatre as well as the numerous student volunteers, for their encouragement and patient support for the stage readings and the four productions, and for their critiques of the translations.

My sincere thanks to María Mercedes Jaramillo for her invaluable contributions, and to Luz Adriana Angel for her art work.

To the friends and colleagues who read through various versions of the translations, offering their comments.

To Emma Buenaventura, for her support, for her guidance through the Colombian maze, for her intellectual values and for the many insights, tales and legends.

The words of the songs in *Lucky Strike* and *Femina Ludens* were translated by J. A. Weiss and Sarah Cardey. Original music by GaRRy Williams is available upon request.

Colombian Theatre
in the Vortex

Introduction:
Death by History: Translating Texts From the Edge of the Vortex

Judith A. Weiss

The Plays

The plays in this collection date from 1966 through 1997. Thirty years, from the earliest works of collective creation (which became models for Latin American theatre artists, for students and grassroots workers, and for the Chicano movement in the United States) to the most recent plays, which are still testimonies of intellectual and artistic commitment to a shared response to history and to social problems. The later plays continue in many respects the earlier experiments in articulating the voices of the collectivity. Beginning with the works of the 1960s and 1970s, optimistic revolutionary times in which lines of conflict were clearly drawn, and continuing down to the products of a time of chaos from which the artist can see little if any possibility of Colombia emerging whole again, these plays together form a chronicle of three decades of social and political disintegration. But they also expose the historical, the economic, and the social roots of the tragedy, and in doing so they continue to equip their actors and their audiences with tools of critical analysis. The theatre thus continues to be a vehicle for making sense of both the causes and the consequences of the violence.

The plays included in this anthology are among the most significant works of the modern Colombian theatre. They are chronicles of a nation marked by violence, paradoxes, and hyperbole; a country both blessed and cursed by its wealth of natural resources and its strategic location in the continent, and unique because of the guerrilla movements that have successfully staved off defeat and have continued to recruit displaced and persecuted peasants and to hold large areas of the country, long after armed revolutionary movements in other Latin American countries laid down their arms.

For the Colombian playwright, the pervasive violence must be demystified and its role understood. The rule of violence has been a part of Colombian society, even though Colombia is often portrayed as "the oldest democracy in Latin America" because it maintained a civilian president throughout vicious civil wars and regionalized conflicts, because it has had an operative and relatively independent judiciary, and because presidential and congressional elections are held every four years. In the tradition of the committed intellectual, the Colombian playwrights represented in this anthology see a need to expose the historical connection between the endemic violence and global and domestic hegemonic forces, whether political or economic. One role of drama is to unmask the inequalities and the tensions that lie beneath the placid image of a nation ruled often by a "gentlemen's agreement" between former rivals within the oligarchy concerned with preventing the consolidation of a popular political movement that will force radical reforms. As progressive artists and intellectuals see it, this united front of elements of the upper-middle classes and the oligarchy has, over the years, closed avenues for social change and resisted carrying out the urgent reforms that could have avoided the slide into guerrilla violence and counterinsurgency operations that cause increasing numbers of civilian casualties.

Whether through documentary dramas based on historical documents and interviews with surviving participants and witnesses of historical events, or through a grotesque metaphorization of the most oppressive paradigms of power relationships, the playwrights of this generation propose alternatives to the "official" (or officially sanctioned) readings of history and socioeconomic issues. They open up breathing spaces for critical re-evaluation and propose models of response; at the very least, they hold up mirrors that return surprising group portraits to individual spectators convinced of the isolating uniqueness of their own experience. In some way and to some degree, this theatre seeks to enable its audiences to address the violence and even, perhaps, to cope with it.

In proposing that theatre respond to every category of violence with an appropriate style and language, these artists engage their role in society: not as commissars, certainly, but not purely as entertainers, either. None of the authors included in this collection has set out to do political theatre as such, but they do not seek to exclude the politics of everyday existence, the politics of a history that defines national identity and community, the politics of the violence that assails every dream of building a sane future: these politics permeate the artists' vision and drive, however subconsciously, the artistic composition.

Although the playwrights have, in the main, rejected the label of "political theatre" for their plays, their work is clearly the product of a developed political and historical consciousness, with strong echoes of Brecht and of later radical theatres. Their methodology (historical and sociological research—including oral history and ongoing relationships with their audience-constituency—improvisation, and actor-centered dramatic methods) and their close connections with, or membership in, theatre collectives and education, as well as the content and the ideological underpinning of most of their plays, are the hallmark of the socially and politically progressive sectors of Latin American society. Popular theatre, as defined by process and by content, is the main medium of the authors represented in this anthology. Chief among the founders of what became known as the *Nuevo Teatro*, the New Theatre, of the 1960s, Enrique Buenaventura, Carlos José Reyes, and Santiago García still stand out as cultural icons, as productive contributors (authors and directors), and as educators of successive generations of theatre workers. The younger generation—Jairo Aníbal Niño, Nohora Ayala, and others—follow closely in this same path.

The two plays that were inspired by watershed moments in the history of the Colombian army (*Soldiers* and *Old Baldy*) deconstruct the primary functions of this important institution in Colombian society. *Soldiers* recalls the period of consolidation of a national army, which cut its teeth in two major series of strikes and protests: the first, in the petroleum fields of Barrancabermeja around the First World War; the second, in the banana plantations of Urabá in the late 1920s. *Old Baldy* tears the lid of silence off the plight of the Colombian veterans of the Korean conflict (1950–1953): the Left considers Colombia's participation in Korea a shameful episode of subservience to U.S. hegemony, but many veterans still consider it a shining moment of bravery, dedication, and loyalty to the cause of freedom. Whereas *Soldiers* draws its plot and characters from the 1962 novel by Álvaro Cepeda Zamudio, and was developed in a process of collective creation documented and published as a model of this method, *Old Baldy* was a playwright's text, drawn from research on the Batallón Colombia.

The two plays which address the problem of the drug trade do so from different perspectives: *Lucky Strike* chronicles the rise of a cartel member in the late 1960s, when cocaine was emerging as a major industry; *Roadhouse* makes an indirect reference to the violence of the cocaine trade while presenting Colombian society in a dead-end situation resulting in part from that trade. *Lucky Strike* is a long epic filled with the vagaries of the rise and fall of Palomino, the protagonist, as he attempts repeatedly to become an independent operator, free of the major players. The shady figures who threaten the fragile peace of the roadside tavern in *Roadhouse* are external players, and the play is relatively short and concentrated.

Pilot Project, much like *Roadhouse*, portrays a human society besieged by corruption and violence, but its subject is as non-specific as are its characters, with a particular emphasis on the dehumanization of all levels of society, allowing little or no space for moral redemption. The dystopia of *Pilot Project* could be read as a sequel to the disintegration, portrayed in *Roadhouse*, of community and stability: *Roadhouse* seems to capture that moment of historic unravelling, a microcosm caught between the struggle to preserve a familiar and nurturing environment and the action of destructive forces, and so the outcome of the characters is open-ended. *Pilot Project* focuses on a similar moment of transition but further along into a generalized dehumanization, as the survivors—a minuscule portion of society—are in some measure already dehumanized—"ratefied."

Femina Ludens represents the experiences of women in the double vortex of the larger political picture and their individual lives. They struggle to affirm their agency and to survive victimization at the hands of the individual males in their lives or of violent political and social forces. Each of the five named characters narrates and acts out her drama, supported by the remaining four actors who become part of her world for that segment of the play. Like *Roadhouse*, *Femina Ludens* is actor-centered, but it is also closer to performance art and the only representation of feminist theatre in this collection.

The Orgy—arguably the best-known of these plays—stands at the crossroads between history and ritual, between archetype and comic type, playing with the delusions of power and status of a character who, having been part of the privileged class, wants to recreate that lost world in her conflictive manipulation of representatives of the traditionally exploited lower classes. Its unpleasant and abusive protagonist, who can also be funny, seductive, and pathetic, may strike some readers as a projection of misogyny, because in this play a female is yet again presented as negativity incarnate. However, in her impoverishment and her obsessions, the character of the Old Lady stands also for the marginalized and the disempowered elements of a bourgeoisie who never quite consolidated their hold on power; she is also the dreamer, the has-been, the former courtesan and world traveller who has now lost her protectors and her freedom of movement and remains confined in her squalid relationship with her mute son and her hired actor-beggars.

The works included in this collection are fairly representative of the range of genres and styles of performance found in Latin America over the past three decades. Each of the scripts presents a different type of challenge to readers, to actors and to potential directors. Because they offer an ideal set-up for role-playing and discussion of important issues, the works can also be of value to groups of readers and academic courses or discussion groups with a focus on Latin American society or on Colombia in particular.

This introduction, and the forewords to each play, do not pretend to be exhaustive studies of Colombia. A representative selection of useful references can be found in the Bibliography.

The Translation

The translations are as faithful to the original Spanish as they could be, without being excessively literal. Translation and staging of Latin American theatre in a foreign context presents two types of challenge: the purely linguistic and the problem of spatial/geographic transfer (*trans-latus*) into a different historical and ideological context. A work of collective creation, however, presents a third challenge: that of the artistic reconstruction, given that collective creation is a subgenre, *sui generis*. The experience of staging four of these plays (*The Orgy*, *Soldiers*, *Femina Ludens*, and *Old Baldy*) at a Canadian university has confirmed this.

The following reflections are based on the experience with full productions at the Windsor Theatre, Mount Allison University, of *Soldiers* and *Femina Ludens*, under the title "Men at war, women at play", in February 2000. I also directed productions of *The Orgy* (translated by R. Rudder and G. Luzuriaga, November 1992) and *Old Baldy* (October 2003) and staged readings of six plays in September 1999.

The Sociolinguistic Challenge

Out of the first level of translation (translation as it is understood in conventional terms), questions arise regarding the permeability of geocultural and linguistic barriers. The linguistic problems of these translations continued to appear until shortly before opening night, even though the texts had undergone three stages of review. Most of the corrections as proposed by the readers were acceptable to the translator. In several instances, however, there were discussions about the intention of a phrase or a lexeme which were resolved rather arbitrarily by the translator. Some examples:

1) Versions of an ambiguous original text. "Se los volvió a poner" can allude to infidelity (poner los cuernos: cuckold) or to bruises. We opted

for "He's worked her over again." Later, while preparing the final version of the text, I decided to replace this interpretive sentence with one whose meaning is more ambiguous, like "He's messed her over again."

2) To de-exoticize or to de-familiarize? In *Femina Ludens*, Amalia describes her husband, who has disappeared. He, says Amalia, "me traía astromelias todos los domingos." I changed "astromelias" to "mountain lilies" to communicate the everyday character, the familiarity of those flowers in their context of origin. What for a Colombian woman is a lovely local flower that grows in the Andes, and whose Latin name sounds quite Spanish, in the northern hemisphere suggests something more exotic, precisely because of the Latin name and because it is a hothouse plant or an import from the tropics. To avoid that exoticism I checked the dictionaries once more and found that simple and deceptively familiar equivalent for our northern audiences.

3) The literal made metaphor. What could be done with the word "rumba", rooted as it is in the cultural geography of the tropics? It would be impossible to communicate all the dimensions of the lexeme, the layers of significance and allusion. The dilemma was solved by gauging carefully the context in which it was used, and ending up with the very pedestrian phrase "dance music", which sacrifices metonymy, metaphor, irony, and other possibilities of the word "rumba".

4) The songs. The words of the songs in *Femina Ludens* and *Lucky Strike* were the most difficult to translate. For the production, this translator rendered the lyrics of *Femina Ludens* aided only by the actors and the composer, Garry Williams. For *Lucky Strike*, the rough translation was reworked on commission by a young writer, Sarah Cardey, who collaborated with same composer. I shall comment only on the *Femina Ludens* experience, for which the songs were seen through rehearsal into full production.

The first thing we lost from the original Spanish was the rhyme, to remain faithful to the meaning. The popular rhythms and the versification of the original songs did not survive, either. But the composer and I decided to translate—transfer—the intentionality. The result: some songs with heavy traces of Eisler and Weill; others, easy, even sentimental, melodies. Each one of them, in our opinion, is faithful to the emotion and the intellectual intention of its Spanish-language counterpart. Even though the songs as a whole suggest a pastiche, they are effective, and were very well received.

The Sociocultural Transference

The central problematic encountered in attempting to present works originally destined for a very different audience from ours involved the actantial subjects of the plays. In the eyes of a North American audience that, consciously or not, enters with a dominant First World perspective on Latin America, the agency, even the worth, of the characters presented as subjects of the play can be diminished as they become simply types from a subordinate society; the experience of seeing or reading the play without its context risks reinforcing the prejudices of that audience. The challenge is to prevent that reinforcement from occurring, and to present a fissure through which the spectators and readers can enter what for many will be an alien reality.

Casting non-Latinos (the only option in that particular university, where there were no Hispanic actors) presented an additional obstacle. Fortunately, this could be discussed with the actors, some of whom already had some understanding (while others came to it later) of the implications of "occupying" characters who are struggling to transcend their historical limitations. The notion of "recolonization" was not difficult for that particular group to comprehend, but it would probably be a difficult nut to crack with many a group of actors or other readers who may be less disposed or able to comprehend neocolonial culture and the contradictions inherent in the relationship between First- and Third-World experience.

The problem, however, is not rooted solely in the representation of the oppressed "other" by an actor identified with relative privilege while also lacking the ease of complete familiarity with the culture in all its ramifications. The challenge lies in being able to justify, somehow, the choice of plays whose social and sociopolitical content is one with which fewer and fewer conventional theatre-goers identify. The challenge goes a step further if we are to justify the staging or study of works by artists who, in the context of galloping global depoliticization, are increasingly seen as a minority even within their own artistic communities in Latin America. The task has become easier, however, with the re-emergence of social movements, transformed into a massive and globalized presence: the subjects and the intention of the plays can be understood anew by greater numbers of people, and the potential audiences may grow as critical responses to problems at every level of society become more necessary.

University theatre especially offers serious implications for scholarly research and for course content. This type of project foregrounds what has become a minority expression of cultural production in societies whose artistic and educational institutions have been systematically depoliticized and alienated from radical thought and critical responses to socioeconomic conflict. By relating the project of studying or presenting these plays to the increasingly familiar paradigms of multiculturalism and of "border" culture (the cultural creation emerging from among the ranks of migrants), some of the inherent ideological issues can be addressed. The concepts of deterritorialization (Deleuze and Guattari) and heterotopias (Foucault) offer a useful basis for analysing what could, in simpler terms, be seen as a product of globalization. This is based, of course, on the presumption that globalization is a much larger phenomenon than the breaking of barriers for economic expansion, as it affects every other aspect of society, including the cultural and artistic foundations of individual societies.

To lend oneself to the recreation of texts born out of experiences that can never really be reproduced, as is the case of Colombia today, can lead into the trap of believing that a transnational, heterotopic discourse can replace a full understanding of the particular experience. In spite of all the influences of globalized culture on the Colombia that generated these plays, these plays themselves are not a product of deterritoralization—on the contrary, they are an expression of a deep national sense and of a set of circumstances whose specificity is demonstrated by the playwrights—but it is, rather, the readers/actors who are placed at those margins. Thus the text calls for a certain openness and ideological permeability among readers or spectators. The analogical intelligence that some people develop through travels abroad and exposure to the ideas of engaged intellectuals and of the new social movements is valuable, and so, too, is the will to examine parallels between other societies and our own. But two elements are essential: familiarity with the Colombian background and also a considerable level of social consciousness.

For the actor especially, works like *Femina Ludens* and *Roadhouse* pose a particular challenge with a stage discourse that is a perfect balance of words, songs, sound, and gesture: how does one translate the gestus, the corporal expression, without falling into parody or stereotype and, conversely, without allowing too much distance to emerge between the new stage discourse and the intent of the original text? Some solutions appeared when we set about dealing with the third challenge.

Reconstruction or Remaking

The character of the dramatic production—its originality, its honesty—can be determined by whether it is attempting to convey only the literal truths of the original, whether it is settling for being a "museum piece" (i.e., an attempt to imitate an original production or simply a conventional approach), or whether it can, with the proper guidance, remain faithful to the spirit of the original while also speaking to its own time and place. With works of collective creation in which the process is transparent, or known through other sources (e.g., production notes), it is both easier and more difficult to effect this balance. Specific subject matter that is rooted in history and social realities alien to the translator–director and the translator–actor calls for more reading and research, parallelling in a way the methods of collective creation. A consultant, a dramaturg, or an assistant director well-versed in the subject should be on hand to assist the cast with background knowledge.

The methodology of collective creation can be of help in forming a new collective with its own identity and motivation, whose privilege would be constituted vis-à-vis the director, a group of performers who emphasize the process and project the voice of the group along with the voices of individual actors. The collaborative nature of the group facilitates collaborative solutions and will protect the integrity of the original project as it is developed by a collective. What type of collective, though?

Soldiers, a prototype of the early collective model, is built on a series of crossed monologues and dialogues, where every character and subgroup is in an impenetrable space; where every speech is a distinct moment along an inexorable progression, or else a chronological rupture defined with a critical, distancing intention. Translating such a transparent and clearly defined text was relatively simple, and the script is quite transparent, requiring little improvisation and research on the part of the actors. *Femina Ludens*, however, is constituted by a flow of situations and identities, with gestures discovered from the response of each actor to a lyrical text and an arcane or suggestive stage direction. The play among the dramatic elements and among the women had the effect of penetrating consciousness at various levels: physical memory, emotion, intellect, identification. In our production, the process adopted from the *Nuevo Teatro* in constituting a new collective enabled the members of this collective to develop their own codes, to guess the intentions of the text much more effectively, and to rework memory, emotion, intellect and movement so that every sound and gesture, every silence and pause, was a successful translation, hence a tribute to the work of the original artists.

Translating and transferring can be more successful, perhaps, if actors employ some form of distancing, of signs that they are consciously mediating between scripts, between cultures, between historically and even ideologically differing societies. The reading and acting of these scripts will not, in all likelihood, be harmed by a touch of irony and self-consciousness, but in the end it would be more important that the director and the actors have the right measure of sympathy for the script and understanding of its pre-text, Colombia in the vortex.

Colombian Theatre

by María Mercedes Jaramillo

THE EVOLUTION OF MODERN COLOMBIAN CULTURE—ITS VALUES and expression as a reflection of social, political, and historical change—can be traced through the various stages of development of its theatre. Colombian theatre, which as recently as the early 1960s was primarily European in theme and form, has evolved into an art form in search of a national identity within its rich cultural and ethnic roots. It includes elements of Native American, African, and Hispanic traditions, revealing the cultural *mestizaje* or transculturation characteristic of the various distinctive regions of this South American nation: the Andean corridor, which has much in common with Peruvian and Ecuadorean culture; the Caribbean coast, with its mix of the most varied influences; the plains (*llanos*); the Amazonian region, and the Pacific coast. The techniques of Western, Asian, or pre-Columbian theatre are used to enrich all these popular traditions, and to recover stories, characters, and issues that are of interest to Colombian audiences.

In pre-Conquest America, there already existed a ritual or para-theatrical form of theatre, where music, dance, and recitations were indispensable elements of the ceremonial act. Some celebrations of a religious character existed in the region of the Chibchas. One such celebration was the ceremony of the Moja, which was practiced by the Muisca Indians in honor of the sun. The sacrifice of the Moja was a ritual event where an adolescent, who had been chosen while still a child, was immolated in the temple of Sugamuxi. Fernando González Cajiao sees these celebrations as pre-Columbian para-theatrical forms, because of the chants, dances, and other elements present in the religious ceremony.

A new conception of theatre that incorporated ethno-cultural elements originated from the cultural shock of the Conquest. Many pre-Hispanic cultural elements had to be mimicked so that they could survive within the civilization of the conquerors. The first American pieces followed the Spanish dramatic forms in a *mestizo* language that united the two cultures in conflict. In Colombia, these works, which still persist in some rural areas, took the form of dances like the *Cuadrillas de San Martín* [Saint Martin's Quadrilles] and the *Juego de los caballeros* [literally, The Game of the Knights; it could also be translated as The Gentlemen's Game]. These performances, which emerged from the tradition of the "Moors and Christians," expressed the culture shock and the encounter of two distinct worlds. This is essentially street theatre with attractive costumes—a playful masquerade that recreates the victory of Christianity over the devil.

The first known play in the history of the Colombian theatre is a piece that mocks baroque language, but remains, nevertheless, within the cultural tradition of peninsular Spain, the mother country. Fernando Fernández de Valenzuela, the first recorded playwright of the Viceroyalty of New Granada, wrote the *Láurea Crítica* [The Critical Laurel Wreath] in 1629. It is a one-act play in baroque verse with typical characters of the period, intended as a satire on the seventeenth-century school of poetry influenced by Luis de Góngora.

In the early part of the nineteenth century, theatrical and commercial activity in Colombia was dominated by the canons of European fashion. This was the century of the Romantic theatre and the opera, the century when Creole descendants of the Spanish identified themselves more with European styles and foreign culture than with the American world. When they took power in an independent state in the early 1820s, the Creole elite strove to retain economic control of the country. They defended this right in the written culture inherited from Europe, while, at the same time, ignoring the oral culture of the illiterate autochthonous peoples.

In 1820, José Domínguez Roche wrote *La Pola*, a play that had at least three productions. The Bogotá production of 1826 involved one of the most famous episodes in the history of the national theatre. So furiously did the audience protest the execution of the famous heroine of the War of Independence that the theatre manager was forced to alter the historical events in the play by changing the death penalty into internal exile. This play, like others from the same period, recreates a mix of styles and tendencies that often came late to the colonies.

Atala and *Guatimoc* by José Fernández Madrid are plays that also follow the European canon, even though they are set in America. The author accepted the criticism of Simón Bolivar, who considered that his plays lacked authenticity because he only cared to follow the scheme of the Italian tragedy. He even changed some of the historical events to reconcile his work with the rigid demands of neoclassical patterns.

The best-known Colombian play of the nineteenth century is *Las convulsiones* [The Convulsions] (1828), by Luis Vargas Tejada. This comedy represents life in the capital after the War of Independence, and it satirizes the conduct of young women who feigned convulsions to escape the severity of family control.

José Joaquín Ortiz Rojas's *Sulma* (1834), a neoclassical tragedy, had a cool reception because it tended toward Romanticism. What is considered interesting about this tragedy is the theme and its dramatization of the cult of the Moja and the ceremonies that preceded the ritual.

Another comedy of manners was *Un alcalde a la antigua y dos primos a la moderna* [An Old-Fashioned Mayor and Two Modern Cousins] (1857) by José María Samper, a play that criticizes the abuse of authority and the foolishness of the village mayor. At the same time, it represents the conflict created by arranged marriage. In this play, we begin to see the elements of a bourgeois ideology, where liberty and love are primary and indispensable elements for the happiness of the individual. In 1864, the entertaining play *El espíritu del siglo* [The Spirit of the Century] by José María Vergara y Vergara was published in *El mosaico* [The Mosaic]. This piece confronts two different moments in Western civilization, in an attempt to criticize the hypocrisy, greed, and vanity of its contemporaries. Adam sends Abel and Cain to visit the world to see the progress of their descendants. Cain and Abel come to realize that men kill each other and greedily search for small golden pebbles, the only sign of value in the world.

Candelario Obeso's comedy *Secundino el zapatero* [Secundino the Cobbler] (1880) presents the vices of the day and the opportunism of city-dwellers. The manual laborers—a workforce that continued to be treated with disdain by the upper class—are lauded for their craft and honest attitudes. *Lope de Aguirre* by Carlos Arturo Torres (1891) reviewed the history of the famous Spanish conqueror and his rebellion against the Spanish Crown.

In Colombia, the early theatre movement did not have the vigor of its counterparts in Argentina or México, where independent theatre groups created an audience, critics, and playwrights. There was no established commercial theatre that would support the development of companies, regularly scheduled performances, criticism, actors, authors, and directors. This forced the few national authors—like Luis Enrique Osorio and Antonio Alvarez Lleras—to occupy themselves with the training of actors. Their plays on national themes had to compete with visiting companies whose repertoire was foreign to the reality of Colombia. This imported theatre was an escape for the elite who had access to artistic creation. Unfortunately, because the national theatre depended on this class for its precarious subsistence, the authors had to make concessions to the elite, regardless of their social and aesthetic differences.

The works of Alvarez Lleras and Osorio, the most prominent playwrights of the first half of the twentieth century, are strong reflections of the social and political currents of the time. Another notable national playwright is Emilio Campos—Campitos—who presented political caricatures within musical vaudeville. Unfortunately, this type of *costumbrista* theatre, a mixture of Spanish comedy and one-act farce, disappeared, for all practical purposes, from rural and provincial Colombia during the period known as *La Violencia*, which profoundly transformed the country (1948–1955).

With the Second World War and the rise of industry, a new phase of Latin American theatre began. Drama opened itself to universal concerns. Theatre of the absurd and existentialist philosophy gained ground in Colombia's theatre. The works of Third World authors reflected the existential anguish, the alienation, the vacuum that developed societies produced in human beings. They also showed the problems of underdeveloped regions devastated by violence and social conflicts. The characters became symbolic and lost their individuality—their names were sometimes transformed into numbers or pronouns. The works reflect inequality and injustice in the countryside and in the city, caused by the State or the Church, by society or the human condition. The contradictions manifest themselves in the characters and the situations, whose antagonistic positions are a projection of the Latin American reality: oppressed and oppressors, slaves and masters, colonialism and self-determination, dependency and political or cultural independence.

At this time, the theatre in Latin American was catching up with European and North American theatre. The new themes demanded a more experimental theatrical discourse. Some authors hoped to restore to theatre its original mythical/ceremonial elements, and they sought nourishment from the country's domestic reality and from genuine expressions of popular culture. The bourgeois theatre—based, essentially, on the mechanical repetition of a discourse that was not responsive to the "here and now"—was rejected. Playwrights incorporated all manner of dramatic trends, from the theatre of the absurd to political theatre, to epic theatre, in order to recreate the historical moment.

Colombian theatre underwent a series of transformations whose origins can be traced in part to the European and North American vanguard movements. But these changes were also a response to the social and political transformations of the country and all of Latin

America. The Cuban Revolution had a profound effect, at the ideological and political level, on Colombia as it did on most other Latin American countries, creating enthusiasm among leftists and among Colombian youth who now envisioned the possibility of significant change in the system of government.

The playwrights and directors especially felt the need to foster a direct and relevant communication with the public through themes of common interest. They did not reject universal theatre but, instead, assimilated the contributions of Bertold Brecht, Konstantin Stanislavsky, and Antonin Artaud. They also adapted the expressive techniques and aesthetic resources of universal theatre to their own reality. The basic objective of the Colombian dramatists was to recover the country's cultural heritage and use it as a shield against the cultural colonialism that threatened (and still threatens) to destroy autonomous values. In this way, the New Colombian Theatre was conceived in the 1960s as a reflection of the political and social changes experienced by the country.

The New Colombian Theatre

Although it was the last "literary" genre to assert its independence from European cultural currents, Colombian theatre soon became a crucible and a bastion of Colombia's cultural and multi-ethnic heritage. The *Nuevo Teatro* [New Theatre] was the crystallization of the popular and marginal cultures that had resisted the repression exercised by the dominant official culture—the culture that controlled all means of communication, regulated the educational system, and defined the country's political culture.

One of the characteristics of the New Theatre that defined its dramaturgy was its close link to the interests of the Colombian public. Findings of a formal nature were directed toward the creation of a new theatrical language, joining it to the social and cultural context in which it was generated. The defenders of the "here and now" confronted the defenders of the imported cosmopolitan culture, a culture that had fostered alienation and a loss of identity within Colombia. The principal objective of the New Theatre was the recuperation of identity. Its practitioners therefore revealed historical, political, and social processes that contributed to strengthening the cultural heritage of the country. Themes emerged from the very real social environment of each community. These were realities that had heretofore been denatured or veiled and it was vital that they be returned to their real significance. Thus, cultural values that belonged to the masses and had for years been confined to oral transmission were being rescued.

The playwrights who lived through *La Violencia* felt the need to bear witness to this dramatic era. Within their works, they analyzed the causes and consequences of this brutality and protested the useless sacrifice of the Colombian people. The significant works of the movement were Manuel Zapata Olivella's *El retorno de Caín* [The Return of Cain] and *Caronte Liberado* [Charon Unbound], Gustavo Andrade Rivera's *Historias para quitar el miedo* [Stories to Take Away the Fear] and *Remington 22*, Enrique Buenaventura's *Los papeles del Infierno* [Documents from Hell] and Jairo Aníbal Niño's *Alguien muere cuando nace el alba* [Someone Dies When Dawn Breaks] and *Golpe de Estado* [Coup d'Etat].

The theories of Stanislavsky and Brecht were brought to the Colombian theatre scene by Enrique Buenaventura, Santiago García, and Carlos José Reyes. They created a national dramaturgy, a critical discourse, and their works represented the New Theatre in the leading independent companies. Buenaventura directed the Teatro Experimental de Cali (TEC) from 1963 until his untimely death, December 31, 2003. His wife Jacqueline Vidal, plans to continue his work. García has directed the collective La Candelaria in Bogotá since 1972. For the younger generation, the theories of Jerzy Grotowski, Antonin Artaud, and Eugenio Barba have driven theatre in new directions, helping to generate different objectives, themes, and attitudes within the national theatre movement. A cultural polemic was initiated, which enabled theatre to evolve, to gain prominence and popularity, to become diversified, and to become more firmly rooted in the national consciousness and in the artistic scene. Despite the divergences and differences between groups and theatre professionals, there are points of confluence and contact, chiefly in their attempts to recover the popular traditions.

Folklore and historical characters have been incorporated into Colombian theatre, and at the same time, the national life-style and events from everyday life are analyzed within dramatic works. Colombian theatre has collected themes, styles, and attitudes that had not been dramatized before. In collective creations, in collective montages, in the versions of other national authors, these themes, styles, and attitudes have found their channel of expression. Colombian theatre has not necessarily produced better works, but it has enriched the theatrical space with new characters, stories, and situations that had been excluded from theatre and cultural creation generally until now. It is a vigorous movement that continues to be nourished by its cultural roots, by its assimilation of universal theatre elements, and by other artistic forms, expanding its horizon into the new millennium.

The history of the New Colombian Theatre can be divided into four stages. The first period involved high school or university theatre, which was undeniably academic. The audiences were shaped by the minority elite who had access to the university and to the culture of the status quo. The second period corresponded to the time of official repression and budget cuts. It was a period of popular/activist theatre, when artists sought out their audiences in poor neighborhoods and in rural areas. It was a time of expansion for the movement, a period when a new public was created.

The third period was marked by the organization of companies into guild or associations, the most important being the Corporación Colombiana de Teatro [Colombian Theatre Corporation]. This organization, which functioned much like a guild or trade union, brought together the independent theatre groups, sponsored festivals, workshops, and publications, and also supported the theatre movement at all levels throughout the country. Moreover, the theatre workers established links with other trade unions. During this stage, the theatre became involved with the process of social development. It involved research into the history of Colombia and themes essential to the community, representing them truthfully to enable spectators to confront their conflicts and contradictions.

The fourth period corresponded to an increased professionalism in theatre, with increased numbers of practitioners who had graduated from drama schools and greater opportunities for authors to stage their plays. The commercial theatre also experienced a resurgence, benefitting from the audience development that was being achieved largely by the popular movement throughout the country. This stage was characterized by pluralism and tolerance. As an example of the vitality of the movement and its broad range of interests, we can mention the presence of theatre schools, independent theatre groups, workshops, publications, specialized criticism, and national and international festivals.

Theatre Schools

At present, there are four degree-granting theatre schools.

1) The Theatre School of the Universidad de Antioquia, where dramatists and directors like Mario Yepes and Henry Díaz work, grants a Masters in Dramatic Art.

2) The Theatre School of the Universidad del Valle, where Enrique Buenaventura has taught.
3) The Department of Dance and Theatre of the Universidad de Nariño offers a Bachelor's degree in Theatre.
4) The National School of Dramatic Art (ENAD), founded in 1951 by Victor Mallarino, has been dedicated to the formation of actors and directors and, in addition to fulfilling an academic function, it has staged a number of plays from the national and international repertoire.

Independent Theatre Groups

There are more than three hundred theatre groups distributed throughout the nation. The more established ones have their own theatre space and others work in rented auditoriums. There are a number of theatres that support important international festivals. In March 1994, Bogotá's Ibero-American Festival presented more than four hundred shows in ten days. Some of the most established theatre groups, whose plays merit attention, are the following:

Acto Latino was founded in Bogotá in 1967. From 1967 to 1971, Sergio González directed some plays of collective creation based on novels by Colombian writers as Gabriel García Márquez's *Los funerales de la Mamá grande* [Big Mama's Funeral] and Jorge Zalamea's *El gran Burundú Burundá ha muerto* [The Great Burundú Burundá has died]. In 1975, the group staged *Cada vez que hablas se te crece la nariz, Pinochet* [Every Time you Speak your Nose Grows, Pinochet], a very controversial play that recreated the coup d'etat in Chile in 1973; it also questioned communisn and fascism. Then, *El coronel no tiene quien le escriba* [No One Writes to the Colonel], and *Blacamán el bueno, vendedor de milagros* [Blacamán the Good, Seller of Miracles] (1980) were staged; these plays, based on the works by Gabriel García Márquez, had an impact because of their ludicrous images.

Historias del silencio [Stories of Silence] (1982) by Juan Monsalve initiated a new stage of investigation and imagery. *El espejo y la máscara* [The Mirror and the Lamp] (1983) was directed by Juan Monsalve and staged with students from the Escuela de Arte Dramático (ENAD); this piece was based on Jorge Luis Borges's texts and Monsalve was exploring the body's memory. The protagonists were to imitate trees, rabbits, stones, ghosts, and so forth, and follow their movements, instincts, and forms. *Ondina* (1985) directed by Juan Monsalve and María Teresa Hincapie, was a montage that explored femininity through the roles of women in society. In 1989, the group participated in the Encuentro Latinoamericano de Teatro Popular

[Latin American Popular Theatre Meeting] with *Punto de fuga* [Point of Escape]. It was a performance by an actress in a store window, where she captured the passers-by's attention with messages written on the glass.

La Candelaria was founded by Santiago García in 1972, with the theatre group of the Casa de la Cultura. It is one of the most well-known theatre groups in Colombia. La Candelaria's plays denounce corruption and human rights violations and defend democracy and freedom. It is a bastion of independent theatre (see Santiago García).

Esquina Latina was founded by Orlando Cajamarca in Cali in 1972. Cajamarca has staged his own works, like *El enmaletado* [The Dead Man in the Suitcase], which recreates the theme of political violence, as well as the works of universal authors. In children's theatre, *Joselito Buscalavida* [Joselito "Lookforlife"] stands out as a collection of popular legends and fables.

Hilos Mágicos is a marionette and puppet theatre founded in 1974 in Bogotá and directed by Ciro Gómez. The group has more than forty plays created with different techniques such as thimble puppets, glove puppets, rod puppets, black and shadow theatre, and Banraku (Japanese puppets). The group has created characters such as Peperepe and Pipirucha that mock human behavior and vices. *El pastel* [The Cake] and *La maga Cuchicuchi* [Cuchicuchi, the Magician] are plays created for glove puppets. The group's better plays are done with marionettes, and they are based on famous fables and fairy tales: *El grano de oro* [The Golden Grain], *El ratoncito azul* [The Blue Mouse], *Lo que caperucita no contó* [What Little Red Riding Hood Didn't Tell], *La gallina de los huevos de oro* [The Goose that Laid the Golden Eggs], *La hormiga y la cigarra* [The Ant and the Cicada]. The group called these pieces "counter-stories" because of the modifications on the original stories. For example, in *La hormiga y la cigarra*, the ant decides to marry the cicada because she missed her beautiful songs and music. In this way, the group shows the importance of art and culture in society, while also praising solidarity.

La Libélula Dorada is one of the most appreciated children's theatre groups in Colombia. It was founded by Iván Darío and César Santiago Alvarez in 1976, two authors dedicated exclusively to theatre and puppets. One of their works, *El dulce encanto de la isla Acracia* [The Sweet Charm of Acracia Island], is a montage of collective creation. This piece recreates the importance of liberty and imagination in the world of children. *Los espíritus lúdicos* [The Ludicrous Spirits] (1990) is a piece where mischievous children get rid of the invincible Lone Ranger, and in a ludicrous way it deconstructs the violence that permeates television. *Los negocios de Don Gato* [Don Gato's Businesses] (1994) was the play selected to participate in the fourth Ibero-American Festival, and it is a metaphor on human ambition. They have also created a magazine of children's theatre, entitled *Quiropterus.*

El Local was founded in 1970 by Miguel Torres. This theatre group has staged national and international plays. In 1971, Torres started to explore physical expression using the techniques of Jerzy Grotowsky. In 1977, after a long period of research in La Guajira, Torres staged *La increíble y triste historia de la cándida Eréndira y su abuela desalmada* [The Incredible and Sad Tale of Innocent Eréndira and Her Heartless Grandmother]. This play has been performed more than a thousand times and recovers elements of Guajiro theatre. *Eréndira* initiated a new era in Colombian theatre by recreating the topic in a ludicrous way and using physical expression to project the environment. It has also been staged in Paris by Augusto Boal.

La Mama was founded in 1968. It has staged plays from the universal repertory as well as from collective creation. The most salient is *Los tiempos del ruido* [The Times of Noise] (1985). This piece is based on real-life events and recreates the routine of large cities. It presents the city's violence, the tragedies that afflict the urbanite, and the loneliness and abandonment of individuals trapped by institutions that govern the city. *Ensueños de Bolívar* [Bolivar's Dreams] by Eddy Armando was the play selected to participate in the fourth Ibero-American Festival in 1994. The piece recalls Bolívar's dreams and projects for Latin America; it takes place in a decadent and polluted city of the future.

La Máscara was founded in 1972 but it was transformed in 1983 by a group of women who sought to analyze the problems of women through theatre (abortion, infanticide, prostitution). Among their works, the following are the most distinguished. *María Farrar* (1983), based on the work by Brecht, does not judge the adolescent for the crime committed (which has already been judged by society) but, instead, it judges the circumstances that lead her to commit infanticide. In 1984, La Máscara staged *Las noticias de María* [News from María], based on *Las nuevas cartas Portuguesas* [The New Portuguese Letters] by María Teresa Horta, María Isabel Barreno, and María Velho D'Costa. The play highlights the conjugal abuse that leads women to leave home. In 1993, the dance and music of *Bocas de bolero* [Bolero Mouths] recreated the monotonous daily life of women who are secluded at home and bound by their domestic duties.

El Taller de Artes de Medellín was founded by Samuel Vásquez in 1975. It is a theatre group that works in collaboration with other artists and this is shown in their works. In 1983, Samuel Vásquez directed *El arquitecto y el emperador de Asiria* [The Architect and the Emperor of Asiria] by Fernando Arrabal. This work stood out because of its rich corporeal expression, which allowed the two characters to assume roles that the isolation of the island imposes, and to (re)create other possible existences. *El arquitecto y el emperador de Asiria* deconstructs complex human relationships by questioning social hierarchies and moral attitudes. *El bar de la calle Luna* [The Bar on Moon Street], staged during the Festival of Manizales in 1989, created a new aesthetic in scenery. This was done by bringing together audience and stage in a shared space. Also, through gestures and attitudes, the characters project the Colombian idiosyncrasy. *Gestos para habitar el silencio* [Gestures to Populate the Silence] was staged during the fourth Ibero-American Festival in 1994. This play reproduces both words and silence through gestures and portrays the urgency and lucidity of the language of the deaf and mute.

Teatro Experimental de Cali was founded by Enrique Buenaventura in 1963. The New Theatre Movement began with El TEC. Its objectives have been always directed toward the recovery and recreation of oral traditions and characters from national folklore. Furthermore, it has developed a theatrical method which has impelled the New Theatre. This method was originated through a close dialogue with the general public, showing the interest of the TEC to recreate the reality and conflicts of Colombian Society (see Enrique Buenaventura).

Teatro Libre de Bogotá (TLB) was founded in 1973 by Ricardo Camacho, Jorge Plata, and Germán Moure. They also had a playwrights' workshop that succeeded in creating important plays, such as *La agonía del difunto* [The Agony of the Deceased] by Estebán Navajas, and *Los inquilinos de la ira* [The Tenants of Rage] and *El sol subterráneo* [The Subterranean Sun] by Jairo Aníbal Niño.

Ricardo Camacho has directed plays by Colombian playwrights such as: *Los andariegos* [The Wanderers] (1983) by Jairo Aníbal Niño, which analyzes the life and troubles of migrant workers; *Un muro en el jardín* [A Wall in the Garden] (1985) by Jorge Plata, which is a piece reflecting the violence and conflicts between the different social classes and their unequal access to economic resources; in 1986, *Sobre las arenas tristes* [On the Sad Sands] by Eduardo Camacho Guizado, recreated the life of José Asunción Silva, a very well known Colombian poet. Ricardo Camacho and Germán Moure together have directed some plays from the international repertoire. Also, the TLB has opened its doors to international companies and playwrights showing plays and new theatre techniques that have not been staged before in Colombia. This has initiated a fruitful exchange for the national theatre movement.

In 1994, during the fourth Ibero-American Festival, the first play written by García Márquez, *Diatriba de amor contra un hombre sentado* [Diatribe of Love Against a Seated Man] (1987) was directed by Ricardo Camacho. In a monologue during her twenty-fifth wedding anniversary, an upset wife reproaches her husband and expresses her unhappiness with her "perfect married life" which she compares to hell. The husband keeps on reading the newspaper and never pays attention to his wife's diatribe.

El Teatro Matacandelas was founded in Medellín by Cristóbal Peláez in 1979. In 1990, it staged a static play based on *O marinheiro* [The Sailor] by Fernando Pessoa. Through the dialogue of the vigil-keepers, the dream world and the possibilities of existence are scrutinized. Their most recent play is *Juegos nocturnos* [Nocturnal Games] (1992), based on the texts of authors like Samuel Beckett, Eugene Ionesco, and Tardieu. This production has been welcomed by the critics.

El Teatro Nacional was founded by Fanny Mickey in 1981 and it has hosted many theatre groups from other countries. This activity has crystallized in the Ibero-American Festival, organized by this tireless theatre worker. It is an important event for world theatre, and it nurtures the development of the national movement. Furthermore, it has created interest among the upper classes who provided financial backing for the event. Among their montages, the work by Martin Sherman, *Bent*, directed by Gustavo Londoño, merits attention. The piece raises the issue of discrimination and the persecution of homosexuals in different periods of history.

El Teatro Popular de Bogotá was founded in 1968 by Jorge Alí Triana, Jaime Santos, and Rosario Montaña. It has always shown an interest in classical works and universal dramaturgy, constantly updating its repertoire. In 1982, Carlos José Reyes integrated El Alacrán into the TPB and worked as director there. One of the classical plays of Colombian theatre staged by El TPB is *I Took Panama* (1974) by Luis Alberto García, directed by Triana. It belongs to the genre of documentary theatre, following Peter Weiss's thesis as it recreates the separation of Panamá from Colombian territory. In the form of a farce, it compares the popular and oral version to the official and written version of the events. García's version introduces humor into the historical play genre.

In 1991, Fabio Rubiano directed his play *María es-tres* [María is Stress/Three] with El TPB. The play is a deconstruction of the famous Colombian novel, *María* by Jorge Isaacs. María and Efraín are divided into three characters analyzing the relationship between men and women in Colombia. María has been the model of romantic love and perfection; she was the pure and secluded girlfriend that died waiting for Efraín. María, is meant to remind us of the Virgin Mary—a model for single and married women that must follow her as the perfect mother and chaste wife. Rubiano desacralizes this myth and creates a new protagonist full of desires and human imperfections. In 1994, during the fourth Ibero-American Festival, Rubiano directed another of his plays, *Amores simultáneos* [Simultaneous Loves]. Again, in this piece Rubiano projects love from different perspectives, and presents, through techniques of the theatre of the absurd, the tragedy and nostalgia created when a loved one is absent.

El Teatro Taller de Colombia, directed by Jorge Vargas and Mario Matallana, was founded in 1972. It has excelled in the street theatre modality. Vargas and Matallana use Colombian music in their performances. They have shown their work in Europe and in the Americas. In 1979, El Teatro Taller de Colombia presented a work by Juan Carlos Moyano, *La cabeza de Gupuk* [Gupuk's Head] (1980) which is based on the *Popol Vuh*. It is a poetic play announcing the end of the tyrant and the birth of freedom. *El inventor de sueños* [The Inventor of Dreams] (1983) is the story of a man, José Isaac, who creates his own dreams which are filled with medieval cavaliers and millenary monsters that chase and torment him. In this play the group shows its skill using stilts and other street theatre props. It was staged in Bogotá and in México. Misael Torres and Moyano have worked together and produced such distinguished pieces as *Memoria y olvido de Ursula Iguarán* [Memory and Oblivion of Ursula Iguarán] (1992), based on the work by García Márquez. This play succeeds in recreating the environment and themes of *One Hundred Years of Solitude*. In 1989, it participated in El Encuentro Latinoamericano de Teatro Popular with *Prometeo* [Prometheus]; this play recreates the suffering and liberation of the Titan. *Popón, el brujo y el sueño de Tisquesusa* [Popón, the Warlock and the Dream of Tisquesusa] was the work selected to participate in the fourth Ibero-American Festival. It is based on a text by Fernando González and it recreates the moment of confrontation between Indians and Spaniards in the land of the Chibchas.

Theatre Workshops

There are a series of workshops in Colombia that seek to train actors, directors, and authors. Other workshops seek an audience of children to initiate them in corporal expression and artistic creation.

It is also a means of subsistence for the theatre groups and schools. For example, El Taller de Dramaturgia, founded in 1975, helped the development of the New Theatre. From here, playwrights were trained and important works emerged. Such works as *La agonía del difunto* [The Agony of the Deceased] by Esteban Navajas, and *La huelga* [The Strike] and *Tiempo de vidrio* [Time of Glass] by Sebastián Ospina, were staged in El Teatro Libre. El Taller de la Corporación Colombiana de Teatro has fomented various investigations and then edited the critical/theoretical results, making them accessible to interested readers. The theatre group Esquina Latina of Cali has developed systematic theatrical workshops in various neighborhoods, which seeks to consolidate groups interested in theatre and integrate them into creative activities. At the same time, the links of the theatre group are strengthened within its medium.

Specialized Publications

Among the periodicals published in Colombia are: *Teatro* [Theatre] edited by Gilberto Martínez in Medellín, and *Actuemos* [Let's Act], a publication by Dimensión Educativa, edited by Jairo Santa in Bogotá. The publications of the group La Candelaria and El TEC have developed a theatrical theory on collective creation and Colombian dramaturgy. With the success of the national and international theatre festivals, other publications like *Gestus* from the ENAD and *Quiropterus* from La Libélula Dorada have emerged. Texts have begun to be published which facilitate the study and diffusion of theatre. In response to the growing demand for specialized works and texts, La Universidad de Antioquia has initiated a theatre collection in its Publications Department.

Theatre Criticism

In addition to the playwrights and theatre directors who have theorized and written about theatre [Enrique Buenaventura, Santiago García, Gilberto Martínez, and Carlos José Reyes], there are a number of Colombian scholars, both in Colombia and abroad, who have made important contributions to the documentation and study of theatre. Fernando González Cajiao, Beatriz Rizk, Giorgio Antei, Héctor Orjuela, Misael Vargas, Gonzalo Arcila, Lucía Garavito, Patricia González, and María Mercedes Jaramillo have written extensively about Colombian theatre. The following critics and reviewers also stand out: Guillermo González Uribe, Eduardo Márceles Daconte,

Hugo Afanador, Juan Carlos Moyano, Juan Monsalve, Adolfo Chaparro, and Iván Darío Álvarez [in children's theatre].

Festivals

University drama festivals were the major catalyst for the emergence of the New Theatre. In addition, the Manizales Festival has helped to develop the national theatre by providing an arena of exchange. The national and regional festivals support provincial theatre groups by giving them the opportunity to show their work. Moreover, the Ibero-American Festival has brought to the country works from the universal repertoire, styles and themes that enrich the national movement. The Ibero-American Festival also allows the work of unrecognized theatre groups to be known at the international level. It fosters criticism and publications and it is an open space for the reexamination of culture, and it has contributed to audience-building.

Soldiers

Introductory Notes

THE PUBLISHED TEXT OF *SOLDIERS* (1966) IS BUT ONE OF SEVERAL VERsions written and staged by Carlos José Reyes and a collective of distinguished actors and playwrights, in what would become one of the landmarks in Latin American popular theatre. The play refers us to a crucial event in Colombian labor and social history and in the development of that nation's armed forces and its labor unions: the great strike of 1928 in the banana-producing region of Colombia.

The banana region of Colombia (centered chiefly in the departments, or provinces, of Magdalena and Urabá) has one of the bloodiest histories of labor relations in the world and remains a terrifying place for peasants and workers. It entered the twenty-first century with an intensified terror, with the army and paramilitaries systematically intimidating and murdering labor leaders and community workers. Conditions defy all international labor laws (to which the Colombian government has subscribed since 1931): fifteen-hour days, exposure to excessive doses of toxic pesticides and fungicides, limited health and disability services, and a generalized violation of human rights, despite which the workers continue to risk death by organizing.

Banana production, centered in the department of Urabá since the 1930s, was originally developed in the late 19th century by French companies and later by U.S. corporations, in the department of Magdalena. The confrontation and massacre described in this play took place in the town of Ciénaga, with related activities in Santa Marta and Aracataca.[1]

The chronology of the massacre can be summarized as follows:

1927–1928. A fledgling union of banana workers is formed, led by socialist organizers with earlier successes in the oil fields of Barrancabermeja. Two previous strikes, in 1918 and 1924, had been unsuccessful.

12 November 1928. General Cortés Vargas, appointed military chief of the Magdalena region by the Colombian government, arrives in the region.

He is welcomed by a delegation of women, who make him swear on the red flag that he would never deploy his troops against the workers.

Last week of November, 1928. News spreads that the Colombian government has dispatched the army to defend national sovereignty by protecting United Fruit Company (UFC) property, in the face of a U.S. government threat to send in the Marines. Workers enter army barracks to win soldiers over to their cause, and many soldiers promise to shoot their commanding officers before they would fire on the strikers.

2–5 December 1928. Striking workers, assembled in Ciénaga, accompanied by local residents, suspend plans for a march on the department capital when they hear that the governor is going to meet with them.

5 December 1928. The governor is persuaded by United Fruit agents and their associates within the army to suspend his trip to Ciénaga because of a threat to his safety. Instead, troops are dispatched to Ciénaga. They surround the main square, where close to five thousand men, women, and children are assembled, awaiting word from the governor. The officers order the demonstrators to disperse in five minutes, but it is clearly impossible for everyone to leave an area enclosed by buildings; officers manning machine guns, some of them pointed at the rank-and-file troops, force the soldiers to fire their rifles at the crowd.

Official figures cite two hundred dead, many of them in armed confrontations outside Ciénaga, although popular lore places the figure at over two thousand; the truth lies somewhere in between, and it is not possible to arrive at a precise figure, because many of the workers were transients from other regions, without roots in the area, and the government and the UFC said that most of the strikers left Ciénaga that night to return home. Stories persist, among the local population, of freight cars loaded with corpses that were taken away and dumped in the sea; the nightmarish version of events was consecrated in the novel *One Hundred Years of Solitude*.

After the events of 1928, the UFC phased out its operations in Magdalena, and, during the Depression, it concentrated on rebuilding the industry in Urabá. One of the organizers of the banana workers' strike, Raúl Mahecha,[2] went underground and remained a hunted man until, in the late 1930s, he emerged as a member of the Communist Party of Colombia. Several of the labor leaders who had been sentenced to jail by courts governed by the military occupation were eventually released.

Alvaro Samudio Cepeda wrote a short novel about the events of 1928, *La casa grande* [*The Big House*, 1962], which combined documentary material with a fictional story line centered around a brothel. The novel reflects a renewed interest in the famous strike among writers and academics from the Atlantic Coast.[3] It was not surprising that a group of playwrights should take their cue from this, and around 1965 the playwrights and directors Carlos José Reyes and Enrique Buenaventura, along with a team of actors, began research and improvisation based on *La casa grande* and other materials. *Soldiers* is of considerable significance in the history and the repertoire of Latin American theatre of collective creation because it was one of the first major works to be developed through a carefully plotted and articulated methodology and also because it is one of the few to become a "textbook" model.[4]

Much of the soldiers' dialogue in this play is taken almost verbatim from the novel, with their story, the personalized version of events, providing a counterpoint to the documentary texts (letters, communiqués, telegrams, military dispatches and orders, and speeches). The stories of individuals lend the power of dramatic discourse to the play, contrasting with the dry, albeit ironic, readings and narratives of the history behind those stories, but standing always as *exempla* of the grand narrative. In the novel, however, the brothel incident which moves the subplot in the play is central and historical facts are assimilated to homogenize the discourse and serve as subtext and background.

The lines of dialogue of the historical characters are spoken by two "wild cards" (to use Augusto Boal's term): the Boatman (*Boga*) and the Drummer, each of whom are also typifications of their role in the banana boom and in the involvement of the army, respectively. The Boatman represents the bargemen and also ship pilots (who also went on strike at one point, affecting crucial transport); the term "boga" is a strong historical referent to the skilled and knowledgeable oarsmen or rowers—initially, African slaves, and later, often Afrocolombians—on barges and other river boats who were essential labor along the waterways that took the place of land roads and highways. The Boatman is an observer of events as well as an instrumental figure. His counterpart the Drummer serves an instrumental role within the army, communicating through drum rolls (an equivalent to the bugle boy's role), and, in this play, taking on the role of announcer and mouthpiece for historical figures.

Notes

1. Gabriel García Márquez, born in Aracataca, was eight months old when the repercussions of the strike and the massacre were felt in his town: labor leaders, workers, and sympathizers in other trades met or hid from the authorities there, planning actions, resistance, or escapes. He claims that the version of the events and

their aftermath that he narrates in his novels and short stories were gleaned from his grandparents' eyewitness accounts.

2. Mahecha began his career as a member of the Catholic Worker movement. He was one of the organizers of the Barrancabermeja oilfield strike and a founding member of the Revolutionary Socialist Party in the 1920s.

3. Samudio Cepeda's *La casa grande* was conceived around the same time as García Márquez's *La hojarasca* [Leaf Storm] and *La mala hora* [In Evil Hour]. These writers were part of the Atlantic Coast circle that reached their maturity in the early to 1960s. Samudio Cepeda was born in Ciénaga in 1926. Jairo Aníbal Niño's play *El sol subterráneo* was published in 1978.

4. See Francisco Garzón Céspedes, *Recopilación de textos sobre el teatro latinoamericano de creación colectiva* (La Habana: Casa de las Américas, 1978).

Soldiers
[Soldados]

A collective creation by Carlos José Reyes, Enrique Buenaventura, Jacqueline Vidal, Jorge Herrera, Sergio Gómez, Gilberto Ramírez, and Guillermo Piedrahita. 1966 version. Translated by Judith A. Weiss © 1998.

Cast of Characters

FIRST SOLDIER, *also* SECOND SOLDIER'S BROTHER, WORKER
SECOND SOLDIER
BOATMAN, *also* BANANA PLANTATION WORKER, UNION LEADER, LABOR INSPECTOR
DRUMMER, *also* ISSUER OF MILITARY ORDERS, GENERAL CORTÉS VARGAS, THOMAS BRADSHAW, MANAGER OF UNITED FRUIT, PRESIDENT MIGUEL ABADÍA MÉNDEZ

1. MILITARY ORDERS. Shoulder arms! On guard! Forward, march!

FIRST *and* SECOND SOLDIERS *carry out the orders. Suddenly, they stop, take several steps forward, independent of commands, and say:*

2. SOLDIERS. Soldiers! The story of a strike.
3. FIRST SOLDIER [*To the audience*]. The first time I heard tell of the United Fruit Company was two years ago, when my brother came to see me at the barracks to say goodbye.
4. BOATMAN [*To the audience*]. I had heard about the salaries that United Fruit paid in the banana region of the Atlantic and I had decided to go and work there.
5. DRUMMER. First soldier, you have a visitor.
6. SECOND SOLDIER [*To the audience*]. I had never heard of United Fruit. In fact, I hadn't even left my father's farm, ever. But one day, all of a sudden, the farm belonged to somebody else: Mr. Próspero Terreros showed us a title and we tenant farmers were out. My father went deep into another forest to carve out another farm. He was all caught up in his dreams of another product: coffee. But I went down to the village. I wanted to see the world.
7. FIRST SOLDIER [*To the* BOATMAN]. As for the folks . . .
8. BOATMAN. They'll be buried on the plantation, but I won't be. [*To the audience*] We had a piece of land on a large plantation and we paid for the rights to grow things on that piece of land by working for the boss from Monday to Thursday. We had Friday, Saturday, and Sunday left to work the land they'd lent us. [*To* FIRST SOLDIER] There's no way to get ahead there, brother. You're like a beast of burden.
9. FIRST SOLDIER. Do you think it's any different with United Fruit?

10. BOATMAN. Of course. At United Fruit you're a worker. You work for a specific number of hours and you get paid for those hours. That's all. You don't have to worry about the cow getting sick or the support beam of the hut rotting away or whether it didn't rain or it rained so much everything rotted. No, sir. You're free.

11. FIRST SOLDIER. But they can fire you. On the plantation you were secure, but over there . . .

12. BOATMAN. What the hell. There are other places. They're building railroads and highways and they're drilling for oil. They need these hands for all of that.

13. SECOND SOLDIER. They carried out a recruiting raid in the village and the Corporal jumped me.

14. DRUMMER. Where are you from?

15. SECOND SOLDIER. From up there, from the mountain.

16. DRUMMER. Are you on the run from some plantation, perhaps, drifting? There are lots of tramps around.

17. SECOND SOLDIER. No, sir, I'm not a runaway. They kicked us off the farm. It turned out that someone else owned the place.

18. DRUMMER. Aha.

19. SECOND SOLDIER [*To the audience*]. A regular army was being organized for the first time in this country, an institution to provide an armed defense for our homeland and our flag.

20. DRUMMER. You're going to be a soldier. Can you read?

21. SECOND SOLDIER. No, sir.

22. BOATMAN [*To the audience*]. The first major strikes had broken out against the Tropical Oil Company in Barrancabermeja. They were recruiting peasants to put down the workers.

23. DRUMMER. Dismissed!

24. FIRST SOLDIER. Well, brother, write to me once in a while.

25. BOATMAN. There, I'll learn to read and write. One of these days, you'll see, you'll be getting a sheet of paper covered in scribbles. You're staying, aren't you?

26. FIRST SOLDIER. I'm all right here. I like fighting for my country. One of these days I'll be promoted and I'll be a corporal . . .

27. DRUMMER [*To the audience*]. Corporals didn't earn much, but the job was pretty secure. He could make sergeant. And if he had what it took, he could even become an officer. There have been a number of instances, like General Cortés Vargas, for example.

28. SECOND SOLDIER. I didn't mind it at all when they took me to the capital and put me in the barracks. In fact, I was glad to go. What I didn't want to do was go back into that bush.

29. DRUMMER. One minute to get ready.

30. FIRST SOLDIER. I never got a letter. Not one. I'm sure he didn't have any spare time left to learn how to write. Two years later they brought a whole lot of recruits and . . . how could I have guessed that we'd be shipped out with those recruits to break a workers' strike at the UFC, no less . . . the company that paid so well . . . United Fruit . . .

SOLDIERS 41

31. DRUMMER. Fall in!
32. FIRST SOLDIER. "On March 30, 1899: the United Fruit Company, a banana company, was incorporated in the State of New Jersey . . ."
33. BOATMAN. The United Fruit Company.
34. DRUMMER. The UFC.
35. SECOND SOLDIER. The UFC.
36. FIRST SOLDIER. "With a declared capital of US$ 20,000,000. This Company will grow bananas and export them, in Santo Domingo, Honduras, Nicaragua, Guatemala, Costa Rica, Panama, Cuba, Jamaica, Puerto Rico, Dutch Guiana, Ecuador, and the banana region of Colombia . . ."
37. SECOND SOLDIER. "As part of its support for Latin American governments, the United Fruit Company is investing part of its profits as follows: in 1927 the Company buys the following tracts of land: Guatemala: 27,000 acres. Honduras: 28,000 acres. Costa Rica: 27,000 acres. Nicaragua: 18,000 acres. Jamaica: 15,000 acres. And in the Republic of Colombia it buys 256,000 acres of land in the banana region and in Urabá for the sum of $30,000,000.00."
38. FIRST SOLDIER. "Conscious of the role that capital investments must play in society, the UFC is also helping the Latin American economy by exploiting the following products: sugar, cacao, hemp, rubber latex, quinine, rubber, softwoods, oilseed, cotton, hardwood and African palm . . . Total annual profits from these products: US$120,000,000."
39. BOATMAN. US$ 120,000,000.
40. DRUMMER. US$ 120,000,000.
41. SECOND SOLDIER. US$ 120,000,000.
42. BOATMAN. Total salaries paid that same year: US$ 2,000,000.
43. MILITARY ORDERS. Set up the platform! On the double! . . .
44. DRUMMER [As PRESIDENT]. ". . . And, upon examining my government's program, it can be said that today the country is clearly and decidedly on the road to progress. There are ample opportunities for everyone. The policy of industrial growth is moving forward at the same pace as the full employment of human resources. It should be said that our country's development is due in large part to the investment plan and to the loans extended by U.S. government aid agencies. This rapid progress of our country's private sector favors the working class in particular. Never before had Colombian workers enjoyed such high salaries and such a high standard of living as the ones they enjoy at present. We can even state quite confidently that the working class in our country is the direct beneficiary of the nation's economic progress. It's because of the conclusions of this study conducted by my government, that, at this gathering of artisans, peasants, and workers in Bolívar Square, and making our voice heard in every corner of our homeland, we once more offer up our beloved Colombian nation to the omnipotent guidance and protection of the Sacred Heart of Jesus."
46. SOLDIERS. Speech by president Miguel Abadía Méndez, October 5, 1928.
47. MILITARY ORDERS. To the barge!

48. BOATMAN. A battalion of 200 enthusiastic soldiers climb aboard the barges that are going up the Magdalena River toward the Banana Region.

49. MILITARY ORDERS. To the barge.

50. SECOND SOLDIER. Hello . . .

51. FIRST SOLDIER. Are you awake?

52. SECOND SOLDIER. No.

53. FIRST SOLDIER. Are you awake?

54. SECOND SOLDIER. Yes. My blanket got soaked in the rain.

55. FIRST SOLDIER. I haven't been able to sleep, either.

56. SECOND SOLDIER. Why is it raining so hard if it isn't the rainy season?

57. FIRST SOLDIER. No. It isn't. Do you have any cigarettes?

58. SECOND SOLDIER. Aw hell. They all got wet.

59. FIRST SOLDIER. It doesn't matter.

60. SECOND SOLDIER. They won't light.

61. FIRST SOLDIER. It doesn't matter.

62. SECOND SOLDIER. They won't light. [*He hands him the cigarettes.* FIRST SOLDIER *shoves him.*] What's the matter with you?

63. FIRST SOLDIER. I've been thinking about what can happen to us.

64. SECOND SOLDIER. Are you afraid? The Lieutenant said they had weapons, but I don't think so.

65. FIRST SOLDIER. Why did they send us?

66. SECOND SOLDIER. Didn't you hear what the Lieutenant said? They don't want to work. They left their farms and they're pillaging the villages.

67. FIRST SOLDIER. It's a strike.

68. SECOND SOLDIER. Yes, but it's not legal, and they also want a raise.

69. FIRST SOLDIER. They're on strike.

70. SECOND SOLDIER. And we've been sent to break the strike.

71. FIRST SOLDIER. That's what I don't like; that's not our job.

72. SECOND SOLDIER. What isn't?

73. FIRST SOLDIER. Strikebreaking.

74. SECOND SOLDIER. We have to do just about anything we're told. I'm glad we came. I've never been to this part of the country, and being in the field is better than sitting around the barracks. There's no muster, no roll call, and they can't throw us in the stockade.

75. FIRST SOLDIER. Yes, they can.

76. SECOND SOLDIER. How can they if we're in the field?

77. FIRST SOLDIER. I don't know, but they can.

78. SECOND SOLDIER. Anyway, it's better than being in the barracks.

79. FIRST SOLDIER. Yes, but it's not right.

80. SECOND SOLDIER. What does it matter whether it's right or wrong? What matters is that we're out in the field and not in the barracks.

81. FIRST SOLDIER. Yes, it matters.

82. SECOND SOLDIER. Your problem is that you're afraid.

83. FIRST SOLDIER. What do mean, afraid?

84. SECOND SOLDIER. So, what are you worrying about then?

85. FIRST SOLDIER. Because if it is a strike, we have to respect it and not get involved.

86. SECOND SOLDIER. They're the ones who should be showing respect.
87. FIRST SOLDIER. For whom?
88. SECOND SOLDIER. For us, for the authorities.
89. FIRST SOLDIER. We're not authorities. We're soldiers. The police are authorities.
90. SECOND SOLDIER. All right, but the police are useless, that's why they're sending us.
91. FIRST SOLDIER. Truth is, the police can't handle them.
92. SECOND SOLDIER. You're afraid.
93. FIRST SOLDIER. Hell no . . . I'm not afraid. It's just that I don't like this business of strike-breaking.
94. SECOND SOLDIER. They don't have the right . . .
95. FIRST SOLDIER. Perhaps they are right.
96. SECOND SOLDIER. They're not right.
97. FIRST SOLDIER. What do you know?
98. SECOND SOLDIER. The Lieutenant said so.
99. FIRST SOLDIER. The Lieutenant doesn't know shit.
100. SECOND SOLDIER. That's true. Help me squeeze the blanket.
101. BOATMAN [*Reading from a document*]

> 1. To recognize us as Company workers through a labor contract and to do away with the system of foremen, in accordance with Colombian law.
> 2. To pay us for our day off, on Sundays, and grant compensation for work-related injuries and provide medical services, as required by Colombian law.
> 3. We are asking for a 50% raise in the minimum wage, which is currently 80 cents.
> 4. To build schools, in accordance with Colombian laws, since the only school there was has been turned into a bar.
> 5. To do away with the company store and the voucher system and allow other stores to open and workers to shop wherever they wish. [*Fade out*]
>
> > La Ciénaga, October 6, 1928. Signed by all the representatives of the Workers' Trade Union of the Company.

102. SECOND SOLDIER. What about your blanket? Didn't you cover yourself with your blanket?
103. FIRST SOLDIER. No.
104. SECOND SOLDIER. You're soaked.
105. FIRST SOLDIER. It doesn't matter.
106. 2ND SOLDIER. What did you do with the blanket?
107. FIRST SOLDIER. I wrapped my gun in it so it wouldn't get wet.
108. BOATMAN. Battalion!

109. FIRST SOLDIER. We're there.
110. SECOND SOLDIER. There where?
111. FIRST SOLDIER. In the banana region.
112. SECOND SOLDIER. This is the banana region?
113. FIRST SOLDIER. Yes, it is.
114. SECOND SOLDIER. I imagined it to be different.
115. BOATMAN. Everyone off the boat!
116. DRUMMER [*As* UNITED FRUIT COMPANY MANAGER]. "Santa Marta, November 12, 1928. Your Excellency Dr. Miguel Abadía Méndez, President of the Republic, Bogotá stop I hasten respectfully to inform you situation developing in Banana Region plantations looks serious stop Behind labor movement and salary demands, irresponsible elements threatening to murder persons who want to work stop Governor willing to help but unable to do so lacking adequate police force stop Commanders Ciénaga, Cartagena, and Santa Marta regiments awaiting your orders and War Minister's instructions stop Company is willing to cooperate with the government to avoid having to take drastic measures stop Yours truly, Thomas Bradshaw, Manager, United Fruit Company, Santa Marta, November 1928."
117. MILITARY ORDERS. Battalion, halt!
117A. THE SOLDIERS. "Work."
118. BOATMAN. The army was now at the Company's disposal: The army . . .
119. DRUMMER. As detailed, occupy your positions in the zone, on the double! [*The* SOLDIERS *take the* BOATMAN *away.*] Fall in!
120. SECOND SOLDIER. Where can we go to get a cup of coffee?
121. FIRST SOLDIER. To the station, maybe.
122. DRUMMER. Fall . . . in!
123. SECOND SOLDIER. What station? Isn't there an army barracks here?
124. DRUMMER. You! Eyes forward!
125. FIRST SOLDIER. What there is here is bananas.
126. DRUMMER. Number!
127. FIRST SOLDIER. . . . Twenty-six. Last one!
128. DRUMMER. Dismissed. One minute to get changed!
129. FIRST SOLDIER. I think they're putting us to work.
130. SECOND SOLDIER. To work? We're not here for that.
131. FIRST SOLDIER. We're here for anything and everything.
132. SECOND SOLDIER. We're on field duty.
133. FIRST SOLDIER. That doesn't matter.
134. BOATMAN. The soldiers were given orders to cut and pack the bananas, with the help of scabs.
135. DRUMMER [*To the* SOLDIERS]. We can't just let the bananas rot. [*To the* BOATMAN] We can't just let the bananas rot.
136. BOATMAN. It's worse to let the people rot. [*The* SOLDIERS *get to work*] [*To the audience*] The strikers were silently witnessing the destruction of their movement.
137. FIRST SOLDIER. Shit! They should pay us for this. It's very hard work.

138. BOATMAN. It's a good thing you realize that, comrade. That's why we're asking for a wage increase.

139. SECOND SOLDIER. I'm not your comrade!

140. BOATMAN. Besides they pay in vouchers. We're asking to be paid in cash. Don't you think that's fair?

141. DRUMMER. Regarding the wage increase, dealt with in item four of the demands: This could not be accepted by the Company because it was not the Company's problem but the contractors'. It is subject to the inexorable law of supply and demand, and neither the Company, nor the president of the Republic, nor God, nor the devil himself has any control over that law. (*Exit*)

142. FIRST SOLDIER. What do you do with the vouchers?

143. BOATMAN. We have to exchange them in the company store for things they bring from over there. That way, the boats that carry the bananas don't come back empty.

144. FIRST SOLDIER. It's a perfect business arrangement.

145. BOATMAN. So it is, comrade.

146. FIRST SOLDIER. Tell me something. Do you know my brother?

147. BOATMAN. What brother?

148. FIRST SOLDIER. My brother.

149. BOATMAN. What's his name?

[*Enter the* DRUMMER.]

150. SECOND SOLDIER. I've told you we're nobody's comrades.

151. DRUMMER [*To the* SOLDIERS]. To the railway cars . . . On the double . . . Left . . . right . . . left . . . right. [*To the audience*] Regarding the company stores, which, according to item five of the petition, should be shut down, this demand was rejected because it conspires against the same law invoked by the petitioners, namely the unalterable law guaranteeing freedom of commerce.

152. BOATMAN [*To the audience*]. How can the region develop if people are forced to buy what the company wants them to buy when and where the company wants them to buy it?

153. SECOND SOLDIER. The fact is, they don't like to work. Carrying big bundles is hard work.

154. BOATMAN [*To the audience*]. If we're asking for a collective agreement it's because we want to work, but not under the conditions they feel like imposing.

155. DRUMMER [*To the audience*]. As for collective agreements, as demanded in item eight of the petition, they were denied, because it was materially impossible to make them conform to current practice.

156. BOATMAN. And you're defending them. You, who are just like us.

157. SECOND SOLDIER. We're not civilians.

158. BOATMAN. Here, read this, and you'll understand. [*Offers fliers to the* SOLDIERS.]

159. SECOND SOLDIER. I can't read . . .

160. BOATMAN. Your buddy can read it to you. He knows how to read . . .

161. DRUMMER. Subversive fliers were printed on the clandestine press belonging to a certain Mahecha, a member of the Revolutionary Socialist Party.

162. FIRST SOLDIER. [*Snatching the paper from the* BOATMAN *and reading aloud*] Don't fear the bayonets, don't fear the guns, because they are in the hands of your class brethren and they will not fire upon you.

163. DRUMMER. The strikers, urged on by agents of subversion, tried to demoralize the soldiers.

164. BOATMAN. Colombian soldier: you know that your leaders and your officers live openly in an evil alliance with the Americans, in their mansions in this zone. With those who first steal our wealth and then take over our land. Don't forget Panama. Turn your weapons against the pirates and against those Colombian Judases who are selling out their country . . .

165. DRUMMER. The owner of the plantation and partner in the United Fruit Company, Eduardo Noguera, was obliged to intervene.

166. FIRST SOLDIER. My brother was going to learn how to read . . . Say: you must know my brother . . .

167. DRUMMER. And this sheet dated December 2nd, signed by the Communist Tomás Uribe Márquez: "We have to organize and establish fraternal links with the soldiers . . . We have to organize a raid on the jail to free our imprisoned comrades . . ." Halt!

168. SECOND SOLDIER. Mr. Eduardo Noguera was going to fire on the strikers, but we took away his revolver before he could shoot and we restored the peace.

169. FIRST SOLDIER. Then the strikers decided to take Noguera and punish him, Captain.

170. SECOND SOLDIER. With no intention of laying a hand on the Army, not on one single button of a single uniform.

171. MILITARY ORDERS. Back to quarters! [*The soldiers begin to hum a song, "Little soldiers, back to quarters".*]

172. BOATMAN. Colonel Páramo, official agent of the United Fruit Company, addresses this telegram on December 5, 1928, to General Rengifo, Minister of War.

173. DRUMMER. "General Cortés Vargas is in an extremely delicate position stop There are four thousand armed strikers stop They have concentrated in the area of Ciénaga, and trains, rolling stock, and single rail cars are in their hands stop Communists in office in every town and village stop I await your orders."

174. BOATMAN. The telegram lied. There were never any communists in authority anywhere . . . The attempts at fraternizing between workers and soldiers caused the higher echelons to panic . . . and the panic led them to make up all sorts of fantastic stories.

175. FIRST SOLDIER. Rub-a-dub-rub-a-rub-a-rub-a-rub-a-dub.

176. SECOND SOLDIER. Soldiers back to quarters.

177. FIRST SOLDIER. Who are they going to defend? Who are they going to punish?

178. SECOND SOLDIER. Can't know, can't ask.
179. FIRST SOLDIER. All peasants report to barracks for the Colonel's calling you.
180. SECOND SOLDIER. Who are they going to defend? Who are they going to punish?
181. FIRST SOLDIER. Can't know, can't ask. To the barracks, without talking, without knowing, without asking.
182. SECOND SOLDIER. My boots are full of water.
183. FIRST SOLDIER. That way they'll get soft.
184. SECOND SOLDIER. And then the leather will harden again in the sun. We should have our coffee here.
185. FIRST SOLDIER. We have to get to the Sevilla station on the double.
186. SECOND SOLDIER. Why's that? Isn't there a train right here?
187. FIRST SOLDIER. Can't you see they've sabotaged it? Over there, they messed up the rails.
188. SECOND SOLDIER. Where the hell are we going to get some coffee?
189. FIRST SOLDIER. At the station, maybe.
190. SECOND SOLDIER. We should camp here and have our coffee. Then we can go wherever they want us to go.
191. FIRST SOLDIER. We have to be at the station when the train gets there.
192. SECOND SOLDIER. What train?
193. FIRST SOLDIER. The one that's taking us to Ciénaga.
194. SECOND SOLDIER. But they should let us have our coffee here.
195. MILITARY ORDERS. Battalion! Fall in!
196. SECOND SOLDIER. There he goes again. He won't let up, that major. Now we'll have to move along on an empty stomach.
197. FIRST SOLDIER. They're forming ranks already.
198. SECOND SOLDIER. Why should we be forming ranks?
199. FIRST SOLDIER. For roll call, again.
200. SECOND SOLDIER. What? Are they afraid that some draftee's been kidnapped?
201. FIRST SOLDIER. No. Not that he's been kidnapped. That he's taken off.
202. SECOND SOLDIER. Taken off?
203. MILITARY ORDERS. Battalion, fall in!
204. SECOND SOLDIER. What's someone going to take off for when he's away from barracks? That doesn't make sense. You take off when you're inside.
205. FIRST SOLDIER. That someone's deserted, I'd say.
206. SECOND SOLDIER. Deserted? You mean there might be a deserter?
207. FIRST SOLDIER. Yeah, same thing.
208. SECOND SOLDIER. But there can't be deserters when one's on detail. Soldiers desert in wartime, and we're not at war, we're just on detail.
209. FIRST SOLDIER. All right. That someone's run away, then, that someone left because he doesn't want to take part in all this.
210. MILITARY ORDERS. Bugle call. [*The soldiers continue marching.*]

211. SECOND SOLDIER. What's with your brother?
212. FIRST SOLDIER. I have a brother in these parts.
213. SECOND SOLDIER. How do you know?
214. FIRST SOLDIER. He came here about two years ago.
215. SECOND SOLDIER. He's probably somewhere else by now.
216. FIRST SOLDIER. Who knows . . .
217. SECOND SOLDIER. Do you think they're armed?
218. FIRST SOLDIER. No. They don't have any weapons.
219. SECOND SOLDIER. This thing's going to be easy.
220. . . .

and

221. BOTH SOLDIERS [*Announcing out loud*]. The station.
222. BOATMAN. December 1928. The United Fruit Company currently owns the following rail lines, which it uses to carry its products: Northern Railway, the Trujillo Railroad Company, the Ferrocarril Central de Guatemala, the International Railways of Central America, the Guayaquil Railroad Company, and the Santa Marta Railroad Company.
223. SECOND SOLDIER. Want some more coffee?
224. FIRST SOLDIER. No.
225. SECOND SOLDIER. I'm still hungry.
226. FIRST SOLDIER. Got any smokes left?
227. SECOND SOLDIER. They're still wet.
228. FIRST SOLDIER. It doesn't matter.
229. SECOND SOLDIER. How can you enjoy chewing it?
230. FIRST SOLDIER. It takes the edge off hunger.
231. SECOND SOLDIER. How do you know that?
232. FIRST SOLDIER. I learned it in my village.
233. SECOND SOLDIER. Wasn't there any food there either?
234. FIRST SOLDIER. No.
235. SECOND SOLDIER. I wonder when the train will get here.
236. FIRST SOLDIER. There's no knowing. The engineers are on strike.
237. SECOND SOLDIER. Why?
238. FIRST SOLDIER. Everybody's on strike.
239. SECOND SOLDIER. So who's going to run the train?
240. FIRST SOLDIER. I guess we'll have to make them do it.
241. SECOND SOLDIER. So we'll make them!
242. FIRST SOLDIER. Why the hell do we have to force them?
243. SECOND SOLDIER. Because if the train doesn't run, then we won't be able to get to Ciénaga to end the strike.
244. FIRST SOLDIER. But we shouldn't have to break the strike!
245. SECOND SOLDIER. Then we'd be stuck in the barracks all the time.
246. FIRST SOLDIER. Better to be stuck in the barracks all the time.
247. SECOND SOLDIER. So they throw us in the stockade.
248. BOTH SOLDIERS [*Announcing out loud*]. The train.
249. FIRST SOLDIER. Did you see the ones riding in first class?
250. SECOND SOLDIER. No.

251. FIRST SOLDIER. Didn't you see that fellow all decked out in the explorer's outfit, riding between Captain Guarín and Captain Garavito?
252. SECOND SOLDIER. Who is he?
253. FIRST SOLDIER. The Company overseer.
254. SECOND SOLDIER. So what?
255. FIRST SOLDIER. So, we're still working for the Company.
256. SECOND SOLDIER. Is the Company very wealthy?
257. FIRST SOLDIER. Yes.
258. SECOND SOLDIER. Is it the wealthiest company in the world?
259. FIRST SOLDIER. Yes.
260. SECOND SOLDIER. Poor people have always worked for the rich.
261. FIRST SOLDIER. But the Army isn't poor.
262. SECOND SOLDIER. Then why is the food they give us so bad?
263. FIRST SOLDIER. Because the officers pocket the money. Captain Garavito's wife has a store where she sells what he takes out of the warehouse.
264. SECOND SOLDIER. Does the Major know this?
265. FIRST SOLDIER. The Major steals too.
266. SECOND SOLDIER. I don't believe that.
267. FIRST SOLDIER. He steals more than anybody else.
268. SECOND SOLDIER. But he steals from the government, not from us, like that Captain Garavito.
269. FIRST SOLDIER. He's stealing from our fatherland. That's far more serious.
270. SECOND SOLDIER. It's not the government that stands for the fatherland. The flag does.
271. FIRST SOLDIER. Had you ever been on a train?
272. SECOND SOLDIER. No. This is the first time. I'd only watched them go by.
273. FIRST SOLDIER. Anyway, it's better than marching on the double.
274. SECOND SOLDIER. Had you been on a train before?
275. FIRST SOLDIER. Many times.
276. SECOND SOLDIER. Have you travelled much?
277. FIRST SOLDIER. Yes. I've been as far as Puerto Colombia.
278. BOATMAN [*As* INSPECTOR MARTINEZ]. I have ascertained the following: despite the fact that their living conditions are shameful, the workers have limited their demands to a reasonable wage increase. The governor approached the manager of the United Fruit Company, offering to act as mediator, but the manager argued that if he raised their wages the workers would keep on going out on strike, because they'd be able to get what they want by striking. The United Fruit Company, according to General Cortés Vargas and through its paid agents inside the Army and the government, are making the strike appear to be a subversive conspiracy ...
279. BOTH SOLDIERS. Military Orders. [*They arrest Martínez*].
280. BOATMAN. And the Labor Inspector of the Banana region was dismissed, arrested and put on trial by order of the Superintendent of the UFC. [*He is taken away.*]

281. BOTH SOLDIERS. "The town."
282. SECOND SOLDIER. The town looks deserted.
283. FIRST SOLDIER. That's because they know what we're here for and they're mad at us.
284. SECOND SOLDIER. Why should they be mad at us? It's not our fault.
285. FIRST SOLDIER. Perhaps.
286. SECOND SOLDIER. The strikers are to blame.
287. FIRST SOLDIER. No, not the strikers. The Company.
288. SECOND SOLDIER. O.K., but not us.
289. FIRST SOLDIER. Perhaps.
290. SECOND SOLDIER. This is a really ugly town.
291. FIRST SOLDIER. They all look the same, really.
292. SECOND SOLDIER. But this one is uglier. I had never seen walls covered in salt. The people here don't have to go and buy salt. All they have to do is scrape the walls.
293. FIRST SOLDIER. You can't eat that salt.
294. SECOND SOLDIER. Why?
295. FIRST SOLDIER. I don't know. You can't, that's all.
296. DRUMMER. Military Orders. [*Bugle call. The two soldiers continue marching.*]
297. SECOND SOLDIER. Do you think we'll get a chance to stop and check out the women?
298. FIRST SOLDIER. I doubt it.
299. SECOND SOLDIER. But *they* can go get drunk with women. Captain Garavito and Captain Guarín had themselves a good time in one of the rail cars.
300. FIRST SOLDIER. They are officers. A uniform's a uniform.
301. SECOND SOLDIER. They weren't in uniform. They were stark naked. The women, too.
302. FIRST SOLDIER. Those women don't come cheap.
303. SECOND SOLDIER. No harm in trying. Where do you think we'll be setting up camp?
304. FIRST SOLDIER. In the Company's fields.
305. SECOND SOLDIER. Isn't there a barracks here?
306. FIRST SOLDIER. I don't know. I heard someone say that they're going to lock us up in the Company's work camps to have us close by.
307. SECOND SOLDIER. Do they eat well in those camps?
308. FIRST SOLDIER. They eat well wherever they go.
309. SECOND SOLDIER. But they have to give us good food because we're going to defend them.
310. FIRST SOLDIER. That's what I don't like.
311. SECOND SOLDIER. Eating well?
312. FIRST SOLDIER. I'd like to be back home in my village, even if I had nothing but shit to eat.
313. SECOND SOLDIER. I wouldn't. Hey, look, there's a whorehouse on that corner.

SOLDIERS

314. FIRST SOLDIER. Where?
315. SECOND SOLDIER. There, next to the sign that says . . .
316. FIRST SOLDIER. "Hotel Europa." What if it isn't a whorehouse?
317. SECOND SOLDIER. It seems to be. I'm going to sneak over there.
318. FIRST SOLDIER. There's roll call at base camp.
319. SECOND SOLDIER. I'll be back in time.
320. FIRST SOLDIER. If they catch you they'll throw you in the stockade.
321. SECOND SOLDIER. They can't throw me in the stockade because we're in the field.
322. FIRST SOLDIER. Well, they'll throw the book at you anyway.
323. SECOND SOLDIER. I'm really quick. Got two pesos? [*The* SOLDIER *disappears with a woman through the door of the house.*]
324. BOTH SOLDIERS. "The massacre." [*The soldiers change out of their uniforms into the workclothes of banana workers. The song "Little soldiers, back to quarters" can be heard. The song fades out.*]
325. DRUMMER [*As a* MILITARY FIGURE]. "There is subversive literature circulating everywhere, printed on the press of the communist Mahecha. And there have already been cases of troops fraternizing with the rioters, although no instance of desertion has been confirmed. Some newspapers are slandering the Army, saying that we are taking orders from the United Fruit Company. The mayor of Ciénaga is protecting the mutineers; the governor is hesitating. The city has been taken over by mobs, who are planning to march 5,000 strong on Santa Marta. If we allow the movement to grow to such proportions, no one can stop it. Alarming news is coming in from everywhere, but I find it hard to issue orders, because the telegraph personnel all sympathize with the mutineers. I have received word that U.S. warships are approaching Santa Marta. My sense of honor as a military officer obliges me to find a way to prevent foreign troops from desecrating our nation's soil. General Carlos Cortés Vargas, Regional Commander."

[*He disappears, then reappears as the* PRESIDENT OF THE REPUBLIC.]

"The President of the Republic, in the exercise of his legal faculties and *Considering*: First.—That the situation in the Banana Region with respect to public order has deteriorated over the past several days due to the conflict among the workers. Second.—That the movement, which was at first believed to involve peaceful workers, has turned to violent demonstrations, looting and armed robbery. Third.—That the civil authorities of the Region have found it impossible to restrain these excesses because they lack the necessary constitutional powers, *Therefore:* Article 1.—General Carlos Cortés Vargas is named Civil and Military Head of the Province of Magdalena. Article 2.—General Cortés Vargas shall be vested with the authority and the power to resolve the problem of public order, taking whatever measures he may consider necessary. Miguel Abadía Méndez, President of the Republic."

[*Drum roll.*]

326. FIRST SOLDIER [*As a* WORKER]. Comrades, it's midnight and the train isn't here yet. What are we waiting for?

327. BOATMAN. Comrades, we have been asked to wait here for the governor, who should be arriving on the next train. The governor has already reached a negotiated settlement with the Company and he is coming here, to the town of Ciénaga, to sign an agreement with us.

328. DRUMMER. The governor only got as far as the place called Red Wells. There he was stopped by Mr. César Riascos, an employee of the UFC, who gave him some alarming news. Armed workers were waiting for him at the station and his life was in danger.

329. VOICE GIVING AN ORDER. Siren.

330. FIRST SOLDIER [*As a* WORKER]. If we are going to reach an agreement with the governor, why are there machine guns on the roof of the station? Why are the troops closing off the streets everywhere?

331. SECOND SOLDIER [*Also as a* WORKER]. We don't have anything against the Army. Our quarrel is with the UFC.

332. FIRST SOLDIER. Why doesn't the Army join us against United Fruit?

333. SECOND SOLDIER. The soldiers' duty is to defend our country.

334. FIRST SOLDIER. Who is our country? We or United Fruit?

335. BOATMAN. We're not fighting the government; everything we're asking for is within the law.

336. FIRST SOLDIER. But the law can be bought and sold. United Fruit bought it.

337. DRUMMER [*As a* COMPANY MANAGER]. The Company wishes it to be known that if conditions for foreign investment are not favorable here, it will be forced to leave the country.

338. FIRST SOLDIER. What is it they need? Slaves?

339. DRUMMER [*As a* GENERAL]. The withdrawal of the Company would bring ruin to the Atlantic Coast and do serious damage to the nation's finances.

340. FIRST SOLDIER. Annual income of the Company: 120 million dollars. Wages paid out: 2 million. All we are asking for is a wage increase. A minimum increase, a fair increase. Let the governor come. Where are they going to find profits like these? Where can they go?

341. DRUMMER [*As* MANAGER]. It's a big world out there, gentlemen, and, as we explained in several articles in *El Tiempo* and *El Espectador*; we can go to Africa, to India, to Indochina, to China or to Cochinchina . . . And you will sink into misery.

342. FIRST SOLDIER. Let them go.

343. SECOND SOLDIER. And who will give us work?

344. BOATMAN. Yes. Who'll give us work? How will we earn a living?

345. FIRST SOLDIER. My question is: Who does the work? Who harvests the bananas? Them or us?

346. BOTH. We do.

347. FIRST SOLDIER. I ask you, comrades, who does the work? Them or us?

348. EVERYONE. We do.
349. FIRST SOLDIER. Who harvests the bananas? Them or us?
350. EVERYONE. We do.
351. DRUMMER [As GENERAL]. "Decree No. 4: After all due consideration by the President of the Republic in the exercise of his legitimate authority, the incendiary and murderous rioters of the Banana Region are hereby declared outlaws. Therefore, the forces of order are empowered to punish by force of arms all those caught in the act of burning, looting or robbing. The Civil and Military Chief of the Province of Santa Marta, General Carlos Cortés Vargas. Major Enrique García Izasa, Secretary."
352. FIRST SOLDIER. Down with that decree.
353. BOATMAN. We don't want any decrees. We want to negotiate with the governor.
354. DRUMMER. Halt. You have five minutes to withdraw from here.
355. BOATMAN. The governor is on his way over here to negotiate with us.
356. SECOND SOLDIER. They've got us surrounded.
357. DRUMMER. One minute is up.
358. SECOND SOLDIER. They've tricked us. [To the BOATMAN] Comrade, let's give the order for the people to leave.
359. BOATMAN. There are more than 3,500 of us, including women and children. We can't be out of here in five minutes. They're trying to scare us.
360. FIRST SOLDIER. We can't turn back. The struggle is just beginning, and we're on the front line.
361. DRUMMER. Two minutes.
362. SECOND SOLDIER. Don't shoot, comrades. Long live the Army!
363. FIRST SOLDIER. Be strong, comrades. Don't be intimidated.
364. DRUMMER. Three minutes . . . Four minutes.
365. BOATMAN. Hey, motherfucker, you can have that extra minute. We're giving it to you. [Shooting breaks out.]
366. FIRST SOLDIER. I fired until my rifle overheated . . . Then they forced us to fix bayonets and roam the streets. The officers went ahead lighting the way with flashlights. Some of them would use their bayonets to finish off the wounded. They had to be cleared away. They made us pile them up like bunches of bananas. Then the trains would carry them up to the coast and they dumped them in the water like rejected fruit. Others were thrown into long, freshly dug ditches. Those death trains just kept on rolling by until dawn.
367. SECOND SOLDIER. . . . Halt. I looked for you everywhere. I didn't have time to get back to camp . . . I was afraid, I was afraid when I heard all that shooting and I stayed with her. Why did they kill them? You were right. They were unarmed.
368. FIRST SOLDIER. General Cortés Vargas was drunk when he arrived at camp last night. Captain Guarín and Captain Garavito were with him. The women who came in with them went into the Company employees' club. They made us line up along the fence as if they were going to shoot us, and the General said: "Now we're going to get this business over and done with

once and for all. The officers will man the machine guns and you are going to shoot. The officers are going to be right behind you, on the roof of the train station. If you don't fire, the officers will shoot you. Understood?

369. SECOND SOLDIER. It's not your fault. You had to do it.
370. FIRST SOLDIER. No, I didn't.
371. SECOND SOLDIER. You had to follow orders.
372. FIRST SOLDIER. My brother was there, I know he was.
373. SECOND SOLDIER. Did you see him? Did you see your brother?
374. FIRST SOLDIER. No, I didn't see him . . . But I know he was there.
375. SECOND SOLDIER. If you didn't see him, he's not there.
376. VOICE GIVING ORDERS. Fall in!
377. SECOND SOLDIER. What for?
378. FIRST SOLDIER. To count us again.
379. DRUMMER. Attention! Shoulder arms!
380. SECOND SOLDIER [*Whispering*]. Are they afraid that someone's deserted?
381. DRUMMER. Number!
382. SOLDIERS [*count up to 26*].
383. SECOND SOLDIER. How could anyone have deserted if they had the officers' machine guns right behind them?
384. FIRST SOLDIER. They all looked like him . . .
385. SECOND SOLDIER. Like whom?
386. FIRST SOLDIER. Like my brother.
387. DRUMMER. Soldier number 2, on the left . . . One, two, three, four . . . On December 5 there was roll call in the camp and you didn't answer . . . Do you know what we call that? Desertion!
388. SECOND SOLDIER. I didn't mean to desert!
389. DRUMMER. Quiet! Do you know what the penalty is for deserting during armed action? Death by firing squad! [*Pause.*]
390. FIRST SOLDIER. Attention!
391. DRUMMER. The duty of a soldier is not only to defend his Country, but also to maintain order, understand?
392. FIRST SOLDIER. Yes, Captain!
393. DRUMMER. After the action, you left the troops and you arrived late at muster with this deserter. Did you feel guilty? [FIRST SOLDIER *doesn't answer.*] Did you feel guilty of anything?
394. FIRST SOLDIER [*after a brief pause*]. No, Captain, Sir!
395. DRUMMER. Take away the deserter's weapons. [FIRST SOLDIER *walks over to* SECOND SOLDIER, *who hands him his rifle.*] Strip him of all Army insignia. [FIRST SOLDIER *takes his helmet, his cartridge case, and his shirt.*] No. 1, aim at the deserter! Ready! [*Pause*] Shoulder arms! [*To* SECOND SOLDIER] You will be brought up before a court martial!
396. SECOND SOLDIER. Me?
397. DRUMMER. Silence! [*To* FIRST SOLDIER.] You will be promoted to the rank of Corporal First Class and, according to your record, you have the potential to rise to the rank of commissioned officer, just like General Cortés

Vargas. Congratulations. [*He shakes his hand.*] You're in charge of the deserter... Understood?

398. FIRST SOLDIER [*Loudly, with the pride of success in his voice*]. Yes, Captain, Sir! [*Exit the* CAPTAIN.]

399. DRUMMER. The fighting force was increased substantially in the region. By order of the Ministry of War the troops' food budget was increased by one peso a head per day. This was a wise measure, thanks to which the soldiers were able to receive healthy and abundant food during the long siege. *Memoirs of General Cortés Vargas.*

400. BOATMAN. "The workers who started work during the state of siege were charged a head tax at the whim of the military authorities. The price of meat went up, the price of milk went up, the price of bread went up. The houses where the workers met in the village were expropriated and replaced with beautification works." *Memorandum of grievances* by Alberto Castrillón, labor leader of the Region.

401. FIRST SOLDIER and DRUMMER. "The courts-martial."

402. FIRST SOLDIER [*In the role of an* OFFICER, *addresses* SECOND SOLDIER). Where were you on the night of December 5th to 6th this year?

403. SECOND SOLDIER. I was there...

404. FIRST SOLDIER. Where?

405. DRUMMER [*to the* BOATMAN]. Who assured the workers that the troops would not fire?

406. BOATMAN. I did. I didn't think they'd fire on defenceless people who were just lying there, asleep. [*To the audience*] It was a mistake. We let down our guard.

407. FIRST SOLDIER [*To* SECOND SOLDIER]. Can't you say where you were? Did you hide? Were you afraid?

408. SECOND SOLDIER. I was not afraid. I didn't try to desert, either. That night I went into a whorehouse... It had been a long time since... you know what I mean, Your Honor...

409. DRUMMER. Didn't you hear the shooting?

410. FIRST SOLDIER. Didn't you hear the voice of duty that called you to your place in battle?

411. SECOND SOLDIER. They slipped me a potion that knocked me out, Your Honor...

412. DRUMMER. Can you recognize the person who gave you the drink in question?

413. SECOND SOLDIER. Yes, Your Honor. [*To the audience*] The defence attorney told me to say that. All that mattered to me was to get out of the Army and be a free man again. I wanted to get as far away as I could from this damned region.

414. DRUMMER [*to the* BOATMAN]. Did you really think that the troops would fraternize with the workers?

415. BOATMAN. Yes, I did.

416. DRUMMER. That is a communist theory.

417. BOATMAN. No. [*To the audience*] The conditions weren't right for fraternizing and we didn't study them carefully enough.

418. DRUMMER. You were one of the people who spoke of the mutineers marching on Santa Marta.

419. BOATMAN. I agreed that we, the workers of the Region, should demonstrate in Santa Marta. That is all. [*To the audience*] The decision to march was made spontaneously, at the last minute. That's why they were able to corner us in Ciénaga. If the march to Santa Marta had been planned ahead and carried out, the strike would have been successful. Of course it would have been successful.

420. DRUMMER & FIRST SOLDIER. The court martial has concluded.

421. FIRST SOLDIER. You are acquitted, because there was neither malice nor premeditation in your actions. Considering, however, that there was neglect of duty involved, you will receive a dishonorable discharge after the appropriate disciplinary sanction.

422. DRUMMER. In accordance with Decree No. 8 of December 18 of this year, covering wrongdoers, those aiding and abetting them, accomplices and accessories after the fact, as well as others who have broken the law because of or in connection with the subversive movement that has been active in this Province of Santa Marta, whatever the nature or disposition of the crimes and according to the declarations made against you by witnesses . . . *(Looks for list of witnesses.)*

413. BOATMAN [*To the audience*]. The witnesses are all high-ranking employees of the United Fruit Company.

414. DRUMMER [*Who has not found the list*]. Well, the witness list will be attached to the sentence . . . You stand accused of . . . wrongdoing, article 248. Crime of sedition, article 245. Arson and looting, article 861, with the aggravating circumstances indicated for criminals by the Penal Code, article 117, adding to your case paragraphs 1, 2, 3, 4, 5, 6, 7, and 8 of the Penal Code and, for the reasons quoted above, the court martial sentenced him to twenty-four years and eight months in prison. [*The four actors step downstage and say:*]

425. BOATMAN. Shortly afterwards, the Liberal party representatives for Magdalena in the Chamber of Deputies denounced the massacre and they managed to have the sentences suspended.

426. FIRST SOLDIER. The hegemony of the Conservatives crumbled.

427. SECOND SOLDIER. The United Fruit Company made a few concessions . . .

428. BOATMAN. And in labor legislation passed subsequently the right to strike and the right to organize were fully recognized.

429. DRUMMER. General Cortés Vargas received the following commendation: "The undersigned, with no distinction between liberal and conservative political allegiance, congratulate the national government for the strong, albeit painfully necessary, manner in which it dissolved the subversive uprising. The people will learn useful lessons from this painful chapter of our country's history that we all deplore while learning to distinguish between the benefits of peace and order and the senseless principles that seek an impossible equality rejected by the very laws of nature that watch over the per-

manent balance among all the forces that move the world." Signed by distinguished members of both political parties.

430. BOATMAN. We too hope that the people will learn the useful lessons they think they can gather from this episode.

—END—

Old Baldy

INTRODUCTORY NOTES

EL MONTE CALVO, A PLAY ABOUT THE PLIGHT OF COLOMBIAN VETerans of the Korean War, was published only thirteen years after the armistice that ended that conflict. It might seem unusual to use that historical footnote as the focus of a play written at the height of student unrest and guerrilla activity and an ongoing war of counterinsurgency—that is to say, when domestic rather than foreign wars were in the foreground. But we should recall that the Vietnam War was at its most intense, generating new opposition to U.S. military adventures, and that the internal war against the Marxist guerrilla armies was itself the focus of much opposition. It was thus a timely example, for those who wanted to draw attention to the exploitation of economically deprived young men by the army, to present the case of the hundreds of Korean veterans, who at the time received little or no recognition or support from the state.

Even at face value, the play speaks for itself. A war veteran and a retired musician-clown are living a hand-to-mouth existence on the margins of society. In the first part of the play, these two figures reminiscent of Beckett's Vladimir and Estragon review their lives while they wait for their own Godot, the Colonel, who, unlike Beckett's, does arrive, but only to bring chaos and death instead of help. The physically maimed veteran Sebastian and the psychologically maimed veteran known as the Colonel, whom Sebastian indulges, are tragic interlocutors of a nonsensical dialogue rooted in the trauma of the battlefield experience. Ultimately, the third protagonist, Canuto, is the victim of this absurdity. The author engages in a scathing denunciation of Colombia's involvement in the Korean conflict in 1951–1953, yes, but the Korean events are a pretext for a veiled criticism of the Vietnam War (the most recent U.S. venture into Asia) and a more overt criticism of social and economic conditions in Colombia. In the dialogue between Sebastian and Canuto, and in the reenacted battle nightmare that follows, two very timely issues are joined: the poverty and social displacement that leads many young men to join the army, and the role that military officers play, first in persuading their recruits of the nobility of their cause, and ultimately in exacting a terrible toll on their own civilian population.

The timing of the play, therefore, is significant. By the late 1960s there were at least three guerrilla groups active in Colombia, soon to be joined by a fourth,[1] and there was also considerable concern among students, intellectuals, artists, and social activists regarding U.S. involvement, the suspension of civil law in region after region of the country, and the effects of the counterinsurgency war on the civilian population caught in the middle. The reference in *Old Baldy* to the commander of the Batallón Colombia who became Minister of Defence is likely an allusion to Alberto Ruiz Novoa, who had cut his teeth as an officer in Korea and now headed counterinsurgency planning.[2]

Colombia had a token participation in the forces fighting under the United Nations flag against North Korean and Chinese troops. A patrol frigate, the 1,300-ton *Almirante Padilla* joined the U.N. fleet operating from Japan in late May 1951.[3] On 20 June, the first Colombian infantry battalion arrived in Korea and on 13 October they took a hill south of Kumsong.[4] This active involvement in the "police action" in Korea was no coincidence. A note in the *New York Times* suggests that Colombia's practical support for the action could have had some bearing on trade opportunities with the United States.[5] In 1951, Colombia was still in the throes of the *Violencia* that engulfed the country in 1948, but the U.S. signalled its support for the government in quelling the Liberal guerrillas, some of whom were already breaking with the Liberal Party over its compromises and forming Marxist guerrilla groups. It also is conceivable that a foreign war could contribute to reinforcing the credibility of the central government and its armed forces.

Four battalions served in Korea, each about one thousand strong: the First, June 1951 to July 1952; the Second, July to November 1952; the Third, November 1952 to June 1953, and the Fourth, June 1953 to October 1954. The Colombian battalions were attached to U.S. Infantry divisions (the twenty-fourth until January 1952, and the Seventh for the rest of their tour of duty). Old Baldy (Hill 266 on U.S. army maps), above the Chorwon Valley, had been the scene of intense battles earlier in the war (in 1952 and 1953) and the hill had changed hands several times, when the encounter described in this play took place, between 23 and 26 March, 1953. The strategic importance of "Old Baldy"[6] lay in the fact that it overlooked "Pork Chop Hill", which was considered an important outpost, until the Eighth Army finally withdrew from there in June 1953.

After dark on 23 March 1953, a company of Chinese soldiers attacked while the Third Colombian Battalion was changing guard and the reserves were moving into position. The Chinese soldiers managed to enter the defenders' trenches, and a U.S. company sent to reinforce the Colombians that night was stopped by Chinese mortars and artillery. The Americans renewed the attack, with a supporting tank, but were finally forced to retreat. This left the surviving Colombians hiding in damaged bunkers, as the battle intensified the next day, with artillery and tank and bombing or napalm strikes on the Chinese positions. It was not until the night of 26 March, when the Chinese left the hill during the air strikes, that the Colombians managed to rejoin the main line of resistance.

The testimony of survivors of those three days of living hell is still fraught with vivid memories, not unlike the memories of Korea veterans of all nationalities.[7]

In this play, the circus, with the dangers it holds for highwire and trapeze artists, is an ironic counterpart of the battlefield, where danger engulfed all its actors. It might be helpful, in establishing the coherence of the play, to see a parallel between spectacle as entertainment (where the audience is an immediate presence and the danger and sadness affect only selected individuals) and war as spectacle (where the details are mediated by official press censorship[8] and the totality of the image is groomed and edited for propaganda purposes by the authorities). Artists, of course, are able to fall back on their own rich resources (even if they are not lucrative) when circumstances force them out of paid employment with a public spectacle where their individuality is valued (even if it is only a façade), whereas the soldier, even as an officer, is so molded in the identity given to him by the state that, once he is rejected, he is triply useless: handicapped, unable to engage in meaningful labor, and psychologically marred by his exclusion from the collective body that had redefined his identity on its own exclusive terms.

As it addresses the interests of audiences of common people, among whom the army recruits its soldiers, the play delivers a strong message. It celebrates questioning and whimsical souls and damns the way soldiers are treated by the military machine. It can remind young men how society discards its fighting men when armed conflict incapacitates their bodies or their minds. The play can only become more relevant in societies where the discarded, the *desechables*, are growing more numerous. If it is true that in the United States up to 40% of the homeless are veterans of Vietnam or the Gulf War; if militarism has left thousands of Vietnam veterans with post-traumatic stress disorder and thousands of Gulf War veterans with a crippling and sometimes fatal ailment known only as the Gulf War Syndrome, then it is also devastatingly true that *Old Baldy* lives on, not only as a reminiscence of a hill whose Korean name was lost to Westerners, a corner of earth where a handful of Colombians confronted wave upon wave of Chinese attackers, but also as an application to military history of the paradigm that Hannah Arendt labelled the "banality of evil."

In the dialogue between the believer (Sebastian) and the sceptic (Canuto/ Whistler) there are echoes of Alvaro Samudio Cepeda's celebrated novel *La casa grande*, on which the play *Soldiers* was directly based. And the end scene, in which Sebastián returns to find his friend destroyed by the mad Colonel, is dramatically akin to the closing scene of *The Orgy*, when the Mute returns to find his mother dead, murdered by the desperate beggars, and he can only mouth his anguished question to the audience. In addition, we have, of course, the possible debt to Beckett mentioned above. Finally, readers should be referred to the protagonist of Gabriel García Márquez's novella, *No One Writes to the Colonel* [*El coronel no tiene quien le escriba*], a veteran of the Thousand Day War (1899–1902) who languishes and starves because his pension never arrives.

Notes by Jairo Aníbal Niño for This Edition of the Play

I began writing the play after reading a note that appeared in a Bogotá newspaper. On a hill of garbage, the corpse of a beggar was found. In the rags he was wearing they found a medal conferred by the United States on war heroes. The medal was genuine and its owner was a veteran of the Batallón Colombia, which had gone to fight in the Korean War. The hero, abandoned, brutalized, persecuted, old, and sick, had finally fallen, in pain and without glory, on the Old Baldy of misery. I then undertook a careful study of several documents. The most profound and moving part of the research was my personal contact with the war veterans. I heard their stories, their dreams, and their ravings and I assumed the responsibility, in this country without a memory, of contributing to the long and ruthless struggle against oblivion. (From an e-mail from the author to the translator, September 2003.)

Two Notes on the Translation

1. After the October 2003 production of this version of "Old Baldy", several people expressed concerns about the anachronistic use of the

term "post-traumatic stress disorder" (which became common currency in the later stages of the Vietnam War) instead of a direct translation of "sicosis de guerra" as "war psychosis" (the term most commonly used after Korea). The decision to keep this adaptation of the term is based on the translator's wish to make this version of the play more accessible to contemporary audiences.

2. This translator has eliminated one line from the original (the Colonel's crazed exhortation beginning "Silence in the ranks! The ideal soldier is brave": "The Virgin tears out her hair in agony and, widowed of her love, hangs it on the cypress tree" is a direct quotation from the Colombian national anthem, recognizable only by those familiar with the anthem. Removed from its original context, it makes no sense.

Notes

1. The Colombian Revolutionary Armed Forces (FARC), the National Liberation Army (ELN), and the Popular Revolutionary Army (ERP) were active in different regions of the country when *El Monte Calvo* was published. All were Marxist, although their ideology and their tactics differed; the official government line was always that the FARC and the ELN were receiving aid and training from Cuba, which justified accepting U.S. aid and advisors, declaring states of emergency, and suspending civil government in different departments or regions, while retaining a civilian national government. The fourth group, the M-19, was formed in the early 1970s.

2. Valencia Tovar boasted that the counterinsurgency curriculum for his armed forces was developed at the Colombian Infantry College in the early 1960s without input from foreign advisors, and it became a model for other Latin American countries (Alape 249). This might seem disingenuous, given that both Valencia and Ruiz Novoa—two of the first graduates of the U.S. School of the Americas—consulted regularly with their U.S. colleagues and also received support for the development of the counterinsurgency program, Plan Lazo, under the Alliance for Progress.

Ruiz Novoa became Commander of the Armed Forces in 1960. In 1962, he invited U.S. Special Forces officers to train Colombian officers under Plan Lazo. In 1964 he became Minister of War, but he was forced to resign in early 1965 on the unfounded suspicion of plotting to overthrow the President.

3. Reference is made to the Colombian battalion in *Américas* 3:9–11 (December 1951), in *Newsweek* 38:52 (19 November 1951) and 37:37 (4 June 1951), and in *Time* 57:43 (28 May 1951).

4. *New York Times*, 14 October 1951 1:1 and 2:3, and 26 October 2:5. The *Times* also reports on 20 December (2:5) that Colombian replacements are on the way.

5. Herbert H. Schell, chairman of the U.S. Inter-American Council and Vice-President of Sidney Blumental & Co., praised Colombia "as an example . . . in encouragement of foreign investment and direct military support of the United Nations in Korea. Both actions were cited as signs of Colombia's democratic progress." Schell spoke at a luncheon in honor of forty Colombian businessmen who were touring industrial centers throughout the U.S.; former president Mariano Ospina was one of the guests. (*New York Times*, 27 October 1951, p. 23 col. 2.)

It is worth recalling that it was in Colombia that the Hemispheric Security Treaty was signed in 1948, shepherded by the United States, to knit the Americas closer together in the event that military action should become necessary for the protection of a threatened member, and one might speculate that there was some pressure for Colombia to show moral leadership in the Korean action.

6. Hill 266 received its nickname after all the vegetation was wiped out by artillery fire from both sides in the first battles.

7. Correspondence from several survivors attests to this. There are, of course, other more nuanced memories, such as experiencing snow for the first time, forging friendships, and meeting Koreans. One extraordinary example of the soldiers' humanity triumphant in a sea of pain is the adoption of a Korean child who appeared to be orphaned or displaced: Yoon Wuchul begged to be taken out of the war zone and the country, and he was smuggled on board ship for the return trip home and hidden in rucksacks and cabins by many members of the battalion; Yoon Wuchul was adopted and raised as a Colombian peasant named Carlos Arturo Gallon; his story was told by the Korean Broadcasting Corporation in 1999, when he travelled to Korea to meet his relatives. These stories did not fit the brief length and scope, and certainly not the optics, of Niño's play.

8. Colombian newspapers were temporarily banned for printing unfavorable reports from the front.

Old Baldy
[*El Monte Calvo*]
by Jairo Aníbal Níño (b. 1941) © 1966
Translated by Judith A. Weiss (© 1998)

Cast of Characters

SEBASTIÁN, *a beggar with one leg and a heavy wooden crutch*
WHISTLER [CANUTO], *a beggar*
COLONEL, *a mentally imbalanced man sporting an officer's uniform*

Set: A railway yard. Piles of crates and boxes. Trash. Nighttime. Enter Sebastián and Whistler,[1] two beggars. Sebastian is missing a leg. He uses a heavy wooden crutch. They enter cautiously as if searching for someone. They sit down. Whistler blows into his hands and rubs them to warm them up. Long pause. A train whistle. Then a sound effect to indicate it passing by. The characters follow it with their eyes. Pause. Whistler takes a reed flute out of his pocket and starts playing a tune.

SEBASTIAN. You and your music.
WHISTLER. It's to trick my gut. Music makes hunger less hard to bear.
SEBASTIAN. It's all the same.
WHISTLER. So, it's the same.
SEBASTIAN. We've had it pretty bad the last few days.
WHISTLER. We're more hard up than a whore on Good Friday.
SEBASTIAN. Yeah.
WHISTLER. You get used to it.
SEBASTIAN. The hunger?
WHISTLER. No, the cold. [*Pause.*]
SEBASTIAN. I hope he gets here soon.
WHISTLER. Who's this guy we're waiting for?
SEBASTIAN. An old army buddy.
WHISTLER. Do you think he'll lend us a few bucks?
SEBASTIAN. I think so.
WHISTLER. We'll have to bum some money off him.
SEBASTIAN. If he has any money, he'll lend it to us.
WHISTLER. What I wouldn't give for cup of coffee with bread and butter and sausage and cakes . . .
SEBASTIAN [*Cutting him off.*] Shut up. [*Pause.*] How would we pay for it?
WHISTLER. Well, let's see . . . ah! I know! [*Triumphantly.*] With my flute.
SEBASTIAN. You won't even get a cup of coffee for your flute.

---

1. Original name: Canuto, equivalent of cañuto, which translates as "reed pipe" and also as "tattle-tale".

WHISTLER. But it sounds great. Listen. [*He plays.*]
SEBASTIAN. Shut up, already!
WHISTLER. O.K. [*Pause.*] It's so goddamn cold! [*He urinates against some boxes. Sound effect of train going by.*]
SEBASTIAN. Cold nights like this one, when I'm hungry, I think of Old Baldy.
WHISTLER. What Baldy?
SEBASTIAN. Don't you read the papers?
WHISTLER. I can't read.
SEBASTIAN. You can't? No wonder everybody's so fucked up.
WHISTLER. Do you know how to read?
SEBASTIAN. Yes I do.
WHISTLER. Well, even so you're just as fucked up as me.
SEBASTIAN. At least I can read about why I'm fucked up.
WHISTLER. Does it change anything?
SEBASTIAN. It does for me. [*With pride.*] I'm a soldier.
WHISTLER. Uh-huh.
SEBASTIAN. A veteran.
WHISTLER. Uh-huh.
SEBASTIAN. A Korean vet.
WHISTLER. So . . . ?
SEBASTIAN. What do you mean, so? I have fought for my country.
WHISTLER. I wouldn't know anything about that. I have fought for something to eat.
SEBASTIAN. You don't understand. You're an animal.
WHISTLER. Old ballsy . . .
SEBASTIAN [*Cutting him off.*] Old Baldy. A bald mountain we defended to the bitter end.
WHISTLER. Did you run away at the bitter end? [*Laughs.*]
SEBASTIAN. Don't you make fun of me.
WHISTLER. I'm not making fun.
SEBASTIAN. It was a place of great strategic importance. And we did our duty.
WHISTLER. Sebastian . . . Could a person work the land or build a little house on that mountain?
SEBASTIAN. No.
WHISTLER. Then I don't understand. There, in that wasteland, is that where they blew off your leg?
SEBASTIAN. Yes. A filthy enemy soldier did.
WHISTLER. What was that enemy soldier's name?
SEBASTIAN. How should I know?
WHISTLER [*Astonished.*] You didn't know him?
SEBASTIAN. No.
WHISTLER. You must have insulted him.
SEBASTIAN. No.
WHISTLER. Called him an s.o.b.?

SEBASTIAN. No.

WHISTLER. So then, why did he blast away at you?

SEBASTIAN. I was fighting for our country.

WHISTLER. [*Still not understanding.*] Uh-huh.

SEBASTIAN. Don't you care about our country?

WHISTLER. I'm feeling cold.

SEBASTIAN. Answer me: Don't you care whether we're ruled by some foreign power?

WHISTLER. I don't know anything about governments or powers. I only know when I'm hungry and cold.

SEBASTIAN. Well, I think you should know that I was a sergeant . . . And I was decorated!

WHISTLER. They had to have given you something to pin on your chest.

SEBASTIAN. Yes, a medal. [SEBASTIAN *rummages through his pockets and pulls out a handkerchief knotted in many places. He undoes the knots one by one and finally pulls out the medal.*] Look! [*He pins it on* WHISTLER'S *chest.*]

WHISTLER. What's it worth?

SEBASTIAN. Not much. It's made of copper.

WHISTLER. Why did they give you that?

SEBASTIAN. [*Solemnly.*] Because I was wounded in action.

WHISTLER. Do you mean to say they gave you that piece of tin for your leg?

SEBASTIAN. That thing you're calling a piece of tin is a very important decoration.

WHISTLER. Couldn't they have given you something better?

SEBASTIAN. I'm a soldier.

WHISTLER. A lame soldier.

SEBASTIAN. Decorated!

WHISTLER. [*Giving him back his medal.*] Anyway, it's better to have both legs in working order than stuff like that hanging on one's chest.

SEBASTIAN. Our batallion received a commendation from foreign generals. They said that we were brave men.

WHISTLER. Where's Korea?

SEBASTIAN. It's very far away. It's across the sea.

WHISTLER. And you travelled all that distance to get your leg blown off?

SEBASTIAN. Yes.

WHISTLER. Couldn't they have blown it off somewhere closer by, so you wouldn't have to cross the sea?

SEBASTIAN. You don't understand. I was fighting for my country.

WHISTLER. Korea your country?

SEBASTIAN. No. This is my country.

WHISTLER. Then why did you travel so far away?

SEBASTIAN. The commanding officer told us that we were the guardians of civilization.

WHISTLER. Civilization . . . what is civilization?

SEBASTIAN. Something to do with books. Things like that.

WHISTLER. So you got yourselves killed to protect some books? I didn't know they were that expensive.

SEBASTIAN. It isn't about the books.

WHISTLER. Oh, it isn't?

SEBASTIAN. No . . . it's because of what's in them. Well . . . I don't know exactly. At least that's what our commanding officer said.

WHISTLER. Did the commanding officer get his leg blown off too?

SEBASTIAN. No.

WHISTLER. That's not fair. If you're lame, your commanding officer should be too.

SEBASTIAN. The commanding officer is a cabinet minister now.

WHISTLER. And you're a beggar.

SEBASTIAN. They don't want lame workers in the factories. Besides, they're afraid of something they call "Post-Traumatic Stress Disorder".

WHISTLER. Must be a disease.

SEBASTIAN. It is.

WHISTLER. Do people break out in sores of different colors and then bust open and die?

SEBASTIAN. They say it's worse than that.

WHISTLER. [*Looking around at the trains.*] It's worse to get ripped apart by a locomotive.

SEBASTIAN. It's a type of madness. Do you know what I mean? They say we all came back crazy. They say we learned how to kill really well, so it could happen that we'd start killing people left and right in the factory, just like that, without any warning. They think that there's a bloody memory stuck in our brains that could get stirred up at any moment. What can I say. They think we're killers.

WHISTLER. Killers aren't welcome anywhere.

SEBASTIAN. Not if they're poor.

WHISTLER. A killer who has no money is a miserable killer, a poor devil. Nobody will lift a finger to help him.

SEBASTIAN. Now we're living in a dump, where no one asks us anything, where we'll forget everything, even hunger, some day.

WHISTLER. The day you forget you're hungry is the day you die.

SEBASTIAN. Do you think that . . . ?

WHISTLER. What . . . ?

SEBASTIAN. Nothing. [*Pause.*] The generals have forgotten all about us.

WHISTLER. Are there many of you?

SEBASTIAN. There were. Few came back. The rest were killed.

WHISTLER. Uh-huh.

SEBASTIAN. Stop saying Uh-huh. They were killed.

WHISTLER. I heard you; what do you want me to say?

SEBASTIAN. You should look sad.

WHISTLER. I'm sad enough without having to hear about dead people.

SEBASTIAN. They were my buddies.

WHISTLER. Were they fighting for their country too?
SEBASTIAN. Yes, they were.
WHISTLER. At least they're at peace now. You have to drag your bad leg around.
SEBASTIAN. A whole lot of guys died.
WHISTLER. People die every day.
SEBASTIAN. Yes, but you should have seen it. Those battles and the fear that freezes you stiff. And the noise of the planes. The machine guns. The gunfire, and you feel yourself all over thinking you've been shot and then there's a sickly sweet smell like burnt sugar and right nearby there's the line of dead bodies and you look closely and sure enough your friends are lying there with their guts spilling out. Others are lying there wounded and bleeding. And screaming.
WHISTLER. [*Pause.*] It's all very sad.
SEBASTIAN. And on the way back, the sea was so wide and lonely.
WHISTLER. Sebastian ... what's the sea like?
SEBASTIAN. You don't know the big rivers, do you?
WHISTLER. Yes, some of them.
SEBASTIAN. Well, it's as if we joined together thousands and thousands of rivers and poured salt into them.
WHISTLER. Why would you pour salt in them?
SEBASTIAN. It's just an example. The sea is salty.
WHISTLER. All that water is salty?
SEBASTIAN. Yes.
WHISTLER. But why?
SEBASTIAN. How should I know?
WHISTLER. You know how to read.
SEBASTIAN. Yes, but I don't know that.
WHISTLER. I don't understand why the water's got to be salty.
SEBASTIAN. It doesn't really matter. [*Pause.*] I want to tell you about the journey. On the way over there everyone was happy. We were singing and laughing. The trip back was sad. Lots of wounded men; some were crippled, like me. Others were paralyzed. Others were crazy or had lost their arms. One soldier used to wander up and down the deck on a little cart. He was a monster, all disfigured. His teeth were all showing; he looked as if he was laughing all the time. He stayed in his cabin all day, and at night he'd go out on his little cart and ride around until dawn.
WHISTLER. What happened to the soldier with the cart?
SEBASTIAN. He was burned. Horribly. It's a miracle he made it out alive, but it was too bad for him he did.
WHISTLER. He got scorched all over.
SEBASTIAN. Yes, it was awful.
WHISTLER. If the man on the cart was scorched all over, I wonder where they'd pin the medal on him. [*The sound of footsteps. The two characters listen closely. The steps fade away.*]
SEBASTIAN. That jerk isn't here yet. [WHISTLER *sits down next to* SEBASTIAN.

He lights a cigarette butt, and they smoke it together.] We thought they'd help us when we got back.

WHISTLER. And they didn't.

SEBASTIAN. No.

WHISTLER. So did you win that war?

SEBASTIAN. I think so.

WHISTLER. You're not sure.

SEBASTIAN. The generals know.

WHISTLER. The only thing you know for sure is that you're missing a leg.

SEBASTIAN. We must have won. They told us the Chinese were evil.

WHISTLER. Oh! So it was against the Chinese.

SEBASTIAN. Yes. They have these long eyes.

WHISTLER. Long eyes?

SEBASTIAN. Yes. Like this . . . they stretch out to the sides. And they're paler than us.

WHISTLER. Must have been because they were frightened.

SEBASTIAN. No. That's the way they are.

WHISTLER. So you killed Chinamen too?

SEBASTIAN. Yes, some.

WHISTLER. And you must have left some of them with no legs, too.

SEBASTIAN. It's possible.

WHISTLER. Did that settle anything?

SEBASTIAN. What do you mean?

WHISTLER. That stuff about our country and all that.

SEBASTIAN. I don't know.

WHISTLER. [*Pause.*] What did you do before?

SEBASTIAN. Before I joined up?

WHISTLER. Yes.

SEBASTIAN. I worked a little plot of land I had near the village.

WHISTLER. And you ate three meals a day.

SEBASTIAN. They were hard times, but there was always enough food.

WHISTLER. You lost that goddamn war.

SEBASTIAN. We won.

WHISTLER. Now you're lame, you're poor, and you're starving. You're a cripple. You lost the war.

SEBASTIAN. The president said we'd won. He used really nice words in his speech.

WHISTLER. Bah . . . Words . . . words. You can't eat words. They've been talking and talking for a long time and they haven't solved a thing.

SEBASTIAN. You don't know what you're talking about.

WHISTLER. Of course. Since I can't read . . .

SEBASTIAN. What did you do before?

WHISTLER. Before what?

SEBASTIAN. Before you started to live like this.

WHISTLER. I've lived like this ever since I was born.

SEBASTIAN. I mean did you ever do anything.

WHISTLER. Anything?
SEBASTIAN. Yes. Some trade.
WHISTLER. Oh! A long time ago. I can barely remember.
SEBASTIAN. What did you do?
WHISTLER. You're going to laugh.
SEBASTIAN. I promise I won't.
WHISTLER. It would be great if you did laugh.
SEBASTIAN. Was your trade funny?
WHISTLER. People sweat and get screwed in every trade. I don't know any funny trade.
SEBASTIAN. It's good to have a trade.
WHISTLER. That's what the bosses say.
SEBASTIAN. So, tell me what you used to do.
WHISTLER. At first, lots of things to earn a few pennies, not to starve; I'd do all sorts of things, but afterwards I hit on something I liked. It's hard to find a job you like. When I was doing it I felt peaceful.
SEBASTIAN. What was it?
WHISTLER [*Leaping onto a box.*] I was a clown. Whistler, the great clown! [*Pause.*] You're not laughing?
SEBASTIAN. Why should I?
WHISTLER. I understand. [*Gets off the box.*] No one finds a has-been clown funny.
SEBASTIAN. Did you wear greasepaint on your face?
WHISTLER. Every clown in the whole wide world wears greasepaint. White cheeks, blue eyelids, and a nose as red as a ripe tomato.
SEBASTIAN. I saw a circus once, in my village. It was small and it seemed poor. The tent was all patched up.
WHISTLER. It could have been ours. It was called the "Andes Brothers". The brothers part was a lie, but it sounded more impressive. [*Pause.*] When we'd get to a village, after raising the tent and setting up the seats, we'd parade down the main street; that made me very happy. Behind the man on stilts went us clowns.
SEBASTIAN. It's exciting. Like when a battalion marches in full dress uniform.
WHISTLER. It was prettier than that. When soldiers go marching by people are silent.
SEBASTIAN. Out of respect.
WHISTLER. Out of fear, perhaps. When clowns march by people laugh and they're happy.
SEBASTIAN. I'd really have liked to see you work as a clown.
WHISTLER. Really?
SEBASTIAN. Yes. Of all the acts in the circus I like the clowns best.
WHISTLER. Wait. I'll show you my most successful number. [*A circus march plays in the distance.* WHISTLER *starts to walk around an imaginary ring. While he speaks his lines and right in front of the audience he puts on a great big red nose and a little blue cap and he sticks a huge flower in his lapel. His tone of voice should be even and impersonal.*]

The ring will be here in the middle. The wind is flapping softly against the tent and it smells like french fries and popcorn. The one elephant we have is very ill and looks at us with its teary eyes. In here it smells of sawdust. In the little tent the bearded lady is praying that it doesn't rain. The clowns ... we're praying that the elephant doesn't die. If he dies we'd have to buy a humongous coffin and it wouldn't fit in the village cemetery. The band plays a waltz and the clarinet player is out of tune, as usual. The elephant is embarrassed. Someone told me that they prefer to die all alone; that they die in the darkest part of the forest. Here he's surrounded by the lot of us. The ballerina's sequins dazzle him. I put my little blue cap on his head. I hope he understands that if we're not leaving him alone it's only because we love him. Because we're afraid. Because we're human beings, not elephants. The lights come on and the show begins.

Change of lighting. Lights on WHISTLER *alone.* SEBASTIÁN *will be in semi-darkness. The typical circus whistle is heard. The march gets louder. The director should give this scene as much of a circus atmosphere as possible. Any elements the director considers appropriate to achieve this may be introduced. Convey the idea of a very popular circus. Do not lose sight of the reminiscent quality of the scene, and therefore use technical elements that help create the necessary distance.* WHISTLER *creates an imaginary hoop that is lowered and on which a parrot is supposed to be sitting. In this pantomime, avoid using real objects; everything must be created solely by the actor.*

WHISTLER *stretches out his hand so that the parrot can sit on it; the parrot refuses. The game is repeated twice.* WHISTLER *tries to grab the bird angrily but it flies to a siding.* WHISTLER *moves toward it stealthily; he pounces and we hear the screech of the parrot as it gets away. The game is repeated at the director's discretion. The parrot perches on top of the tightrope tower.* WHISTLER *gestures to it to come down; he threatens, pleads, etc., etc. He decides to climb up the rope; when he reaches the top he tries to catch the bird by throwing his cap at it; we hear the bird's screeching as it escapes and perches on the front tower.* WHISTLER *looks down and is scared of the height. He calls the parrot, threatens it, pleads. He decides to go along the tightrope and does so in a very comical manner. He gets to the other side, grabs the bird and scolds it. He places her on his shoulder and climbs down the rope. He bows deeply, sits on a box and continues to scold the bird. He puts it on his knee, lifts up its little tail feathers and spanks it. The parrot screeches. It gets angry and pecks his nose; the clown reacts by squaring off as in a boxing match, but the little parrot starts to peck him all over. The little clown runs around in circles trying to shield his buttocks from some very heavy pecks. The music gets louder and the clown blows his whistle from the middle of the ring, as he bows, pointing to his partner. He pretends to stretch a wing and laughs. Suddenly he looks at the audience and stops laughing, and little by little his expression changes, becoming infinitely sad. He places the little parrot on the palm of his hand and tells it to fly away. He drops and sits down slowly. The only non-mimed element of this scene is the parrot's screeching. Lights up. Music stops.*

SEBASTIAN. [*Applauds and laughs.*] That's wonderful, Whistler. You're a very funny clown.

WHISTLER. Was.

SEBASTIAN. Why did you give it up?

WHISTLER. Life.

SEBASTIAN. Did they fire you?

WHISTLER. I quit. [*He takes off his clown trappings.*]

SEBASTIAN. You quit?

WHISTLER. Yes. The last night I worked in the circus I gave it my very best effort. I did a new routine for the first time. With this routine, after working his whole life long, a clown finally accomplishes something good—super, even. In short: it was one of the good things that have been invented in this lousy world. When I did it that night, do you know what happened?

SEBASTIAN. They burst out laughing.

WHISTLER. No. They just sat there, really quiet. Just as you're hearing it now. Quiet. And then I sat on the big colored ball and started to cry.

SEBASTIAN. You cried in front of everyone?

WHISTLER. Yes. When the people realized that I was crying, they started to laugh. Very softly, at first; then, louder and louder until all you could hear was one big laugh. Everyone was laughing and clapping. They were happy. Do you understand. They were laughing. I quit, that night. I left the circus. [*Pause. Pulls out his flute and plays.*]

SEBASTIAN. Where did you learn that tune?

WHISTLER. I made it up. [*Pause.*] I'm tired. That work-out made me hungrier. Do you think your friend will be much longer?

SEBASTIAN. He shouldn't be. The Colonel is punctual.

WHISTLER. But . . . is he a real colonel?

SEBASTIAN. No. He's a sergeant who went crazy. He thinks he's a colonel.

WHISTLER. Ah! The pissed-traumatic stress.

SEBASTIAN. Post-traumatic.

WHISTLER. Same difference. He lost the war, too.

SEBASTIAN. Shut up.

WHISTLER. All right. Don't get angry.

SEBASTIAN. Something inside him was thrown out of kilter by the concussion from the hand grenade.

WHISTLER. What sort of crazy is he?

SEBASTIAN. What do you mean, what sort of crazy?

WHISTLER. I mean, crazies can be sad, happy, furious, dangerous . . .

SEBASTIAN. The Colonel is a . . . how do I define it . . . he's an army crazy.

WHISTLER. Do army crazies lend a hungry man some money for a hot cup of coffee?

SEBASTIAN. I hope so.

WHISTLER. [*Sitting down next to* SEBASTIAN.] It's been a really bad day.

SEBASTIAN. Terrible. People don't give they way they used to.

WHISTLER. Tomorrow we'll go to the church downtown. It's the first Friday of the month so there will be lots of prayerful old ladies. [*Pause.*] Yesterday I made up a religious song.

SEBASTIAN. You did? That's a sacrilege.

WHISTLER. Why? Just because I'm not a priest does that mean I can't serenade God?

SEBASTIAN. You don't know what you're saying.

WHISTLER. It's a pretty song. I like it. [*He sings.*]

> Hey God, good buddy,
> My pal,
> Do you laugh too
> With your red nose?
> Or are you sad because of the death
> of the baby elephant?
> Good buddy God,
> It's your own fault if you're all alone
> Because your house is so far away.

SEBASTIAN. If they hear you they'll excommunicate you.

WHISTLER. For singing?

SEBASTIAN. You'd better forget that song if you don't want to get into trouble.

WHISTLER. What could they do to me?

SEBASTIAN. They'd jail you for heresy.

WHISTLER. They won't let me in the jail. The cops don't like me to play my flute. [*Takes out his flute. Plays. Enter the* COLONEL. *He is wearing a ragged uniform that was once a showy dress uniform. His chest is covered with grotesque medals.*]

COLONEL. Troops! . . . Attention!!!!

WHISTLER. The "pisstraumatic", I mean, the Colonel. [*He and* SEBASTIAN *stand at attention.*]

COLONEL. Report, sergeant.

SEBASTIAN. No news, sir.

COLONEL. Troops! Two thousand four hundred sixty eight years, three months and two days of history are looking down upon you!

SEBASTIAN. Colonel . . .

COLONEL. Colonel, sir, soldier. Colonel, sir. Even if it takes a little longer to say.

SEBASTIAN. Yes, Colonel, sir.

COLONEL. Request permission whenever you wish to speak . . .

WHISTLER. Permission to speak, Colonel, sir.

COLONEL. Denied! A great responsibility lies in your hands. Troops! You are about to write a glorious page in history.

WHISTLER. I don't know how to write, Colonel, sir.

COLONEL. In order to write glorious pages in history one doesn't need to know how to write, soldier. It's enough to know how to fire at the right moment. I'll make great soldiers of you. The army will be proud to have you in its ranks. Ready for review. Fall . . . in!!! At ease . . . Attention . . . Eyes forward!!! [*Everything goes very silent as the* COLONEL *begins to review the troops.* WHISTLER *tries to imitate* SEBASTIAN'S *military moves, but he does so clumsily.*]

COLONEL [*To* SEBASTIAN.]

Congratulations! Your boots are sparkling. Don't forget that we have to die with our boots on. [*To* WHISTLER.] What do those horrible buttons mean?

WHISTLER. They're from a trash can, Colonel, sir.

COLONEL. Three days lockup.

WHISTLER. But Colonel, sir . . .

COLONEL. [*Cutting him off.*] Silence! Five days lockup.

WHISTLER. These buttons . . .

COLONEL. [*Cutting him off.*] Ten days on bread and water.

WHISTLER. Colonel, sir . . .

COLONEL. [*Cutting him off.*] Don't answer back! Three months in a dark cell.

WHISTLER. I think . . .

COLONEL. [*Cutting him off.*] Twenty-four years in prison, no parole!

SEBASTIAN. Permission to speak, Colonel, sir.

COLONEL. Denied! In a few minutes the general will make his triumphal entrance accompanied by the army general staff. You are going to march past in honor of those prominent visitors. Troops!! At ease . . . Attention . . . Eyes front . . . March!! [*They start marching around in a circle. The sound of a train is heard, getting louder. The sound of the train gradually changes into the sound of machine guns, airplanes, bombing, etc. The* COLONEL *runs around the stage in terror, trying to hide. He must give the impression of being like a frightened child. He falls down and hides his head in his arms. The sound effects fall silent.*]

COLONEL. Leave me alone! . . . What have I done to you? . . . Why are you hitting me? I want to go home! . . . Why don't you pick on someone your own size?

WHISTLER. [*To* SEBASTIAN.] Tell him to lend us some change for coffee.

SEBASTIAN. This isn't the right time. Wait a little while.

WHISTLER. I'm hungry.

SEBASTIAN. So am I.

COLONEL. [*Getting up.*] Silence in the ranks! The ideal soldier is brave and disciplined. [*Stepping forward with a martial bearing.*] My country, I love you in my mute silence and I am afraid of profaning your holy name. [*Hallucinating.*] There they are!!! . . . They're climbing up the hill like red ants!!! . . . They're poisonous scorpions! . . . They're crawling all over the place!!! . . . There they are!!! Sergeant!

SEBASTIAN. At your orders, Colonel, sir.

COLONEL. Patch me through to the general.

SEBASTIAN. Yes, Colonel, sir. [*Pretends to establish communications over the radio telephone.*] I have the general on the line, Colonel, sir.

COLONEL. [*Picking up the receiver.*] Hello . . . ! General? Yes, General, sir, good morning, general, sir, How are you? . . . I'm glad . . . And your wife? . . . And how are the children? . . . I'm glad . . . It's a splendid morning . . . Yes. Yes. Yes. Oh, General, sir, you know I hold you in such high regard . . . Yes . . . Yes . . . Of course. Nothing like the country air . . . Yes . . . naturally . . . Yes. Just a small favor, General, sir, I am so sorry to disturb you, but you know we're in right in the middle of a war . . . Yes, yes. We're surrounded by enemy soldiers . . . Would you be so kind as to provide us with some artillery support? Thank you. I am so sorry to inconvenience you . . . Yes. Please give my regards to your fine wife and to the children. It has been a great pleasure to hear your voice . . . Goodbye, General, sir . . . Yes . . . yes . . . Goodbye, General, sir. [*Hangs up.*] Sergeant!!

SEBASTIAN. At your command, Colonel, sir.

COLONEL. Hand me my field glasses.

SEBASTIAN. [*Gestures as if he were handing them to him.*] Here, Colonel, sir.

COLONEL. Thanks, sergeant. Although one eye is more than enough, for what there is to see. [*Looks out at the audience through the binoculars.*] There they are! . . . Like rats! They're climbing like leeches ready to devour our guts . . . It's the Apocalypse! Troops! Prepare to repel the attack! We'll give them a run for their money . . . Attaaaack! Fire!! . . . [SEBASTIAN *starts firing using his crutch as a rifle. He signals* WHISTLER *to join him; the latter does so reluctantly but little by little the game excites him. They shoot, running about the stage. It should be a sort of violent and grotesque ballet. The* COLONEL *advances downstage, but when he hears an imaginary explosion he runs, terrified, toward backstage. There, crouching behind a crate, he directs the attack.*]

COLONEL. Forward!! . . . On to victory!! Hit 'em hard!! . . . Remember that we are a nation of lions!! But a dead colonel is worth more than one who turns and runs . . . !! For our country!! For freedom!! . . . Fire!! [*The characters continue playing the previous game.*] Troops . . . !! Cease firing. Let the vanquished surrender unharmed!

WHISTLER. I'm tired. Let's go.

SEBASTIAN. We can put up with him a little longer. After all, what do we lose?

COLONEL. [*Singing.*]

> When Tom Cat went marching off to war,
> how sad, how sad.
> When Tom Cat went marching off to war
> he never came back, came back.
> Do-re-mi. Do-re-fa.
> I don't know if he'll be back.
> He might be back by Easter,
> rub-a-dub dub, rub-a-dub dub,
> He might be back by Easter,
> or by next Christmas Day.

> Oh Tom Cat went marching off to war,
> and he'll never be back this way.

COLONEL. [*Pause.*] I must congratulate you, troops. You will be cited in the order of the day. The world has been made safe again! Troops ... The watchword. [*To* WHISTLER] Give me the watchword.
WHISTLER. What watchword?
COLONEL. Don't you know the watchword?
WHISTLER. No.
COLONEL. You spy! You filthy, lowdown spy, infiltrating the ranks of our glorious army! [*To* SEBASTIAN.] Sergeant!
SEBASTIAN. At your command, Colonel, sir.
COLONEL. Arrest this soldier.
SEBASTIAN. As you order, sir.
WHISTLER. [*To* SEBASTIAN.] Your friend's as crazy as a coot.
SEBASTIAN. Yes. I feel sorry for him.
WHISTLER. Tell him about the money, already.
SEBASTIAN. Let's just wait for him to calm down.
COLONEL. Quiet! You're in solitary confinement. You'll be brought up before a court martial. The council of war is now in session. The accused over there, please. [*He points to a seat on one side.*] As the judge, I will sit in this armchair. [*He sits on a high crate, center stage.*] Attention, please. In accordance with the Geneva Convention, the accused may choose the manner of his execution. Now I shall read the charges: Spying for a foreign power. High treason. Conspiracy to commit a felony and distribution of subversive literature. [*Pause.*] Do you have anything to say in your own defense?
WHISTLER. Colonel, sir, I ...
COLONEL. [*Interrupting him.*] You don't have to say it. It's nothing but nonsense anyway.
SEBASTIAN. Permission to speak, colo—
COLONEL. [*Cutting him off.*] Quiet! Or I shall have to clear the courtroom. The jury is now going out to deliberate. [*Climbs solemnly off the crate, walks toward backstage and urinates. Then he stands on the crate.*] I will read the verdict: Guilty as charged!! I will hand down the sentence. The enemy soldier, accused of spying for a foreign power, of high treason, of conspiracy to commit a felony and distribution of subversive literature, is hereby condemned to death by firing squad. Inform the concerned party in writing and send copies to the newspapers and other media. [*To* SEBASTIAN.] Sergeant, this man is on death row.
SEBASTIAN. As you command, Colonel, sir.
COLONEL. [*To* WHISTLER.] Enemy soldier. This is your last night. Every condemned man is granted a last wish. So they won't say we are barbaric in victory, but magnanimous. What is your last wish?
WHISTLER. A hot coffee, sir.
COLONEL. Just a coffee, or something to eat too?
WHISTLER. Something to eat, too.

COLONEL. [*To* SEBASTIAN.] Sergeant.
SEBASTIAN. At your command, Colonel, sir.
COLONEL. Bring this man a hot coffee. [*He hands him several banknotes.*]
WHISTLER. Can I go along with him to the cafeteria?
COLONEL. Are you forgetting that you're a prisoner, condemned to death and in solitary confinement? You can't leave here.
WHISTLER. [*To* SEBASTIAN.] Buy a really big roll . . . with butter.
SEBASTIAN. We'll have enough left over for breakfast tomorrow. Just humor him. I won't be long. [SEBASTIAN *starts to exit.*]
WHISTLER. And a piece of salami . . .
SEBASTIAN. All right. [*He exits. The scene is silent. The* COLONEL *starts to walk around.*]
WHISTLER. Colonel, sir, do you think that singing is a sacrilege?
[*The* COLONEL *doesn't answer. He continues to walk about.*]
WHISTLER. Have you ever made up songs, colonel, sir? [*The* COLONEL *looks at him with profound contempt.*]
WHISTLER. Why is it that people don't like the sound of my flute? [*The* COLONEL *stops.* WHISTLER *looks at him. The* COLONEL *draws a pistol and fires several shots.* WHISTLER *starts to fall, slowly. The* COLONEL *gives a military salute and exits. Enter* SEBASTIAN. *At first he thinks that* WHISTLER *is asleep. When he realizes that he is dead, he turns his head violently toward the place where he had left the* COLONEL. *He turns toward the audience, and the melody that* WHISTLER *was playing on his flute at the beginning can be heard as the curtain falls.*]

—END—

Lucky Strike

Introductory Notes

With the 1980 collective creation *LUCKY STRIKE* Teatro La Candelaria confronted their audiences with Colombia's new identity as a major player in the international drug trade. The play is of singular historical importance because it pointed to a shift in the type of drug business in the late 1970s and to the way in which this business was conducted. At the same time, by framing it as a morality play (the medieval Spanish *auto,* which has persisted in Latin American folk drama) and presenting the specific conflict and characters as allegorical types, they were able to point to the wider implications and propose a model of moral conflict that would continue to apply to Colombian society as the future of the drug trade unfolded.

Marijuana was the export drug of choice until the mid to late 1970s, at which point the production and export of the more dangerous and destructive cocaine—which was also far easier to conceal and ship and far more profitable—emerged as the dominant illegal export. More significantly, however, the relative simplicity of marijuana cultivation and its straightforward marketing and transport contrasted sharply with the international tentacles of the cocaine trade. The coca leaf was imported from Peru or Bolivia, which required dealing with suppliers there—producers and sometimes middle men, often underworld figures and corrupt government and army elements—and arranging transportation of the raw material to Colombia. Then, processing plants or factories had to be established in the least detectable areas, to produce the cocaine in Colombia; the cartels often chose locations in guerrilla-controlled territory, which meant negotiating terms of protection and taxation. The processing also wreaks havoc with the delicate Amazonian ecology, as by-products are routinely dumped into the rivers of the region.

Cocaine production requires a variety of chemical reagents and catalysts in the production process; because most of them have to be imported (from the U.S. or Europe), this meant that legitimate front companies had to be established or agents planted in existing pharmaceutical companies that enjoyed an untarnished reputation. Sophisticated operations (which included drug lords, complex offshore banking, political and military connections, and small private armies) known as cartels were identified with major cities (chiefly Medellín and Cali); in practically every aspect of their structure and operation, they contrasted radically with the looser networks associated with the marijuana trade. Finally, the cartels became engaged in turf wars for the extraordinarily lucrative trade, and had to keep finding ever more sophisticated—and often cruel—means of evading detection as they transported the product out of the country.[1] Because the families of the cartels' *capos* (the drug lords), with their conspicuous wealth, became targets of kidnappers, the drug lords resorted, first, to arming and training bodyguards in addition to their hit men, and took the initiative in attacking the left-wing guerrillas suspected of plotting against them (to kidnap their family members for ransom, or to support the peasants being persecuted or exploited by drug lords). Drug traders thus became allies of the army and of right-wing politicians against the rebel armies and their sympathizers. Some of these politicians came out of the ranks of the cartels or their associates.

The United States, which in the mid 1960s had Special Forces troops assisting the Colombian military in their air and ground attacks on guerrilla-held territory, also had an office for their military attaché within the Colombian Ministry of Defense. Throughout the 1980s and 1990s, extradition remained a contentious issue, with the U.S. insisting on the obligation of the Colombian judiciary to turn indicted drug lords over to U.S. courts for trial. Colombia entered the twenty-first century with several hundred advisors operating throughout the country, officially engaged in the war on drugs. The figure of the enigmatic American in Lucky Strike, while caricatured in the style of the 1970s, retains its symbolic strength even in today's context. With only one female character, the sexism in the play is glaring, though not altogether anachronistic; intelligently acted, however, Popy can be a powerful foil for the men.

When *Lucky Strike* was produced, the implications of the shift to cocaine and U.S. involvement in Colombia were not yet widely known or of widespread concern. The action is set in the late 1960s (as seen by the references to the Vietnam War), in part to shift the historical perspective to the nascent stages of the problem. Yet the play resonates with events of the following decades, through the upheavals associated with the rise of the cartels around the cocaine trade, and it continues to ring true because of the clarity of line with which the pattern of patronage and construction of power is laid out, and because of the universal nature of the principal genre that defines the play, the morality play or *auto sacramental*.[2]

Overall, the play integrates a variety of styles and genres besides the *auto*. A Brechtian overlay involves the use of songs, breaks in the action, and a chorus, providing the intellectual/critical elements. However, most of the play relies on popular genres and forms to draw in and retain a broad-based audience. Thus, elements of melodrama and soap opera open the show (the hospital scene, the kidnapping scene); broad farce is introduced in the stereotypes, the costuming, and some acting styles. Obvious agit-prop touches, like the Statue of Liberty, link the political dimension of the play with the entertainment value of their theatricality.

The individual characters and the figures of the chorus embody virtues and vices associated with a variety of social types. The modern-day fight, in which wrestlers—often masked and flashily costumed—assume names connotative of good or evil, mirrors the folk drama and its forerunner in religious drama, the *auto*, in which devils and angels often did battle in spectacular actions with elements of suspense, horror, and comedy combined. In bridging the gaps between the secular and the sacred, between the timely and the timeless, this play proposes an original fusion that serves to anchor theatre *qua* theatre and to rejuvenate it. The circus-like environment, the implied salute to sacrality found in references to ritual and sacramental forms, the embracing of the liminality of sport (in this case, wrestling) as both spectacle and virtuous struggle: these paradigms occupy an increasingly important place, internationally, in late-twentieth-century theatre, and they situate *Lucky Strike* on the cutting edge of the theatre of its time.

Although the text is long and, on the surface, it may invite cuts, the play is strong as a composite of its parts and constitutes an interesting challenge, a tour de force for director, actors, and designers. The scaffolding makes for a deceptively simple, even portable, set. Original musical scores capture the spirit of each song.

Notes

1. It was most common to use human "mules" who carried cocaine in their body cavities, risking death. There have been some extreme cases discovered, including the use of the body of a dead infant or a shipment of tropical fish, to transport the drug.

2. The *auto sacramental*, or "sacramental act," most often performed in the religious festival of Corpus Christi, is a Spanish medieval counterpart of the Everyman play or the miracle play. It remained a staple of religious drama through the seventeenth century and is found in folk drama in the Americas.

Lucky Strike
[Golpe de suerte]

A collective creation by Santiago García and Teatro La Candelaria
(c) 1980 Translated by Judith A. Weiss (c) 1998

FIRST PART
I. The Operating Theatre

Dark. An amplified heart beat will provide the background sound for the entire scene. Voices, sobs, and shouts in a hospital emergency room. Two NURSES *arrive carrying a wounded man (*PEDRO PABLO PALOMINO*) on a stretcher. They are followed by a man and a woman:* MARTA, *the wounded man's wife, and* JULIÁN MATAMOROS, *his friend. They are stopped by the* DOCTOR *at the entrance to the operating room. Meanwhile,* NURSES *and* OPERATING ASSISTANT *prep the wounded man on the operating table.*

MARTA. Is he going to make it, doctor?
DOCTOR. Are you his wife?
MARTA. Yes, doctor.
MATAMOROS. Is it very serious, doctor?
DOCTOR. I think so. The wound is very close to the heart. [*Marta sobs.*] Calm down, ma'am. Rest assured that we'll do everything we can.
MARTA. Oh, save him, doctor! Save him!
MATAMOROS. Calm down, Marta. Everything is going to work out.

The operating room lights go on as the doctor enters.

DOCTOR. Ready?
ANESTHETIST. Ready, doctor.
ASSISTANT. What happened?
DOCTOR. A precordial wound, no less.
ANESTHETIST. How did he get it?
DOCTOR. A bullet. No exit wound.
ASSISTANT. So we're in it for the long haul. Pressure?
ANESTHETIST. It dropped from 50 to 30.
DOCTOR. Blood.
INSTRUMENT NURSE. One thousand.
DOCTOR. Too little. Send for more. Pressure?
ANESTHETIST. Too low. He's going into shock, doctor.
DOCTOR. Let's not waste any time. We're going in.
INSTRUMENT NURSE. How did it happen?

DOCTOR. They say he got into a fight with some thugs.
INSTRUMENT NURSE. Poor man. He's so young.

The light of the operating room goes off. Light on MARTA. *She is cursing, then:*

MARTA. Oh God, save him! Here, on my knees, I'm begging you, Lord, master of destiny and of the lives of human beings, save him! How could a misfortune like this befall him, when he's been the best father in the whole world, the best husband! A man's life cannot be worth less than the life of an animal. I told him that, and I told him that guard's job would be the death of him. But what could he do? How could he turn it down, if we've been eating and breathing poverty, unemployment, and homelessness?

Don't take him away, Lord! Reward him for his courage, for his loyalty. Grant him the destiny he deserves. He has the right to be happy! Save him, Lord, save him!

[*Dark. Lights on, in the operating room.*]

DOCTOR. Scalpel.
ASSISTANT. Compresses.
INSTRUMENT NURSE. Hemostat.
ANESTHETIST. More compresses.
ASSISTANT. Electrocoagulator.
DOCTOR. Mop my brow. I can't see very well.
ASSISTANT. Suction.
DOCTOR. Kelly forceps.

Operating room light off. Background to the shootout follows. Dim light. This is a recollection of the wounded man, PALOMINO: *On a tall platform, a man (the* EMPLOYER) *wearing a uniform with a pocket watch and a gun on his belt. Below the platform,* PALOMINO *and his friend* MATAMOROS. *The sound of the heartbeat continues.*

MATAMOROS [*To the man on the platform.*] Sir, this is my friend, the one I told you about. He's an honest man. He has superb references. For the business he would be . . .
EMPLOYER [*Interrupting him.*] Name and surname!
PALOMINO. Palomino. Sir, I . . .
EMPLOYER. Age?
PALOMINO. Thirty-five. Listen . . .
EMPLOYER. Just answer my questions! Married or single?
PALOMINO. Married.
EMPLOYER. Any children?
PALOMINO. Three.
EMPLOYER. Healthy? How's your eyesight? And your heart? Are you fearless? Can you see a shadow in the dark?
PALOMINO. Well, I think I . . . I mean, I don't have any illnesses.

MATAMOROS. Sir, my friend is an accountant, so he could . . .
EMPLOYER. Quiet, Matamoros! We don't need your suggestions. You are needed to do what you were hired to do. To be a chauffeur. In Mr. Palomino's case, to be a guard. The job carries a great deal of responsibility, Mr. Palomino!
PALOMINO. A guard? That's very dangerous. Besides, I'm an accountant, or rather, an assistant accountant.
EMPLOYER. That's what we have to offer you. Take it or leave it. It's a very responsible job! You would be in charge of looking after the company's interests.
PALOMINO. That would be a very low-level job for me, with my background.
EMPLOYER. On the contrary. You'd be taking on more responsibility. You're a lucky man.
MATAMOROS. Take it, Palomino. If you hesitate someone else will. There are hundreds of people after this job.
PALOMINO. [*Hesitates for a moment. Looks toward the operating room.*] All right, I'll take it. But it is very dangerous.
EMPLOYER. All right, Mr. Palomino. Keep a sharp eye and a sharp ear and stay alert on the watch. You have a great deal of responsibility on your shoulders! The early bird won't be let the worm get away. Here's your gear: Your uniform, a guarantee that nobody will dare take what belongs to us . . . [*He tosses him a guard's uniform.*] With this watch, you'll count out every hour you're on guard for us. [*He tosses him a guard's watch.*] And the most important thing, the gun. [*He tosses him a holster with a revolver in it.*] Keep your eyes open at all times! You are taking on a great deal of responsibility with the company. You will defend these sacred interests from the hundreds of enemies who threaten us in the night. Sharpen your aim and don't allow any strangers into the world we have built. Don't be afraid of pulling the trigger when you see the shady criminal approaching. The law is on our side, Mr. Palomino. It is a job with heavy responsibilities!

The image disappears. Lights on operating room.

    DOCTOR. We're losing him!
    ASSISTANT. Compresses! Quick!
    INSTRUMENT NURSE. Where is it?
    DOCTOR. Right next to the pulmonary artery.
    INSTRUMENT NURSE. Holy Mother of God! Look at all that bleeding!
    ASSISTANT. Suction!
    DOCTOR. I can't. More blood!
    ASSISTANT. Vascular clamp. Electrocoagulation.
    DOCTOR. Silence! I've got it tamped. Quiet now!

Lights off. Another memory image of PALOMINO *appears: a* NANNY *with a* BABY *in a carriage.* PALOMINO *(as guard) with his friend* MATAMOROS *watches. The* NANNY *sings absentmindedly.*

NANNY. ". . . Just live for today, what do we care about the past. Today there's time, and tomorrow might . . ."

Suddenly two KIDNAPPERS *accost the* NANNY. *One of them stuffs a handkerchief into her mouth and forces her to lie on the ground. The other one takes the baby from the carriage.* PALOMINO *and his friend notice the kidnapping. Freeze. Offstage, the* EMPLOYER'S *voice.*

VOICE OFF. Don't be afraid of pulling the trigger when you see the shady criminal approaching! . . . The law is on our side!

PALOMINO *draws his gun. He wounds one of the* KIDNAPPERS. *One of them shoots* PALOMINO, *who, although he is wounded, grabs the* LITTLE GIRL *while the* KIDNAPPERS *flee. Light shifts to operating room.*

DOCTOR. [*Wiping perspiration.*] He made it!
ASSISTANT. How do you think it was possible, doctor?
DOCTOR. Because he's a lucky man.
INSTRUMENT NURSE. It was God's doing.
ASSISTANT. You saved his life.
DOCTOR. Here's the bullet. He is a lucky man. [*The* SURGEON *leaves the operating room and addresses* MARTA, *the wounded man's wife.*] Your husband made it. He is a lucky man.
MARTA. Thank you, God, thank you! I know that his fate was in your hands, and you do reward the brave! Thank you, Lord!

Lights off. When they come on again, PALOMINO *is lying in a hospital bed.* MARTA *and* MATAMOROS *are next to him. Near the head of the bed, one of Don Félix Bastidas's* MEN *and a* NURSE.

MAN. In a little while you'll be receiving a visit from Don Félix Bastidas, the father of the little girl you rescued. He's a very important man and a generous man. But, like any important man, he is easily irritated. My advice to you is, Don't contradict him. You're lucky to have Don Félix for a benefactor and I can assure you that very few people enjoy such favor.
MARTA. Will there be a reward, sir? Palomino almost got killed for rescuing the girl.
MAN. Don Félix pays extremely well for favors he receives.
MARTA. Is he very rich?
MAN. If he weren't rich, they wouldn't have tried to kidnap his daughter.
PALOMINO. Marta, don't ask so many questions.
MARTA. The house! We could buy the house.
MATAMOROS. The workshop, Palomino! This is our big chance! What do you say?
NURSE. Don't make him talk. He hasn't fully recovered yet.
MAN. Here's Don Félix now!

LUCKY STRIKE

DON FÉLIX *arrives, accompanied by his mistress* POPY, *an elegant and sophisticated woman. They are escorted by* BODYGUARDS. POPY *stops at the door.*

POPY. I'm not going in, Félix. Bloody scenes depress me.
DON FÉLIX. You're very sensitive, Popy. All right, then, wait for me out here. I'll be right back. [DON FÉLIX *enters the room.*] Aha! . . . So this is our hero! I am Félix Bastidas. I wanted to come and show my gratitude in person.
MARTA. I am Marta, his wife. Palomino was in critical condition. He fought like a hero . . . and they almost wounded Julián.
MATAMOROS. We both did our best, but it was really Palomino who ran the greatest risk, because he jumped right in.
DON FÉLIX.
You rescued my daughter. It was an act of great courage. For me a man's courage is worth more than a fortune. Men like you are what this country needs: real men, who aren't afraid of fear! If anything had happened to my daughter, this city would have been showered with lead. Here, Palomino: three round trip tickets to Miami and some spending money in U.S. dollars.
MARTA. But sir . . .
DON FÉLIX. I'll take care of the medical bills . . . This is just for openers.
MARTA. . . . You are very kind, sir.
DON FÉLIX. Sometimes, ma'am. Sometimes.
MATAMOROS. Thank you, sir.
DON FÉLIX. Thank Palomino. He's a lucky man.

Freeze. MATAMOROS *moves downstage centre.*

MATAMOROS. [*To the audience.*] What I expected as a reward was a sum of money that would enable Palomino and me to gain some independence. And they give us a ticket to Miami. I won't deny that the offer is tempting. Palomino and Marta might take the trip. I, personally, prefer to sell the ticket and use that money as a down payment to set up my workshop.

Matamoros's Song

> It's fine to think only of the here and now
> but the future is far more true and safe.
> A life that's so close to death makes you think
> and reconcile yourself to a time beyond today.
> It's fine to think only of the here and now
> but the real blessing's in the future.
>
> A balance
> between moments of sheer good fortune
> and single strokes of bad luck that bring you down:
> Great moments are transformed by one mischance.
> A single stroke of luck can change it all.

The future holds the best, the safest bet.
To be swept away by a wild wind is crazy—
it's the path that requires the least of our efforts.
Shortcuts, to be honest,
aren't necessarily the straightest way to reach your goal.
It's fine to think only of the here and now
but the real blessing's in the future.
Embrace too much and you'll end up with very little
in the end.

II. The Airport

During MATAMOROS'S *song the scene changes to an airport departure lounge. Upstage, a check-in counter. Throughout this scene the key ambient element will be the public address system (P.A.) announcing flight arrivals and departures.*

P.A. Attention, please. Dreams and Drums Airlines announces a delay in the departure of its flight D-333 to Happyland, La Sigilosa-Stealthsville and Puerto Olvido-Forgotten Harbor.

Center stage, a PLAINCLOTHES DETECTIVE *is giving orders by means of hand signals to others who are standing in a circle. They move off in different directions.* PALOMINO, MARTA *and* MATAMOROS *enter in a hurry, each loaded down with baggage. At the counter, a* PASSENGER *is arguing with the* CLERK. *There is a* PLAINCLOTHES POLICEMAN *standing next to the counter.*

MARTA. Give me the passports, Pedro Pablo, I'll look after them.
PALOMINO. But I already gave them to you.
MATAMOROS. In your handbag, Marta, look inside your handbag.
MARTA. Oh, yes, here they are! [*They go to the counter and call out.*] The Miami flight, please! Who's working here?
CLERK. [*Entering.*] The Miami flight leaves in two hours, ma'am. And please, don't shout.
MARTA. I'm not shouting. That's how I usually speak.
PALOMINO. Calm down, Marta.
MARTA. How can I calm down? What if the flight doesn't take off? Do something, Palomino, don't just stand there!
MATAMOROS. Take it easy, Marta, it's an international flight.
DETECTIVE. All the flights are delayed. Why don't you go into the departure lounge? [*Marta tries to say something.*] Madam, please don't make a scene.
PASSENGER. What kind of country is this? Nothing works the way it's supposed to. Demonstrations, strikes, thieves, plainclothes police everywhere, every day. How can you stand it?

PALOMINO, MARTA *and* MATAMOROS *go and sit down in the departure lounge. On a terrace upstage a* SINISTER MAN *appears, carrying a briefcase and walking up and down.*

P.A. Attention, please: passengers bound for Bangkok, Casablanca, Bari, and Copenhagen, please proceed to the Buccaneer Air Lines counter.
PALOMINO. You should be coming with us, Matamoros. Fifteen days in Miami. Only the rich can afford that.
MARTA. Take out your passport, Julián. We'll be expecting you in Miami. Don't pass up this opportunity.
MATAMOROS. I've already made up my mind. I'm selling my ticket... The workshop business is a done deal, Palomino.
MARTA. That workshop business is insane. Take our advice.
MATAMOROS. What I want is to become independent. It's what I've dreamed of all my life. I don't want to be somebody's chauffeur.

During the conversation, POPY *has entered. She circles the stage before going over to where* PALOMINO *and his party are sitting. A* YOUNG MAN *enters, who starts to distribute flyers surreptitiously. He hands some out to our characters. They read them.*

MATAMOROS. [*Reading the flyer.*] Mr. Adams, leave the country. Your very presence insults our sovereignty... Get out of Vietnam...

A PLAINCLOTHES DETECTIVE *who has seen the* YOUNG MAN *walks toward him very fast. The* YOUNG MAN *tries to get away. Other* DETECTIVES *appear, and he is arrested and beaten.* PALOMINO, MARTA, *and* MATAMOROS *stand up, frightened, hiding the flyers they are holding.* POPY, *too, is a little frightened. Then the* DETECTIVES *apprehend the* YOUNG MAN *with the flyers and take him away.*

P.A. Smile and Shine Airlines announces that its flight 039 to Chantecleer and Costa Azul has been delayed.

The characters sit down again.

POPY. [*Addressing all three.*] Are you going to Miami?
MARTA. [*Somewhat surprised.*] Yes... yes, ma'am.
POPY. Is this your first trip to the U.S.?
PALOMINO. Yes, it is. We've never been. And you?
POPY. I've been at least twenty times. You might say I live over there more than over here.
MARTA. Oh, so you're not a foreigner?
POPY. No. It so happens that I own a boutique. I buy merchandise over there and sell it down here.
MARTA. Oh yes? How so? Are things very cheap over there? And isn't it all in dollars?

POPY. Of course. But things can be bought very cheaply over there, and customers down here go crazy for them. It's an amazing business! Incredible! Of course, the exchange is the best part: taking handicrafts from here and bringing back electrical appliances and clothes. Are you going shopping?

MARTA. . . . No. I mean, we're just going as tourists, to see the place.

PALOMINO. Yes, we're getting away for a rest. So tell me: what's it like? Is it as nice as they make it out to be?

POPY. Much nicer than you could even imagine. It's a real paradise. Nothing can compare with it! Sunshine, wonderful hotels, swimming pools! You know?

During this conversation, the MAN *from the terrace approaches the group. He takes a package out of his bag discreetly and leaves it on the bench, then leaves.*

MARTA. Oh, so you speak English! Did you learn it over there?

POPY. Of course. One could say I speak it better than Spanish.

MARTA. Do you, now? Tell me, how do you say "How much" in English? [POPY *pretends to discover the package that the man has left, and picks it up.*]

PALOMINO. What's the point of asking, Marta, if we don't have any money?

POPY. Look, you dropped this package. You should be more careful with your stuff. Well, I'll be off now. [*She exits hurriedly.*]

PALOMINO. [*Getting up.*] Hey! This package isn't . . .

MATAMOROS. [*Stopping Palomino*)] Be quiet! Don't you realize it's not hers? There could something valuable inside.

Just then, PLAINCLOTHES DETECTIVES *enter, looking around and checking everything in sight. Two of them approach the trio.*

FIRST DET. Have you cleared customs yet?

PALOMINO. No. We're not arriving passengers. We're leaving. Travelling to Miami.

SECOND DET. You are? What are you carrying there? Open those suitcases. Quickly!

POPY *runs in, interrupting the inspection.*

POPY. [*Greeting the detectives.*] How do you do, gentlemen? Oh, my package! What a shame, I'd left it behind. Thanks. [*She takes the package from* PALOMINO'S *hands.*] It's perfume. "Bon Voyage" by Yves St. Laurent. Thanks so much.

FIRST DET. [*To* POPY.] Is there a problem, ma'am?

POPY. No, these people are friends of mine, travelling to Miami. [*Exits.*]

SECOND DET. Well, you can't stay here. Please hurry! Take your bags and move over there.

The trio withdraws to a corner of the stage. The PLAINCLOTHES DETECTIVES *stay to stand guard.* MR. ADAMS *enters from the other end of the stage. He is a strange character, dressed all in white; he is in a wheelchair which is being pushed by a* NURSE *who is also his interpreter. He is accompanied by a group of* REPORTERS.

FIRST REPORTER. Mr. Adams, how do you see the situation in Latin America, as you head back to the United States?
MR. ADAMS. [*Appears to mouth words without sound.*]*
INTERPRETER. After inspecting the terrain, Mr. Adams says that the future is full of risks that can startle the bravest hearts.
SECOND REPORTER. 1968 promises to be one of the most convulsed years of this decade. Mr. Adams, what does the U.S. government fear most about Latin American countries?
MR. ADAMS. [*Appears to mouth words without sound.*]
INTERPRETER. Mr. Adams says that it all depends on whether the balance can be maintained. Otherwise the U.S. would have to withdraw altogether.

At that moment, PALOMINO *tries to approach in order to get a better look at* MR. ADAMS. *Two* PLAINCLOTHESMEN *appear immediately, training their guns also on* MARTA *and* MATAMOROS.

INTERPRETER. [*Moving in front of* MR. ADAMS *in a protective stance.*] What's wrong?
PALOMINO. I only wanted to get a better look at the gentleman.

MR. ADAMS *whispers something to the* INTERPRETER. *The latter addresses the* PLAINCLOTHESMEN.

INTERPRETER. Let him go! Mr. Adams says he can get close, that he wants to greet him.

PALOMINO *approaches* MR. ADAMS, *who offers his hand.* PALOMINO *shakes it timidly. The* PHOTOGRAPHERS *snap pictures.*

The INTERPRETER *signals to* PALOMINO *to leave. He returns to his place next to his wife and* MATAMOROS. MR. ADAMS *continues on his way.*

SECOND REPORTER. Mr. Adams, why did you cut short your visit to the university campus?
FIRST REPORTER. Were you afraid of demonstrations against the war in Vietnam?

---

*Having Mr. Adams mouth inaudible phrases was one way around the problem of translating sections in which characters actually speak English. Another solution, used in *Femina Ludens*, was to reverse the English and the Spanish, but this could not be done here.

SECOND REPORTER. Why did the Alliance for Progress fail in Latin America, Mr. Adams?

The group exits along with the PLAINCLOTHESMEN *and the previous atmosphere is reestablished. The trio of characters returns to the little departure lounge.*

P.A. Northeast Air Lines announces the departure of flight 007 for Tierra del Sol, from the usual gate.
MATAMOROS. Man, why did you shake his hand? Didn't you read the flyer?
PALOMINO. So what? What can happen to me because I shook hands with a gringo? Lay off, will you?

POPY *rushes in, headed toward the group again. She is carrying the package.*

POPY. Oh, what a pity! It seems the package is yours, after all. I just happen to have one very much like it. Look here. [*She opens her bag and shows them a similar package inside the bag*] I'm so sorry!
MARTA. [*Accepting the package with some hesitation.*] But this package isn't . . .
POPY. It *is* yours. Now, don't you leave it lying around. [*She slips away quickly. The three characters are left looking perplexed.*]
MATAMOROS. This is really strange. First she hands us the package, and then when the police show up she takes it back, and now she gives it back to us. I don't understand a thing.
MARTA. I'm going to look and see what's inside.
PALOMINO. Not here, Marta! What if the owner shows up?

At that very moment, the MAN *from the terrace appears with his briefase and addresses* MATAMOROS.

MAN. Excuse me, are you Mr. Matamoros?
MATAMOROS. Yes, I am. What can I do for you?
MAN. You're wanted at the information desk.
MATAMOROS. Me? What for?

The MAN *from the terrace points in the direction of the information desk and then leaves.*

PALOMINO. Go on, Julián. It could be something urgent.
MATAMOROS. . . . Well, all right, I'll be right back. It might be a good idea to see what's inside the package. It could be something valuable. [*Exits.*]
MARTA. I'm going to the bathroom. I have to see what's inside that package.

MARTA *starts out for the bathroom but* POPY *intercepts her.*

POPY. Oh, it's so wonderful to run into you again! Come with me, I'd like to show you some marvellous handicrafts you can take to Miami. You could make a super profit!

MARTA. [*Hesitating.*] But . . . I don't have enough money.

POPY. Don't worry. Come on . . . don't hold back. Be impulsive for once! [*She practically drags her offstage.*]

From one end a BLIND MAN *appears and from the other end, a* MAN *who offers to help the* BLIND MAN.

MAN. Would you like to sit down, sir?

He leads him to the seats where PALOMINO *is. The* BLIND MAN *sits down next to* PALOMINO *and the* OTHER MAN *sits on the other side of* PALOMINO, *hemming him in.*

BLIND MAN. Palomino?

PALOMINO. [*Surprised.*] Oh!? Yes, that's me. And you . . . ?

MAN. Don't be afraid. The package that your wife has . . .

PALOMINO. [*Nervously.*] Look, sir, that package isn't ours . . . It seems that . . .

MAN. There's no risk involved at all. You won't have any problem with customs.

PALOMINO. No, gentlemen, I don't . . . the package . . .

BLIND MAN. The risk is minimal.

MAN. If you deliver it, you'll be able to spend fifteen fabulous days in Miami.

BLIND MAN. With this money. [*He pulls a wad of bills discreetly out of his inside pocket, and shows them to* PALOMINO, *who is surprised to see so much cash.*]

PALOMINO. It's just that I am not . . . that's very dangerous . . . No, I can't . . . Besides Don Felix gave me some money.

MAN. Don't worry, everything's been taken care of. What do you say? Can you use the money? Your wife can buy anything she wants over there. Make up your mind. There isn't much time.

PALOMINO. All right, just a minute . . . What I need to know now . . .

BLIND MAN. They'll recognize you at the airport over there if you wear this hat, this coat, and these glasses. Your wife has to wear this hat. [*He hands him the accessories.*]

PALOMINO. [*Hesitating.*] But gentlemen . . . I've never done anything like this, believe me.

BLIND MAN. Quick: yes or no? Here's four grand. [*He places the wad of bills on his leg under the hat. At that moment* MATAMOROS *enters, catching a glimpse of the money the men have given* PALOMINO *and realizes what a strange situation he is in.*]

PALOMINO. What?

MAN. Dollars!
BLIND MAN. And our eternal gratitude! [*He smiles.*]

The TWO MEN *get up and leave quickly.* MATAMOROS *looks at everyone in surprise.* PALOMINO *gets up and tries to follow the* TWO MEN. *He calls out after them.*

PALOMINO. Look here, gentlemen! . . . I still hadn't . . . These things . . . must be thought through more carefully . . . Oh Lord! [*He puts the money away in his jacket decisively.* MARTA *hurries in.*]
MARTA. Pedro Pablo, this package is very suspicious . . . I think the best thing would be to . . .
PALOMINO. To take it!
MARTA. What? Who knows what's inside? That woman practically forced me . . .
PALOMINO. Be quiet! [*He shows her the cash.*]
MATAMOROS. [*Approaching.*] What's the matter? Who were those guys? There was no one asking for me at the information counter. That package . . .
MARTA. The package? Palomino decided . . .
PALOMINO. We decided, Marta! We decided!
MARTA. Yes . . . we decided . . .
PALOMINO. To take it! We decided to take the package. It's an assignment. Nothing dangerous. [*To* MARTA.] Put it away! [*He gives her the package.*]
MATAMOROS. What kind of assignment? From whom?
PALOMINO. What do you mean, from whom? From . . . from don Félix, of course. Who else?
MATAMOROS. Don Félix? When did he give the order? How do you know? . . . What's the matter with you, Palomino? You two are acting very strange. Those men are very suspicious. You're getting in way over your heads.
MARTA. [*To* PALOMINO.] Matamoros is right, Pedro Pablo. I'm really scared. What if . . . [MARTA *gives the package back to* PALOMINO. PALOMINO *struggles with* MARTA *to force her to keep it. The dollar bills fall out of his pocket. Frightened and looking around, he hurries to pick them up.* MARTA *helps him.*]
MATAMOROS. [*Surprised to see the cash.*] Palomino! Don't get involved! It's a dirty business. I'm sure that there's some of that . . . [*He lowers his voice.*] . . . disgusting stuff in the package. You could still . . . Palomino, if you are my friend you'll throw away that package. [MATAMOROS *snatches the package from* PALOMINO, *who snatches it back and hands it to* MARTA.]
P.A. Attention, please. S.A. Air Lines announces the departure of flight 577 for Miami and New York. Passengers please board plane No. HK-294 in the international departures area.

The announcement continues in Spanish, more softly. Several PASSENGERS *travelling on that flight cross the stage.* PALOMINO *puts on the hat, drapes the coat over his arm and picks up his bags.*

MATAMOROS. Palomino! Throw away that package! You'll regret this for the rest of your lives!

PALOMINO. It's my life, isn't it?

MATAMOROS. You've gotten yourself involved in something you'll regret for the rest of your life. What's wrong with you, man? For a few lousy dollars?

PALOMINO. Mind your own business, Matamoros. I don't owe anybody any explanations, least of all you. I've made up my mind and that's that!

MATAMOROS. Palomino, it's not too late!

MARTA. Pedro Pablo, Julián is right . . .

PALOMINO. You keep your mouth shut! We're taking it! It's an errand for don Félix.

MARTA. It can be dangerous.

PALOMINO. Put on this hat!

MARTA. I don't want to.

PALOMINO. Put it on, goddamn it! [*He forces it on her head.*] Let's get going.

P.A.. Last call for flight 577 to Miami. Passengers should be on board airplane No. HK-294, at gate No. 2, in the international departures area.

MATAMOROS. Palomino, you're no longer my friend! If you get involved in that business, you can forget that you ever knew me!

PALOMINO. [*Putting on the glasses the men gave him.*] I don't give a damn! [*He gestures his wife to follow him; they turn and enter the customs area.*]

After observing them, MATAMOROS *makes a gesture of frustration in the direction of the audience and leaves.* POPY *enters from one end of the stage and the* MAN *from the terrace, carrying the briefcase, from the other end.*

POPY. Did they take the hats?

MAN. Yes. *The orchestra begins to play and* POPY *sings while the actors change the set for the next scene.*

The Song of Decent Folk

Decent folk think only of the present.
My life is adventure and pleasure.
It's easy, in a business deal—
what matters is now, what's right in your grasp
many decent folk have had their chance—

important folk take what's best at hand.
Decent folk think only of the here and now
my life is adventure and pleasure.

It's easy in a business deal—
what matters is now, what's right in your grasp
many decent folk have had their chance.

My advice to you is this:
polish your dreams of happiness now
while you wait for your turn
while you wait for your chance

I wish you good sense, and be wise, my friend

III. The Building

Noises of construction work on a mansion. WORKERS *are putting the finishing touches on* PALOMINO'S *house. The* FOREMAN *is diligently checking the work. A* WOMAN *is energetically scrubbing the floors. One worker is singing a popular song of the day. A* MAN *wearing dark glasses and looking like a goon enters. He's one of* PALOMINO'S *bodyguards.*

BODYGUARD. [*To the foreman.*] I need a couple of men to help us bring in some boxes! Quick, *doctor** Palomino will be arriving any minute!

The FOREMAN *sends two* MEN*. They bring in box after box of whisky, leaving them all in the middle of the stage. From outside we hear a car horn that plays "La cucaracha": It is* PALOMINO'S *automobile.*

FOREMAN. Doctor Palomino is here! See what I told you! Goddamn it! And this goddamn job isn't done yet.

Enter PALOMINO *followed by two bodyguards. He is wearing flashy clothes. One of the bodyguards keeps freshening up the glass of whisky that Palomino holds at all times. The workers drop what they are doing and gather silently.*

PALOMINO. Let's see, have you finished? Or is this trip of mine going to be a waste of time?
FOREMAN. No, doctor Palomino, of course not!
PALOMINOI. I'm not a *doctor* yet. I'm just beginning my studies! [PALOMINO *and his* BODYGUARDS *laugh heartily.*]
FOREMAN. Don Palomino . . . the problem is that . . . the finish turned out to be very complicated, but the whole thing is practically ready. That is to say, in a couple of days I'll be handing you your house with everything completed. And the back, doctor Palomino, in a couple of months, as we had agreed.

They start to inspect the construction.

---

*The title "doctor" is an honorific widely used in Colombia to assign status to university graduates (those with an undergraduate degree) and to high-ranking officials, sometimes whether they completed university or not. Its use became increasingly widespread in the last several decades, until it became almost absurd.

PALOMINO. My wife wanted to move in right away. We arrived from abroad today and we're tired of living in hotels. Let's see how this looks.

They approach center stage, where there is supposed to be a large sculpture.

PALOMINO. Ah, the fountain! It looks pretty good. Of course, I wanted the fish in the middle to be smaller and the nymph to be bigger.
FOREMAN. But Doctor Palomino, that's why I asked you . . .
PALOMINO. All right, it doesn't matter. Who put the finishing touches on it?
FOREMAN. [*Calling one of the* MEN.] Ramírez, come over here! *A* YOUNG MAN *approaches shyly.* PALOMINO *offers to shake his hand.*
PALOMINO. Very good, kid, I like that work. You're an artist. [*To the bodyguards.*] Two boxes of whisky for this young man.

The WORKER *walks away skipping with joy.* PALOMINO *goes over to one of the* WOMEN, *who is pregnant.*

PALOMINO. What are you doing here? You shouldn't be working in that condition.
WOMAN. I need the money, sir.
PALOMINO. [*To his bodyguard.*] These things break my heart. [*He pulls out a wad of dollar bills and hands some of them to the* WOMAN. *He turns to the* FOREMAN.] Place her on paid leave until the child is born.
FOREMAN. Whatever you say, doctor Palomino.
WOMAN. You are a very kind man, Doctor Palomino.
PALOMINO. Sometimes. [*He continues his walkabout.*] Let's look at the veneer on the porch. How did it turn out?
FOREMAN. This section is all that's left to finish now, *doctor* PALOMINO. We couldn't get it all done because they wouldn't let the Dutch tiles through customs in Curaçao. But they're here, at last. And they're wonderful, as it turns out. They look just like mirrors.
PALOMINO. Not bad. My wife loves anything shiny. Well, and who finished this?
FOREMAN. [*Calling one of the* WORKERS *over.*] Manolo, come over here!
PALOMINO. [*To his bodyguards.*] A box of whisky for Manolo. What about the security glass panes?

They walk over to where the security glass is stacked.

FOREMAN. They got here before any of the other stuff. They're German, *doctor* PALOMINO. Far better than the Canadian ones you thought of getting. What do you think of the colors? Aren't they a beauty?
PALOMINO. And do you think they're secure enough?

FOREMAN. [*Laughing.*] You couldn't smash through them with a cannonball. Test them if you wish, *doctor* PALOMINO.

PALOMINO *puts his hand to his belt and starts to draw his pistol. Everyone pulls back in fear.* PALOMINO *changes his mind and holsters the gun.*

PALOMINO. No! We'll leave that for the house-warming party. [*Laughs with his* BODYGUARDS.] After the trip to Miami. [*To his men.*] Three boxes of whisky for the people who worked on this! It's a hell of a good job! You really outdid yourselves, boys! What will don Félix say when he sees this palace? He'll die of envy, because this marvel is ten times better than his mansion. His little puppy dog is all grown up now. [*To the* FOREMAN.] Let's see the swimming pool.
FOREMAN. The only thing left to do is the lighting on the bottom. [*To a* WORKER *who is on that job.*] Hey, you, the electrician! Are you done? Where are those colored lights?

The ELECTRICIAN *approaches. It's* JULIÁN MATAMOROS.

MATAMOROS. That's a very complicated job. With all the fancy stuff these moneybags want to put in. But I think that by tomorrow ...

MATAMOROS *stops, surprised, looking at* PALOMINO. PALOMINO *recognizes him, too.* PALOMINO *takes off his glasses.*

PALOMINO. Matamoros! Julián Matamoros! [*He lets out a belly laugh.*] You've got to be kidding, man! What are you doing here? [*They embrace, looking quite moved.*]
MATAMOROS. Palomino! Pedro Pablo Palomino! How can it be? [*Looking him over.*] What happened to you? Damn, but you've changed! With that getup and those glasses, I swear no one can recognize you now.
PALOMINO. Luck, Matamoros, luck. A stroke of luck! I'm a businessman now. Import-export. [*He laughs.*] Remember don Félix? He turned out to be quite an amazing fellow. Of course, I've had a few differences with him lately. What about you, Julián? Where have you been hiding? I've looked for you everywhere. How's life treating you?
MATAMOROS. Remember the workshop? It went under after only six months The competition ...
PALOMINO. The big fish swallows the little fish. Isn't that true?
MATAMOROS. So they say.
PALOMINO. Some times, of course. Well, if it wasn't a hell of a coincidence to run into you like this, Julián! [*To the foreman.*] Scotch all around! We've got to celebrate this! [*He starts to change clothes with* MATAMOROS. *He gives him his jacket and takes* MATAMOROS'S *hard hat.*] Gentlemen, this is my friend Julián Matamoros! My life-long friend! One day I lost him and now I've found him again! Shit, isn't life full of surprises!

While PALOMINO *is talking, the* FOREMAN *has ordered his* MEN *to set up a table and take the whisky out of the boxes.*

PALOMINO. This is a great day. Cheers!

They all drink. Suddenly the FOREMAN *notices one of the workers hiding a bottle of whisky.*

FOREMAN. [*To the worker.*] You there, why the fuck are you stealing the booze? Put that bottle back!

WORKER. What bottle? I haven't stolen anything.

FOREMAN. You damn well have! What kind of fool do you take me for? I saw you. You were hiding that bottle!

[PALOMINO *orders his* BODYGUARDS *over to where the* FOREMAN *and the* WORKER *are arguing. They grab the* WORKER *and the bottle.*]

PALOMINO. What's going on there?

FOREMAN. Look, *doctor* Palomino, this guy was stealing liquor. One can't be too careful with these people. It's the same with the tools, with the building materials, with everything! [*The workers protest.*]

PALOMINO. All right, quiet, everyone! [*To the worker.*] Come here. [*The* BODYGUARDS *take the* WORKER *over to him.*]

WORKER. Really, *doctor* PALOMINO, I didn't . . . I mean, I thought that the whisky . . . that we could . . .

PALOMINO. Ah! So you think that anyone can do whatever the hell he wants with isn't his?

WORKER. No, on the contrary, *doctor* PALOMINO . . . it's just that . . . as there were so many bottles . . .

MATAMOROS. Listen, Palomino . . . I'll pay you for that bottle.

PALOMINO. Don't be a dummy! It's not about the bottle. It's what he did!

FOREMAN. [*To the workers.*] It's the attitude!

PALOMINO. That's right . . . it's the attitude! [*To the workers.*] No one, do you hear me? No one is going to steal even the smallest piece of string from me! Hell, ask me for anything! But don't steal from me! Pedro Pablo Palomino will give you whatever you ask him for. But I won't let some asshole suddenly try to steal what I've earned the hard way. What I've earned with the sweat of my brow. Not the tiniest bit of string! Everybody hear that? Not one lousy bit of string! [*He grabs the* WORKER *and pours the contents of the bottle over his head.*] You wanted whisky, huh? Well, there you have it, you louse! Now, get out of my sight! Right now! You can collect what's owed you, then vanish!

The BODYGUARDS *throw the* WORKER *out.*

MATAMOROS. Palomino, you can't do that! . . . What that boy did . . .

PALOMINO. He's a common thief! And I won't stand for that here. He's out of here, and that's that!

MATAMOROS. But you can't treat people like that.

FOREMAN. [*Interrupting them, he takes* PALOMINO *aside.*] *Doctor* Palomino, your friend Matamoros . . . I'd like to warn you, because I consider it my duty. Your friend Matamoros is a dangerous fellow. He's what they call a . . . subversive. He's always making trouble here . . . It's thanks to him I got stuck with the union here. That says it all, *doctor* PALOMINO.

PALOMINO. And what the hell makes you think you have the right to speak ill of my friend Matamoros?

FOREMAN. No, *doctor* Palomino, don't get me wrong.

PALOMINO. Julián, come over here! [*To the* WORKERS.] Gentlemen, I'd like to introduce the new boss of this building project! [*They all laugh.*]

FOREMAN. Just a minute, *doctor* Palomino! You can't fire me just like that. These are my workers and I've been directing this building project for a year and a half. Besides, don't forget that we still have two months left on our contract.

PALOMINO. [*Laughing.*] Our contract, eh? . . . You were in charge of this project . . . till today. Now the boss, or rather, your boss, is Matamoros. And I'm not firing you. I'm simply changing your title.

FOREMAN. You can do whatever you want with your friend but you're not going to fuck me so easily. [*To the* WORKERS.) Hey, guys, what do you think? Something like this has to be discussed with the union first.

A WORKER. Now you find the union convenient.

ANOTHER. So join. Better late than never.

[*The* WORKERS *laugh.*]

FOREMAN. Go to hell! That's not what I'm talking about. [*To* PALOMINO.] I'll lodge a complaint with the government. With the main office of the labor ministry.

PALOMINO. You can complain to whoever the hell you feel like complaining to. You don't know me. I'll buy your labor ministry, your union, and anything else you can think of.

FOREMAN. I'm going to hire a lawyer. This is going to cost you!

PALOMINO. You get a lawyer after me and I'll send five after you, you big fool! [PALOMINO *pulls a wad of dollar bills from his pocket and walks up to the* WORKERS.] See this? Look at it really closely! It rules the world. With this a man can buy whatever he wants! With this we're going to build a different world, a world without thieves, a world without rats like you. [*As he turns to the* FOREMAN *and tosses the wad of bills in his face.*] And now, get the hell out of here!

FOREMAN. [*Pocketing some of the bills that have fallen on him.*] You can be damn sure I'm getting out of here and I'm leaving your lousy house just the way it is! You may have a whole lot of money, but I've got my self-respect, and that's worth more than all your dough. [*The* BODYGUARDS *shove him out.*]

PALOMINO. Well, it's over. Let's get back to celebrating this reunion. Go on, drink up, boys, nothing happened . . . Nothing's happened here.

[*The workers start leaving, one by one.*]

MATAMOROS. Hey man, Palomino, what's the matter with you? How could you kick that man out like that?
PALOMINO. [*Half drunk.*] You shut up, hear? I do as I please. Is it my house or isn't it? It's my money! So, don't bug me!
MATAMOROS. O.K. And you don't have to yell at me, either.
PALOMINO. Oh, hell! Now this jerk's putting on airs. You may be the foreman now, but I don't need to remind you that you can tell the workers what to do, but you can't tell me. Show some respect!
MATAMOROS. What I'm trying to say is that you can't fire people just like that.
PALOMINO. Don't you threaten me, Matamoros! Get the hell off my case and don't threaten me! [*The* BODYGUARDS *approach* MATAMOROS.] Let him be! It's sad enough that he doesn't have a penny to his name, but he's an idiot too.
MATAMOROS. Well, you can take your foreman's job and stuff it, because I won't stand for that crap! I'd rather die! [MATAMOROS *takes off* PALOMINO'S *jacket, tosses it on the floor and starts to sing the Money Song.*]

The Money Song

> Those who have nothing know money is king
> but it's commonly known to all who would see
> that all that glitters is not gold
>
> You can buy anything, you can sell anything—
> purchase a friend or disarm a foe.
> Money can calm, it can dazzle and woo
> money is festive, joyful and fun
> money can cure you and bring you fame—
> the dwarf grows taller, is raised in stature
> the hateful man learns congeniality
> hands are restored to the amputee
> but oh what a false idol money can be
>
> But if hope is as green as a new dollar bill,
> all that glitters is not gold.
> You can buy anything, you can sell anything—
> purchase a friend or disarm a foe.
> It rocks the rich to pleasant dreams
> from the poor it steals their sleep
> Money is festive, joyful and fun.
> It buys supporters and soothes the lonely.

Money's the madness of so very many,
but all that glitters is not gold.

Matamoros finishes the song and walks out. Palomino is left alone and drunk, walking around the stage area.

PALOMINO. Julián! What's the matter with you, Julián? Have you gone soft, or what? Do you know what that rat was telling me? That you're a subversive, that you wanted to turn this place of mine inside out. I want to help you, you dope, but you won't let me. Open your eyes, Julián Matamoros! Everything's got its price! You can buy or sell anything! . . . Matamoros! Where are you? Hey, old pal . . . You miserable bastards! Hey buddy! You're a damned bunch of ingrates . . . Julián . . . my only friend . . . He doesn't have any money, and he's an idiot, too . . . Fine, then . . . To hell with you! . . . Scram . . . I don't give a damn if I'm alone . . . all alone . . .

He falls across the table, drunk out of his mind. The lights have faded, except for the special on PALOMINO'S *table. The mood changes to a dream-delirium of* PALOMINO. *High above him, the American from the airport, as a* GOD.

GOD. A great confusion is upsetting your spirit, Palomino! You search for happiness, but it slips through your fingers like the desert sands. I have pointed out a path to you, but you're too dizzy and conceited and seek it elsewhere. I like you, Palomino, but don't try to upset my inscrutable ways. Don't presume to organize the world. That is my reason for existing. What would I do with an orderly world? Do you want to deprive me of my job? Your friend Matamoros has the same intention. In another direction, of course. He makes me even angrier . . .

He keeps talking, in an increasingly incomprehensible murmur. PALOMINO *gets up and tries to go toward the* GOD. *Enter* DON FÉLIX *pushing a baby carriage. He is laughing silently and starts to take money out of the baby carriage and throw it at* PALOMINO, *who lunges at him and strangles him.* DON FÉLIX *keeps on laughing as he falls to the ground. A soft music plays.* POPY *appears, dancing seductively.* PALOMINO *tries to grab her, but she vanishes and reappears dancing in another spot, until she disappears altogether. We now hear religious music. A group of* BEGGARS *appear.* PALOMINO *goes over to help them. Just as he is about to give them some money,* MATAMOROS *comes out of the group in the form of a huge bird that attacks him, cawing and pecking.* PALOMINO *flees and the bird pursues him, until* PALOMINO *falls exhausted across the table. The nightmare disappears. Lights come up as before. Enter* MARTA *with a* BODYGUARD. *They wake him.*

BODYGUARD. Don Palomino, don Palomino, wake up! Aren't you feeling well?

MARTA. Why are you doing this to me? Don't you realize how dangerous it is to live the way your life the way you're living it? Someone's going to kill you when you least expect it. You're so inconsiderate! You don't the right to jeopardize this God-given fortune.

The BODYGUARDS *take* PALOMINO *away. Marta stays behind. She looks around the place and then leaves.*

IV. Squealing

A dark alley. Two of DON FÉLIX'S THUGS *are lying in wait. Another* THUG *arrives, kicking and insulting one of Palomino's* BODYGUARDS, *whose hands are tied behind his back.*

FIRST THUG. [*Hitting the prisoner.*] We finally got you! Clipped your wings, you little insect. Now you're mine and I'll squash you if you don't loosen that tongue right now. Tell me! Who's the contact? Talk! Or would you rather have your wings clipped? You're making me nervous, you cockroach, and when I get nervous I get out of control. You bastard! Talk, goddamn it! [DON FÉLIX *enters right then, and he stands there watching the* THUGS *and the* PRISONER *on the ground.*]
DON FELIX. What happened?
FIRST THUG. He didn't want to talk, boss.
DON FELIX. Untie him! I told you not to hit him. [*They untie the prisoner.* DON FÉLIX *signals the first* THUG *to leave. He takes out a handkerchief and wipes the* MAN'S *face.*) They're s.o.b.'s, but deep down they're good people, just like you. Look, it's really pretty straightforward. I only want to know one thing: the name of the contact. You give it to me and you walk away. What do you say? [*He puts a wad of dollar bills into the* MAN'S *pocket.*] Here, let me make it a bit easier, kid . . . I can help you . . . Tell me . . . Who is Palomino's contact? It wouldn't be . . . Mr. Adams, by any chance, would it? [*The* PRISONER *nods.*] Aha! . . . Very good. You're a doll. [*He orders his* THUGS *to let the* MAN *go and then he exits.*]

Making sure his money is safely in his pockets and dusting off his clothes, the beaten GOON *leaves slowly and cautiously. One of Don Félix's* MEN, *who was leaning against the wall, calls him. The "Insect" stops, raises his arms and turns slowly. Don Félix's* MAN *puts his index finger to his lips to remind him not to breath a word of all this. The scene freezes for a moment, then changes.*

V. Pay-Back

A casino in Miami. A jazz band is playing. Several PLAYERS *are betting at a roulette table. Upstage, a* CROUPIER. DON FÉLIX *is placing large bets.* POPY *is next to him.*

DON FELIX. Eighty-five on the red. Sixty on the green, O.K.?
CROUPIER. That's fine. Play! One more.

The roulette turns. DON FÉLIX *picks up the chips.*

DON FELIX. Double or nothing. Who's playing? Nobody?
MOBSTER. No, Félix, you're number one.
DON FELIX. Yes, I know. One hundred.
POPY. You're number one, daddy. No one can measure up to you, no one.
CROUPIER. Mr. Félix Bastidas wins again. It's fantastic! Attention, please! Place your bets!
POPY. If you go on at this rate, you're going to break the bank, daddy.
DON FELIX. I want to go on playing, but not alone. Isn't anybody playing? Two hundred on 34 red. One hundred on 22 green. O.K. Nobody?

PALOMINO *makes an ill-timed entrance. The music stops. He is dressed just like* DON FÉLIX.

PALOMINO. I'll play you, Don Félix. Where are the bets at?
DON FELIX. What a pleasant surprise, Palomino. You flew over here all alone. What's the occasion?
PALOMINO. Business, Don Félix. Personal business.
POPY. Palomino! I'm so glad you came over to see Don Félix. [*She hugs him and gives him a kiss.*]
DON FELIX. You two seem to know each other quite well, don't you?
POPY. Sometimes, daddy.
DON FELIX. Popy, you know your place. [*He takes her by the arm and brings her over by his side, then turns to* PALOMINO.] Wanna try your luck, Palomino? O.K.? Go ahead, don't be afraid. Gon on, place a bet. If you're going to take a risk, you might as well risk it all. That's my creed. [*The* PLAYERS *start to withdraw. Only* PALOMINO, DON FÉLIX, *and* POPY *are left.*) Personal business, then. Fine. [*To the* CROUPIER.] Two hundred!
PALOMINO. No, no, monsieur. Two fifty! O.K.?
DON FELIX. O.K.

The CROUPIER *spins the wheel.*

CROUPIER. O.K., O.K., we'll see who's number one.
DON FELIX. Who are you going with, Popy?
POPY. With the winner. [*She sings a song. While she is singing, the two* PLAYERS *continue to place bets in slow motion.*]

The winner's song

> Two men after the very same treasures—
> glory, money, power, profit, pleasure
> they seemed as close as kin, as close as blood—
> but underneath their thin façade the veil of lies was woven
> one a spy, the other forever a betrayer

two men after the same treasures—
glory, money, power, profit, pleasure.
Turned into rivals by their mistrust—
they played for success, with happiness their ante.
You can't rely on luck when it's power you're after.
The stronger man will win, so you have to choose—
it's you or me, my friend, it's me or you.

VI. Secret Airfield

Dark. Downstage, several MEN *are signalling skyward with flashlights. They quickly place flares along the ground to outline a landing strip. Sound of an approaching airplane. Upstage, in the previous setting of the casino,* PALOMINO *is making a telephone call. At the secret airfield a* MAN *answers.*

PALOMINO. Call to Colombia, please! Call to Colombia!
MAN. Everything's in order. The record's almost over. There's only one song left.
PALOMINO. O.K. Stay alert! Just a little longer now, and we won't be hearing another sound out of super stereo. [*He hangs up.*]

The airplane lands. Four MEN *walk from the proscenium toward backstage. They are wearing leather jackets and carrying a briefcase. Two of them are heavily armed. They stop at center stage. Another four appear from the back, carrying packages. It's the cargo.*

CARGO MAN. Satisfied?
Leather JACKET. Satisfied.

Several MEN *who had been surrounding them appear right then and machine gun the cargo men.*

Leather JACKET. Nobody understimates Don Félix. They wanted to fly on their own? Now they're free to do what they wanted. Assholes! [*The* MEN *in the leather jackets recuperate the briefcase containing the cash and exit.*]

VII. Miami Bar

Light over the bar. PALOMINO *and* DON FÉLIX *are facing each other. The roulette is turning. The* CROUPIER *raises the cup. They both rush to see the results.*

POPY. You've won, Palomino!
DON FELIX. That's life, kid. It's your turn now. Take advantage! But remember, Palomino, that you mustn't try to fly any higher than your wings can carry you.

PALOMINO. I accept your advice, Don Félix. Everything I have I owe to you . . . and I am sure that includes everything that's coming to me, too. [*He laughs.*]

POPY. Say, what's the matter? Aren't you going to go on playing? [*To* DON FÉLIX.] Are you calling it a night? I don't believe my eyes. It's the first time you've ever done this. [DON FÉLIX *starts to put on his coat.*]

DON FELIX. From now on you'll have to learn to dress for yourself, Palomino. You don't need to imitate me any more. Find your own hat, your own jacket, your own style, and your own women. From this day on, you're a free man. Was that what you wanted, Palomino?

PLAINCLOTHES POLICE *rush into the bar without warning.*

FIRST DETECTIVE. Silence, everybody! Hands above your heads! Which one of you is Palomino? Pedro Pablo Palomino?
PALOMINO. What's going on? I am Palomino. [*The* DETECTIVES *frisk him.*]
DETECTIVE. Come on. Follow us!

They take PALOMINO *away as he is. They don't allow him to put on his jacket or his hat.*

POPY. [*Running after Palomino.*] Palomino, what's the matter? Why are they taking him away? He hasn't done anything! [*She returns crying next to* DON FÉLIX.] Why did you let them take him away? Why didn't you say anything?
DON FELIX. He wanted to fly too high, Popy.

VIII. Prison

In the foreground, a GUARD *in front of prison bars. Another* GUARD *shoves* PALOMINO *on stage. They make him change into a prison uniform. They put his clothes away in a duffle bag. The gate slides open and* PALOMINO *goes in. He proceeds to walk around the stage where gates and cell doors open and shut. It is like one big maze. As he walks through, the* JUDGE'S *voice can be heard over the amplifiers. (The actor who plays* GOD *also plays the* JUDGE.) *The* JUDGE *stands at one end of the stage and questions* PALOMINO.

JUDGE. What's your name?
PALOMINO. Pedro Pablo Palomino.
JUDGE. Where are you from?
PALOMINO. What do you mean?
JUDGE. Nationality. Colombian?
PALOMINO. Oh, yes, Colombian. Married. I need a lawyer, please.
JUDGE. Once more. You have conspired against the laws of the United States.

PALOMINO. I'm innocent. I have no idea what you're talking about. I need a lawyer!

JUDGE. What can you tell us about cocaine and marijuana?

PALOMINO. I'm innocent! I know nothing! I'm going to file a complaint with the representatives of my country!

JUDGE. Your victims are American citizens! Your cocaine and marijuana business undermines democracy! It violates our laws! It goes against God's law! If you are found guilty, as I know you will, the United States Government will sentence you to a minimum of ten years in federal prison. Ten years!

As the trial ends, PALOMINO *is locked in a cell upstage. Downstage,* POPY, DON FÉLIX *and two* BODYGUARDS. POPY *says goodbye to* DON FÉLIX.

DON FELIX. I'm not going in, Popy. Prison scenes depress me.

POPY. You're very sensitive, Félix.

DON FELIX. All right, Popy. Tell him that I paid the bail, and that I don't ever want to have anything to do with him again. Anything at all! Let him pull himself back up on his own, and when he gets up, we'll see.

POPY. You're a kind man, daddy.

DON FELIX. Sometimes, Popy.

FÉLIX *is left alone, waiting, at one end of the stage.* POPY *goes over to the cell and shows her identification to a guard.*

VOICE OFF. Mr. Palomino, you have a visitor!

SECOND GUARD. [*Escorts* PALOMINO *and places him behind the bars facing* POPY.] Five minutes, O.K.? [*He leaves.*]

POPY. I've come to see you.

PALOMINO. To see what's left of me?

POPY. Don't talk like that.

PALOMINO. Well, how do you want me to talk to you? You led me into this and now what am I supposed to do?

POPY. Do you know who posted your bail? Félix Bastidas.

PALOMINO. Félix? And why, why did he do it? He wants to buy my freedom.

POPY. He can't forget what you did for his daughter. Besides, he's touched by your silence. He says that once you get out you can do whatever you want. I'll take care of that part! [PALOMINO *moves close to her and grabs her around the neck.*] I love you, Palomino!

PALOMINO. All I did was imitate him and you encouraged me, Popy. And now, what? My family, my reputation . . . I've lost everything . . .

SECOND GUARD. Your five minutes are up!

POPY. Are you going to accept the bail money?

PALOMINO. Do you think I could refuse it?

POPY. We could go abroad, start over. Build a happy life together. [*A* GUARD *takes* PALOMINO *away.*] What do you say?

PALOMINO. I love you, Popy!
POPY. Palomino!
PALOMINO. See you in Colombia! [*He is taken away.* POPY *walks out through the maze. Walks over to* FÉLIX.]
DON FELIX. How is he?
POPY. Not well at all.
DON FELIX. And how are you? [POPY *looks at him and smiles.* FÉLIX *takes out a diamond necklace and puts it around her neck.*] This will make you feel better.
JUDGE (OFF). Palomino, you are a free man.
FIRST GUARD. Palomino, you are a free man.
SECOND GUARD. You're a free man!

PALOMINO *leaves the prison. At one end of the stage, the* GOD *dressed up as the Statue of Liberty appears.* MARTA *is waiting for* PALOMINO. *He falls on his knees before the statue.*

STATUE. [*Shining a flashlight on him.*] You're free now, Palomino. Fight for your wealth. Only the power that gold confers on you will make you free, and in this dirty war on which I'm shining my light all that matters is winning. I have stood square in the heart of the world for many years, and it makes sense that I should be the symbol of the most powerful nation on earth.
MARTA. [*She approaches* PALOMINO *and helps him up, then helps him put on his coat.*] What's the matter, darling? Are you sick? [*She embraces him.*] They pushed you down to rock bottom. But we'll start over. The money I managed to put away is in a clean business that's successful too. Come, don't look back. The dirty past will be buried forever . . .

As they are about to exit the STATUE OF LIBERTY *calls out to* PALOMINO.

STATUE. Palomino! [*He turns around.*] Remember, time is money and money is freedom.

The cries of seagulls. They exit.

INTERMISSION

SECOND PART
IX. Interlude

Dressed as GANGSTERS *and* WHORES, *the actors are dancing around a boxing ring, singing the song "The Rich Man's Reasons".*

The Rich Man's Reasons

I pay no heed to the poor and the good—
though virtues are very lovely
I heed the reasons the rich possess
held up by our banks and our money.

What you need most of all
is to know how to cheat
to survive in this crazy world
Dupes and deceit are so hard to beat
where whatever you eat is a lie.

I know that our life is a bloody trick
no room for the good and the honest
I bypass the rules if I want to make good
or I'll never get what I'm promised.

Don't wander unarmed or you just might get shot
don't wander the path of the just
Your law is your money, so guard what you've got
self-interest is a definite must.

I'm not at risk as the first one to strike
just trust my loaded weapon
Because if I'm weak,
who'll feed my family next week?

Enter POPY, *dressed as* DEATH, *blowing a referee's whistle.*

DEATH. Ladies and gentlemen! We have a wonderful evening in store for you! We would like to present the Interlude of the Battle between Good and Evil! Palomino must purge his guilt if he is to rejoin lawful society.

PALOMINO. [*Crossing the stage, he addresses the* GOD, *who is sitting on the scaffold to one side of the action.*] Save me, Lord! Teach me the path of righteousness! I know I have fallen low, but I was blinded by ambition. Now my penitent spirit wants to return to the righteous path. Grant me a second chance. I promise I won't throw my luck away.

GOD. I knew you would come back, Pedro Pablo. I see you have repented, for I recognize the sound of sincerity in your words. That is good. Humility will always deliver the most troubled souls. The path of happiness and success is a very difficult one indeed. Many have embarked upon that journey and they have failed. The proud man fails because he is blinded by conceit; he fails because he is unable to see the path of righteousness beneath the mud. I will help you one more time, but I warn you: this will be the last time. Open your spirit to the great lesson: you will have to pass like the camel through the eye of the needle.

Behold, a ring: you will do battle with evil, thus showing the men in black hats your true repentance. During the fight you will learn the arcane art of recognizing actions that lead to victory. Take off those clothes and put these on. [*He hands him a wrestler's costume.*]

PALOMINO. I am afraid, Lord. Where are you, Marta?

MARTA. [*Appears next to the ring.*] I'll stand by you, my darling! You represent hope. The people still believe in goodness!

DEATH. Ladies and gentlemen, the fight is about to begin! The judges in the black hats are entering right now. They are two famous captains of industry whose reputation is without reproach.

TWO MEN *in tails and top hats enter, smoking cigars. They sit on a bench set diagonally from the ring.*

CAPTAINS OF INDUSTRY. [*Together.*] We're here this evening to have a good time, because the real pleasures in life are not having to suffer and being able to do whatever we want! Life hasn't been easy: our homes, our families, our construction industry. But today we want to enjoy ourselves, with the noise and wildness all around. We're laying bets on Palomino. We'll test him here to see how useful he can be to us, but we'll also place a few bets on Evil, just in case. You should never bet on only one contender!

DEATH. The regulars, the fight fans, are taking their seats and . . . the bets are on!

The FANS—*gangsters all—go over to the* GOD *figure and place their bets with the* MEN *in top hats. There is a minor scuffle, then they all go to their seats.*

PALOMINO. Where are you, Matamoros? I'm afraid, Lord! Please, I beg you to have my friend Matamoros present at this fight! [MATAMOROS *appears. He tries to turn back, but he is stopped by the* GANGSTERS.] Stay, Matamoros! Remember when we used to climb trees together, and when you got me that job, and the kidnapping? Do you remember? [MATAMOROS *is now* PALOMINO'S *trainer. He massages him.*]

DEATH. [*Drum roll.*] The fight is on, ladies and gentlemen! It's a fight between the powerful forces of good, represented by . . . Pedro Pablo Palomino! [PALOMINO *walks in with* MATAMOROS, *blinded by the lights.*] And the dark forces of evil, represented by the green devil, Félix Bastidas! [DON FÉLIX *appears, wearing a green wrestling mask.*] Accompanied by a deputy of Mr. Adams, a trainer of the most famous and undefeated wrestlers! [DEATH *puts the microphone to* PALOMINO'S *lips.*]

PALOMINO. I would like to dedicate this fight to my wife Marta, who has always stood by me!

DEATH. In this corner, with all the weight and burdens accumulated in dishonorable activity, Félix Bastidas, a kingpin of drug trafficking, extortion, and death, an undefeated fighter and master of evil headlocks and deadly tricks. [*Brings the microphone up to* DON FÉLIX.]

DON FÉLIX. I will wager all my money on myself! It will be a clean fight, gentlemen! I dedicate it to Death, one of my closest partners! [*Kisses* DEATH.]

FANS. Hit him hard, Félix! Send him six feet under! Hey, Félix, break every bone in his body!

DEATH. And in this corner, the sorcerer's apprentice, his disciple: Pedro Pablo Palomino! In this fight to the death he will test his luck and his fate. He weighs in at what he's worth and his worth is measured by what he has.

The fighters shake hands.

CAPTAINS OF INDUSTRY. Go, Palomino! Rip his heart out!
FANS. [*Laughing.*] What heart? He doesn't have one!
FELIX'S TRAINER. He ate it ages ago! [*Laughs.*]
DEATH. First round!

The gong is struck. The fight is on. PALOMINO *is terrified, but he wins the first round.*

MATAMOROS. Don't waste your blows. Sharpen your aim!

DEATH. First break! You may still place your bets! [*Everyone bets again.*] The fight will go an unlimited number of rounds. It will end only when one of the two contenders has been clearly eliminated, which of course involves the death of one of them.

FANS. Go, Death, go!
MARTA. No, death, no!
DEATH. Second round!

Gong. In this round, PALOMINO *rips the mask off* DON FÉLIX BASTIDAS's *face. A furious* DON FÉLIX *gets a number of different tools from his trainer and he starts to torture* PALOMINO. MATAMOROS *rages into the ring.*

FANS. That's it, Félix! Harder! Grind him up!

Gong. End of the second round.

CAPTAINS OF INDUSTRY. Low blows, especially, and violence, lots of violence!

MATAMOROS. They're cheaters, every one of them! The fight was fixed. They're going to kill you!

CAPTAINS OF INDUSTRY. Get him out of here! The man's an idiot. He wants to change the rules!

MATAMOROS. There's something I want to say!

FANS. [*Dragging him away.*] Don't worry, we'll get him out! No one is allowed to change the rules. This man's an intruder!

MARTA. Don't take him away!

CAPTAINS OF INDUSTRY. It was just a minor incident. Let the fight go on!

FANS. Let it go on! Hey, Death, let's have some order here!

DEATH. Third round of the evening! A man was removed for attempting to change the rules. Everything is back to normal. The match goes on. The bets are closed!

Gong. The spectators are silent. The fighters circle each other in the ring.

DON FELIX. You brought this on yourself. Why?
PALOMINO. I want to make a fresh start.
DON FELIX. You always were a dreamer.
PALOMINO. It doesn't matter.
DON FELIX. I'm going to crush you, to make a man of you again. I'm sorry, don't say I didn't warn you.

In the third round DON FÉLIX *knocks* PALOMINO *down.* MARTA *jumps into the ring holding a revolver. Death snatches it away from her and deals her a karate blow.* DON FÉLIX *takes the revolver away from* DEATH *and shoots* PALOMINO *in the head five times.* MARTA *is out cold. The* MOBSTERS *and the* JUDGES *go to collect their winnings from the* GOD. *Meanwhile,* DEATH *holds up* DON FÉLIX's *hand in victory.* DON FÉLIX's *trainer picks up the tools and they leave. Silence.*

FANS. This place stinks. His name was Pedro Pablo Palomino and he thought he could be honest and rich at the same time. What a dreamer!

A MOBSTER *tosses a flower to* PALOMINO. DEATH *pounces on* PALOMINO, *taking him by one arm.*

CAPTAINS OF INDUSTRY. His repentance was genuine. He fought like a hero. His only mistake was to believe in honesty.
DEATH. [*Trying to take him away.*] At last he'll be mine, all mine!
GOD. That's what you think, you fool!
MARTA. [*Taking* PALOMINO'S *other arm.*] My God, why have you deserted him?
GOD. Such a lack of faith, girl! Wait, I have to concentrate. Death, I order you to leave him alone! [DEATH *runs away.*] Palomino, get up, you did your duty! [PALOMINO *comes back to life.*] Even though you were defeated, I hope you've learned your lesson. The lessons that leave the deepest mark upon the spirit are those learned in defeat.
PALOMINO. I don't understand, Lord. The judges encouraged Don Félix to use dirty tricks.
GOD. Nothing's perfect in this world, Palomino. Start over, Palomino. Get back in the ring. Do you see those two men? Do you remember them? They wagered on you. They are examples, but they're not necessarily the right examples for you, because, even though they live in peace and comfort, they're not happy. They helped you. You must obey them always, and outdo them. Because you will be able to attain happiness. If you want to get to the top you'll have to do a hell of a lot and then some. [*The two* MEN *in top hats approach* PALOMINO. *They give him a suit, which he puts on, and a briefcase.*]

You'll find your instructions in that briefcase. They involve donations to the sacred interests of the Construction Company. A great deal of responsibility.

PALOMINO. And what does that "and then some" mean, Lord?

GOD. Don't be impatient, you'll find out soon enough. Oh, I almost forgot. Don't forget to call your friend Matamoros to offer him a job. I don't think he'll turn it down. He's out of work right now. Remember that capital and labor must work closely together. But your friend believes that there are more important things than wealth. Well, I'm off . . . I don't know why I get so involved in your life.

X. The Legitimate Business

Four scaffoldings of different heights placed in different parts of the stage make it look as if a big city is going up. PALOMINO *appears on the tallest scaffolding, in the middle. On the other three,* POPY, *the* CAPTAINS OF INDUSTRY, *and* MARTA, *respectively. A cabaret-style M.C. appears.*

M.C. [*While the set is going up.*] Wealthy and respected at the same time. Just as his benefactor promised! . . . Palomino goes to work at a large construction company. He starts out as a management assistant and ends up as the general manager.

Up, up, Palomino, rise to the highest positions! [PALOMINO *climbs up the scaffolding.*] There are no obstacles in his path to happiness . . . Luck, which sometimes is unruly and adverse, is smiling on him now. The construction company's flexible capital is growing by the minute, under a skilled new hand. But suddenly—oh prosperity, you treacherous veil that blinds the wisest man!—he decides to invest all the company's earnings in the purchase of 30 percent of an Investment Company . . . one of those fashionable enterprises that multiply your capital three, five, one hundred times in the twinkling of an eye. It's a stroke of daring behind his partners' back. [*Looks at* PALOMINO, *on the scaffolding.*] But now that Palomino is up there, let the events speak for themselves . . .

PALOMINO. [*Speaking agitatedly on the telephone.*] Hello? You must be wrong! Very wrong! We, the construction company, bought 30% of the shares of that Corporation. The others, the owners of the other 70%, are small shareholders. They can't make decisions about dividends . . . They are private shareholders . . . [*Calls his secretary.*] Margarita!

[*His* SECRETARY *appears.*]

SECRETARY. Yes, *doctor* Palomino?

PALOMINO. Call the Investment Company right away. Find out if there's any truth to this business of freezing the dividends.

SECRETARY. Yes, *doctor* Palomino. Mr. Matamoros has been waiting for you for more than an hour. What shall I tell him?

PALOMINO. Let him wait!

POPY *appears on one side of the stage, in a blue light. She is carrying a suitcase in one hand and airline tickets in the other.*

POPY. Pedro Pablo, we have to talk about us . . .

PALOMINO *starts to climb down the scaffolding. Another scaffolding is lighted and the* CAPTAINS OF INDUSTRY *appear.* POPY'S *area goes to black.*

CAPTAINS. [*Together.*] We just found out, Palomino! How could you have done something like that?
FIRST CAPTAIN. How could we have trusted you the way we did?
SECOND CAPTAIN. Do you realize what it means to lose the dividends?
FIRST CAPTAIN. Do you realize?
PALOMINO. [*Approaching the* CAPTAINS OF INDUSTRY.] I'm making enquiries as to who is buying up the shares . . .
CAPTAINS OF INDUSTRY. Too late, though! What kind of world are you living in? Read this! [*They toss him a newspaper.*]
PALOMINO. [*Reading aloud.*] Seven unknown buyers take over 70% of the shares of the Investment Company, Inc. There is speculation that it involves . . . That's impossible!
CAPTAINS OF INDUSTRY. [*Together.*] But true! Now they are the ones making the decisions. And they have frozen the dividends.
FIRST CAPTAIN. How are we going to fulfill our outstanding contracts?
SECOND CAPTAIN. Without a single dividend!
FIRST CAPTAIN. And on top of all of this, there's the problem with the union!
SECOND CAPTAIN. We're up to our necks in lawsuits!
FIRST CAPTAIN. And not a single dividend!
SECOND CAPTAIN. You've wiped out our capital! We authorized you to invest part of the earnings.
FIRST CAPTAIN. Not all of them!
PALOMINO. But I thought it was a splendid opportunity for the Company . . .
CAPTAINS OF INDUSTRY. [*Together.*] And it turns out to be just the opposite, complete ruin! There's no way out of this!
FIRST CAPTAIN. Without a single dividend!
PALOMINO. I did it for everyone's benefit. I'll pull the company out ahead. I swear I will!
CAPTAINS OF INDUSTRY. [*Together.*] Traitor!
SECOND CAPTAIN. Do you know what's coming to you to if we don't get out of this mess?
FIRST CAPTAIN. Do you?
PALOMINO. No, I don't.
CAPTAINS OF INDUSTRY. [*Together.*] Jail.
PALOMINO. Not again, no.

POPY *appears in her blue area.*

POPY. Palomino, don't you see where your crazy scheme of being rich and honest is leading you?
PALOMINO. [*Runs toward* POPY. *Takes off his jacket.*] They think everything's lost, Popy, but there's hope yet. I'll save the Construction Company. The thing that matters in business is to be daring. They're not daring and I am.
POPY. You're such a dreamer! You're in this up to your neck. You should call it quits right now.
PALOMINO. Just the opposite! It's the right time to rescue the whole thing!
POPY. It's a trap! Come along with me as we'd agreed, darling. Let's get away from here. [*In the background, a* BAND *appears playing Hawaiian music, bathed in a bluish moonlight.*] Let's go far away, where we can be happy together. Right now you and I are the only ones who matter. Leave everything—your ridiculous friends, your messy money problems, your wife's insatiable ambitions . . . Why are you hesitating?
PALOMINO. Oh, Popy . . . Popy! Give me a just a little longer, a few days, that's all. I can't leave this now . . . It's not the right moment . . . the timing couldn't be worse . . . We have to give it time . . .
POPY. With the money you've already got and with what I have we could set up a paradise for ourselves. I have it all planned. Look: here are the tickets. Let's get away, as far away as possible from this hell, Palomino! . . . Every minute that goes by is another step closer to hell for you. I don't want to lose you. Come with me!
PALOMINO. [*Running desperately from one side to the other.*] Popy . . . why are you doing this to me? . . . Wait just one or two weeks longer . . . I understand what you're saying . . . but . . . once I see this through we'll . . . we'll have twice as much, three times as much as we need to be happy . . . not just for a few years . . . but for our whole life.
POPY. [*Looking at him in silence.*] You don't love me anymore!
PALOMINO. That's not true, Popy!
POPY. Then come with me, right now!
PALOMINO. Please don't . . . you're tearing me up . . . Popy, I . . . the Company . . . Just think of it . . . It's millions . . . you don't understand anything about business . . . you don't know where money comes from. Besides, deep down it's not just about money . . . it's about my good name, too.
POPY. Palomino, it's over! You just didn't measure up. Deep down inside, you're a coward . . . and just so you understand that I know where money comes from, I'll tell you something. Do you know who bought the 70% of the shares of the Corporation? Do you know who bought the shares, one by one? Félix Bastidas, that's who.
PALOMINO. What? Félix?

The Hawaiian BAND *disappears.*

POPY. You're trapped. You see the spider's web being woven around you and you're not even aware of it. Come along with me!
PALOMINO. [*Shouting.*] I can't!
POPY. You fool!

POPY'S *light fades quickly to black.* MARTA *appears in another area of the stage. She is sitting at her dresser putting on make-up. She disappears.* PALOMINO *climbs up his scaffolding quickly.*

PALOMINO. So it was him. Félix Bastidas! He was the one behind it all . . . Margarita! [*The* SECRETARY *appears.*]
SECRETARY. Yes, *doctor* Palomino?
PALOMINO. Call my proxy!
SECRETARY. Yes, *doctor* Palomino. Mr. Matamoros is still waiting.
PALOMINO. Let him wait!
CAPTAINS OF INDUSTRY. [*They appear on their scaffolding and speak as a chorus.*] Palomino, Palomino! How could we have trusted you? We're going bankrupt because of you! Do something!
FIRST CAPTAIN. The instructions in the briefcase weren't supposed to be followed to the letter.
SECOND CAPTAIN. [*Together.*] They were subject to interpretation!

They vanish. MARTA'S *scaffolding is lighted.*

MARTA. Palomino, I've been waiting for you for more than an hour to go to the candidate's luncheon. Where have you been?
PALOMINO. [*Climbing down.*] What candidate? Oh, the candidate! [*He climbs back up.*] I can't just now, Marta!
MARTA. What? Is this how you treat your political obligations? This is one opportunity we can't afford to pass up. You, of all people, should know how important it can be for us to be there when the candidate launches his campaign.
PALOMINO. I don't have time! We're about to go bankrupt and I have to figure out a way out of this mess!
MARTA. But if you don't build up a strong relationship with the political machine, how far do you think you'll get?
PALOMINO. Right now, Marta, what's important is strengthening my financial position. There will be plenty of time for politics later. I don't have any time for all that right now!
MARTA. Oh, so you don't have time! [*She explodes.*] You don't have any time for me but you do have all the time and money in the world for that woman. For me, for your lawfully wedded wife, you don't have time, but for that slut you do! Of course! The manager is very busy, the manager can't see his wife or talk to her because the manager is very busy with that shameless slut. You swine! What do you have up your sleeve? To whom do you owe everything you've achieved? To those people or to me?
PALOMINO. What people? Are you crazy? [*He starts to climb down.*]

MARTA. You don't understand how important it is that we show up at the campaign luncheon. Instead, you prefer . . .
PALOMINO. I understand that political stuff . . . how important it is . . . the backing . . . how important the future is. But right now the present is what matters.
MARTA. Now it's becoming very clear to me! That woman has cast a spell on you!
PALOMINO. That's not true! I'm through with her. With all of them, if that's what you're thinking. You know that, Popy . . . sorry, Marta.
MARTA. Whom do you intend to deceive now? Palomino, look at me: how do you plan to get out of this financial disaster if it's not with the political backing I'm working on? When are you going to get it through your head, Palomino? Politics first, business after! Let's go to the campaign luncheon. It's the only way out!
PALOMINO. That might be true . . . it might be. But the way things are . . . [*He hesitates.*] You go alone, Marta. I can't. [MARTA'S *light goes to black.* MATAMOROS *appears on* PALOMINO'S *scaffolding and sings the song of happiness.*]

Song of Happiness

If happiness seems to be out of your reach
ignore it: it's only a false escape.
There are far finer things in this world than wealth.
Prosperity won't make you happy.

Don't try to steal every free afternoon
Don't try to grab everything around you
Don't clutch what's precious in your tightened fist
Share life with your friends for its beauty.

You'll tear up your world to ensure your place
Don't throw off your life for illusions.

Chorus:
    Life is hard, but it still *is* life
    put aside your melancholy now—
    to climb the hill, you have to sweat
    every day is rough and tedious

    Life is hard, but it still is life
    put aside your melancholy now
    there may be no such thing as happiness
    but you'll never be all alone.

Aristotle, who didn't mince words,
said the rich man's character is like the happy fool's

there are far finer things in this world than wealth prosperity won't make you happy.

MATAMOROS *enters, followed by the* SECRETARY. *He climbs up* PALOMINO'S *scaffolding.*

SECRETARY. He forced his way in!
PALOMINO. That's all right, leave us alone. [*The* SECRETARY *exits. Like a cat,* PALOMINO *starts to climb up the scaffolding and stops near* MATAMOROS.] Matamoros, I was looking for you! I need you now more than ever. You're the only friend I have, Julián! Do you hear me? The only friend! So, in the name of that friendship, I'm asking you to stop the union's petitions right away.
MATAMOROS. Just a minute, Palomino! I'm here representing . . .
PALOMINO. I know, I know! Representing your comrades . . . Comrades! Why can't you speak for yourself, for once in your life?
MATAMOROS. And do you speak for yourself, Palomino? Aren't there other interests lurking, perhaps, behind your words?
PALOMINO. Perhaps. But at this moment I am speaking in the name of our friendship. I brought you into this company. I gave you the job you needed. Did I or didn't I? I never objected to your work with the union and with my help you can still rise very, very high, Julián. Well, right now I'm asking you . . . I'm demanding in the name of that friendship, that you help me! The firm is broke . . . There's no time left to lose!
MATAMOROS. I too am speaking in the name of our friendship. That is to say, in the name of the good old days, Palomino. You're the one who has to help us. This is the right moment to accept the workers' demands. Don't forget where we came from. [PALOMINO *hesitates.*] All that stuff about bankruptcy is a lie. They withdrew the capital to buy shares in the Financial Corporation. And it's our money, Palomino!
PALOMINO. That's not true!
MATAMOROS. We checked the books! The list of demands can be accepted! With the earnings of the construction company, which were invested so irresponsibly, we can get the miserable increases we're asking for.
PALOMINO. Who gave you the right? Who gave you permission to pry into my accounts? You give them an inch and they'll take your hand! You're not the Julián I used to know!
MATAMOROS. Our jobs and our benefits are on the line! Help us, Palomino!
PALOMINO. What do you mean by that? I'm the one who needs help! . . . I'm about to go to jail . . . The bankruptcy is almost a done deal, Julián . . . my wife left me . . . and Popy. [*He takes out a handkerchief.*] You're all I have left in the world.
MATAMOROS. Enough, Palomino! Stop whining! I'm here to present the union's final offer . . .

PALOMINO. Don't threaten me! Don't you threaten me!

MATAMOROS. I'm not threatening you. I'm warning you . . .

PALOMINO. [*Exploding.*] This guy is getting on my nerves! Beat it! I don't want to see you around this office ever again. Get out!

MATAMOROS. I am leaving, yes. But I'm not leaving the firm. The times when you could fire people just like that . . . or buy them, those times are over. I'm staying and we'll see this through to the bitter end! This round is going to be a long one! [*Exits.*]

PALOMINO. To hell with you, you ungrateful prick! You're all a bunch of ingrates. I'm alone, I'll take care of this alone, as I always have: alone, all alone. [*He thinks. Suddenly he remembers.*] The instructions! Where are they? [*He opens his briefcase and reads them.*] "If your right hand is detrimental to what the left hand is doing, cut it off" . . . I don't understand . . .

The GOD *appears on his scaffolding.*

GOD. I warned you that it was the last time I was going to help you. I did everything I could for you. There you have the road to happiness opened for you. If you don't get there it's because you don't deserve it. "Ho tes hodos aretés traheiais stín": the path of virtue is a tragic one. I have more important business to attend to. Very urgent business! This world's becoming harder and harder for me to manage. The disorder is widespread. Unbearable! The day they least expect it . . . I'll retire for good.

PALOMINO. But, Lord, the way things are, it would be best if . . .

GOD. Yes, son, if you put all this in order. I'll be going now, I'm very tired. Goodbye, son. [*He disappears.*]

PALOMINO. Don't abandon me in this situation! Wait, don't go! [*He makes a phone call.*] Hello . . . Don Félix, how are you? It's me, Palomino. How is your daughter? She must be quite a young lady . . .

DON FÉLIX *appears on his scaffolding.*

DON FELIX. Aha! Are you in trouble, Palomino? What's the matter, son?

PALOMINO. It's hard, Don Félix, but I'm trying: You see, we invested all the Construction Company profits in the Financial Corporation that promised . . .

DON FELIX. All the profits? Why, Palomino? You're always rushing into things. You were doing so well with the construction company.

PALOMINO. We thought we could . . .

DON FELIX. And once again you thought you could fly higher than your wings could carry you?

PALOMINO. Don Félix, in spite of our differences, you and I . . .

DON FELIX. No speeches, son. There's no need.

PALOMINO. You bought the shares. Without the dividends the construction company will die. If you help us we could pay interest . . .

DON FELIX. You are the interest.

PALOMINO. Me?

DON FÉLIX. Look, son: This is my first big investment and there will be others. We have friends: the friends from New York . . . We can be partners like before, but on different terms. Terms that you never even dared to dream about.

PALOMINO. I don't understand, Don Félix.

DON FÉLIX. You'll understand, little by little, if you follow the instructions. First of all, you have to get rid of the Construction Company. Liquidate it. Declare bankruptcy. A phony bankruptcy. Meanwhile I'll look after your shares. They're safe in my hands. As far as your partners are concerned, they'll be forced to sell their share. We're laundering the money, do you understand? And this is a great opportunity. I'm not interested in showing off. I own other businesses.

PALOMINO. But that would mean betraying the partners. I think . . .

DON FÉLIX. Don't be so naive. In business you don't think, you act. That's why you're there. Or do you think it's by God's good grace that you're there? What do you say, son? Do you accept? [PALOMINO *withdraws and sings the song of the cat and the mouse.*]

Song of the Cat and the Mouse

In the game of Cat and Mouse
One of the players is lost.
(There are roads of no return):
The fly in the cobweb who struggles will lose:
too tangled to win, too tangled to move
if she waits, is she's quiet, she is just as lost:
in cloudy conditions, discernment is tough.

[Spoken] Life is like this sometimes:
If you head East
You'll end up in the West
and when you retreat
you'll be in the South,
there's no true North to guide you.
The path of goodness is a trap
and evil will bear you no good.

Easy flattery is deceptive
but it's foolish to opt for the worst.
Perhaps life lacks sense,
Perhaps all is lost from the start
In this foolish game of black and white.

What's it to be?
[*sung*]

In the game of Cat and Mouse,
one of the players is lost.

Who is right?
Everything's permissible and nothing matters.
Another wind may blow tomorrow,
bringing in a different world.
Still . . .
If you fight the trap, you'll fall in far deeper.

When he finishes the song, PALOMINO *is standing facing* DON FÉLIX, *at the extreme end of the stage. He opens his arms wide and is silent for a moment.*

PALOMINO. All right, Don Félix. I accept.

XI. Apotheosis

Upstage, DON FÉLIX. *The scaffoldings have been assembled upstage to form an allegorical picture of happiness and triumph, with the figures of several characters: Don Félix's* DAUGHTER, *a high-ranking* MILITARY OFFICER, *the two* CAPTAINS OF INDUSTRY, *the* STATUE OF LIBERTY, MARTA, *and, at ground level, two* GANGSTERS *armed with machine guns. At the other end,* PALOMINO *stands with arms wide open.* DON FÉLIX *sings his song in an operatic style.*

Don Félix's song

Come to me, Palomino,
son of all your guilt,
your betrayals and your errors
that have all been in vain.
Son, I forgive you.
Come to the bosom
of your real family,
even though you did forget us
occasionally.
Now that you know everything
you're joined to us forever.

A gong sounds and the CHORUS *of all the figures assembled in the allegorical tableau can be heard.* PALOMINO *walks slowly toward the group.*

FIRST CHORUS.

Palomino moves forward as boldly as he can
overcoming shoals,
and winds,

and hurricanes,
and the very jaws of the lion.

Gong. PALOMINO *stops. The lighting changes. The* CHORUS *is silent.* MARTA *appears, ghost-like. She takes a revolver out of her purse and walks toward* PALOMINO. *Just as she is about to shoot him, she puts away the gun and takes out a handkerchief. She walks away weeping and climbs up the scaffolding. The lighting changes and the chorus continues.*

SECOND CHORUS.

He has learned that in this crazy rise
shark's teeth are earned
only by biting,
and kicking,
and snapping.

Gong. The CHORUS *stops. Change of lighting.* PALOMINO *stops. A* CABINET MINISTER *appears, with the* STATUE OF LIBERTY *leading him by the hand. They cross the stage slowly.*

MINISTER. Palomino has stripped us all of our wealth, all those who produce the country's wealth without a trace of dishonesty. With the dollars he earns from such dealings, this upstart is taking over the political structure of the country. I have irrefutable proof, with names and surnames that have just been delivered to me!

A MESSENGER *enters carrying papers. He raises them, as if to hand them over. A shot is heard and he drops to the ground. The* CABINET MINISTER *covers his face with his hands. The* STATUE OF LIBERTY *exits, horrified. The* MINISTER'S *face is pale with terror.*

[*Stammering.*] In this moment . . . of chaos . . . and uncertainty . . . we must appeal . . . to the spiritual resources of those who bequeathed us . . . faith and trust . . . in law . . . and order. [*He exits from upstage. The lighting changes. The* CHORUS *continues and* PALOMINO *keeps advancing.*]

THIRD CHORUS.

Step by step he's closer to his goal,
smiling,
proud,
sweating,
without a tear in his skin.

The CHORUS *stops. Change of lighting.* POPY *appears dead on a sheet dragged by two* GOONS. *She has a revolver in her hand. They pass by* PALOMINO. *They exit. The* CHORUS *continues. Change of lighting. Now all the characters form the allegorical picture of happiness, with* DON FÉLIX *in the center.* PALOMINO *is already very close to them.*

    FOURTH CHORUS.
        Palomino is about to exchange
        his dreams of fights,
        of terrors,
        of evil
        for the happy, triumphant life
        that's practically in his grasp.

From upstage, the sound of footsteps approaching. They get louder as they move downstage, as a voice calls PALOMINO. *The* CHORUS *is interrupted. The voice and the footsteps are* MATAMOROS'S. *He arrives downstage and the* CHORUS *stands paralyzed and they all put up their hands.*

    MATAMOROS. I have something to say.

PALOMINO *slowly slides his hand to his side, takes out a revolver and aims it at* MATAMOROS. *The* GANGSTERS, *too, aim their guns at him.* PALOMINO *raises his forefinger to his lips and signals* MATAMOROS *to be silent.*

—END—

Roadhouse

INTRODUCTORY NOTES

OF ALL THE CHRONICLERS OF COLOMBIA'S DESCENT INTO CHAOS, the most consistent—and the most coherently critical—are probably Santiago García and his Teatro La Candelaria. For this group, the decade between *Lucky Strike* and *Roadhouse* also involved a return to literary sources from seventeenth-century Spain. From the latter, they dramatized searing satirical testimonies of a society in crisis, dominated by a materially and morally bankrupt aristocracy, widespread economic misery, thieving, filth, and the wandering homeless who achieved immortality as the anti-heroic protagonists of the picaresque novel; works like *El diálogo del Rebusque*, based on Quevedo's novel *El Buscón*, are reminiscent of Gay's *Beggar's Opera* and Brecht's *Threepenny Opera*.

The decade of the 1980s in Colombia was marked by the consolidation of the power of the drug cartels, the failure of civil institutions,[1] and the continuation of the state of war between the revolutionaries and the state. Peace talks led to the demobilization of the M-19 guerrillas and their integration into political life, while at the same time a third party was formed, the left-wing Unidad Popular (UP), which brought together intellectuals, unions, farmworkers, and other popular sectors, and many former M-19 and FARC guerrillas. By the end of the decade, however, it was open season on the UP, and over one thousand of that party's candidates for public office, including their presidential candidate, were assassinated. Thousands more of their supporters were killed or terrorized and displaced from homes and farms by a systematic campaign waged by paramilitary groups and by the armed forces. Apart from the UP and trade union leaders, distinguished victims of unidentified killers included the academic deans and professors of the school of public health and the medical school in Medellín, assassinated in all likelihood because they promoted social consciousness and community medicine.

At around the time when *Roadhouse* was being developed and produced, hundreds of well-known persons were forced to wear bulletproof vests and to hire bodyguards, after their names appeared on hit lists or they received direct death threats. Patricia Ariza, a founding member of La Candelaria, was targeted because of her suspected association with a FARC operative, and she opted to leave the country for several months—a luxury that few of the others under death threats could afford.

Municipal governments, congressional offices, police departments, army units, the media, and sports teams were systematically infiltrated or intimidated by the drug cartels. In contrast with the methods of the Medellín cartel, the modus operandi of the Cali cartel was considerably less violent, as it involved political contributions, support for community projects, and even marrying into respectable old families, with money laundering, bribery, and political and social camouflage as their main objectives. The Medellín cartel, whose bosses remained outsiders, was notorious for its open war with the police, which caused innumerable civilian deaths. During that decade, too, the drug trade expanded, on the one hand with the establishment of large cocaine processing factories and of coca plantations in territory controlled by the FARC (to whom the drug lords paid taxes and protection money, while the FARC also protected the welfare of the coca plantation workers), and, on the other, with the expansion into other areas of the economy such as cattle ranches[2].

Kidnappings continued, increasing in number as the deteriorating economy, coupled with an ineffectual or simply indifferent state, made such crimes easier and more attractive to criminal elements. Common criminals and paramilitaries would deliberately try to confuse the public into thinking that their kidnappings had been carried out by guerrillas. Meanwhile, guerrilla factions were sporadically in disagreement with one another over strategies and tactics, and one notorious faction of the FARC carried out summary executions and is suspected of being responsible for major human rights violations, contravening the FARC's operational rules. Drug enforcement agents from the United States were assumed in many cases to be interested mainly in helping to recuperate territory held by the guerrillas, although they were busy redesigning the problem as one of "narco-guerrillas", that is, shifting the entire blame for drug traffic squarely onto the FARC. The worst human rights offenders in cases of civilian massacres, torture, or assassinations were often elite battalions trained by U.S. personnel.

La Candelaria's portrait of this topsy-turvy world was the result of many months of collective research, improvisation, and rehearsal. Rather than an easily accessible script that followed dramatic conventions, *Roadhouse* was, in the end, a text that read either like an obsessively choreographed narrative dominated by stage directions or like a choppy backwater of flotsam and jetsam dialogue and sound effects. It could strike a director as a potential nightmare, but such fears are unwarranted if it is developed as a collective, actor-centered exercise. Every gesture leaves an invisible trail of alternative moves not made; every fragment of dialogue rises into audible speech as part of a continuum to which the audience is not privy. Each fragment rises out of an intimate conversation, out of the very private thoughts of an individual, or out of a pre-existing relationship that reveals part of itself in snatches of speech or gesture. Mediating between drama and performance, the stage directions, while precise and calculated, also offer the freedom of a loose narrative on which the actors can build their characters.

Every character can be said to represent a different sector of Colombian society, trapped on the set of a strange drama where the routine, even the comfortable, enters into conflict with the unusual, the unexpected. As a microcosm, it shows little, if any, of a productive working class; the Prostitute, the Taxi Driver, and the Waiters represent the service sector, and two of them are probably self-employed. Don Blanco represents the old dominant class, the landowners with undisputed authority until the arrival of the new forces: the drug lords and the paramilitaries.[3] At least one of the Musicians has spent ten years in prison; although his crime is not revealed, he still stands as a marginal character. The Lovers are entirely out of place, a bourgeois pair engaged in an extramarital affair that has brought them well beyond their geographic limits, to the very edge, literally.

The cast could fit the archetypal patterns of *commedia dell'arte* or the opera. This reader, for one, also heard fragmentary traces of the tavern scene in *Rigoletto* and saw broader strokes from *Huis clos* [*No Exit*]. The dialogue/counterpoint between speech and act, between meaningless words and meaningful silence, between noises and sounds, carries the play. The recorded opera music, which for one character is a haven from the barbaric environment and a protest against it, dialogues with the popular music of the two musicians. The fragments of conversation alternate with the installments of the letter that Chela is dictating to Doris (suggesting perhaps that she is illiterate?), in which she chronicles the disintegration of a rural community. The rain is a constant background for the music, the barking, the slamming of doors and drawers, the sounds of the cars and the helicopter, and, of course, the gunshots, which kill the two truest representatives of the old established order of an unchanging Colombian countryside: Don Blanco and the dog.

NOTES

1. The crowning moment, more horrific perhaps than the murder of presidential candidates, was the physical destruction of the Supreme Court by army tanks and shells, with the death of most of the justices and scores of personnel in the ensuing fire. This followed the hostage-taking of justices and personnel of the Court by M-19 guerrillas and a refusal by the army to continue dialogue with the guerrillas.

2. Some of these ranches were generally suspected of being major investments of some drug lords, and others, simply opportunistic land-grabs at the expense of small farmers, displaced by the private "anti-guerrilla" war of the land-grabbers. These families armed and equipped paramilitary groups, ostensibly to protect the landowners from guerrilla kidnappers, but in practice they were used most often to terrorize small farmers and farm union organizers, and eventually to carry out the more sordid work of the armed forces against suspected guerrilla sympathizers.

3. The third possible element operating in the countryside, the guerrillas, are not likely to be a part of this particular scenario. The code of the strangers' costumes and their conduct would preclude us from recognizing them as guerrillas. On dress codes in *Roadhouse* and in *Lucky Strike*, as well as for an excellent application of speech–act theory, see Lucía Garavito (1997).

Roadhouse
[El paso]
A collective Creation of Teatro La Candelaria (Bogotá) © 1988
Directed by Santiago García
Translated by Judith A. Weiss © 1992

The place: The authors use the terms taberna *(saloon) and* parador *(wayside inn) to describe the locale where the main action of the play takes place. It can be best conceived as a general store on a country road, where liquor is sold and music is featured at night, a meeting place that serves the needs of a scattered rural population.*

The title: "paso" can be translated variously as a crossing, a step or pace, a passage or course, a very short theatre piece, each of the stages of Christ's Passion, and an event or incident. "Crossing" and "incident" seem to be the most appropriate. To avoid excessive betrayal of a perfectly polyvalent title, the title of the translated version is changed entirely, to focus on the location of the events, the roadhouse.

Cast of Characters (in order of appearance)

EMIRO, *the shopkeeper's companion*
CHELA, *the shopkeeper*
FIRST MUSICIAN
SECOND MUSICIAN
DON BLANCO, *farmer*
DORIS, *the shopkeeper's daughter*
OBDULIO, *waiter*
The TAXI DRIVER
The LADY
The LADY'S LOVER
The PROSTITUTE
FIRST STRANGER
SECOND STRANGER
MAN IN BLACK

In the half light of the stage, we see a roadhouse—a tavern and general store—situated near a river crossing. Two MUSICIANS *with guitars.* EMIRO *at his accounts and* DON BLANCO *leaning against the counter.*

The MUSICIANS *wait, motionless, on a small riser. Suddenly they start playing a song: "Por el camino verde" [Along the green road].* DON BLANCO *is nodding off.* EMIRO *continues to work at his accounts, by candlelight.* CHELA *appears from the back, fixing her hair. She walks to the front of the stage. She looks up fixedly at the sky. The day is dawning. It is beginning to rain. She stretches out her hand to make sure. She walks around the store, stopping at the counter.* DON BLANCO *asks for two drinks. The song ends.*

DON BLANCO *goes up to the* MUSICIANS *carrying the two drinks. The* MUSICIANS *drink with him.*

CHELA. [*To* EMIRO]: So, what's up? Did you find the five hundred pesos?

EMIRO *ignores her and keeps on looking over his accounts. All of a sudden he starts to scratch the paper furiously and stands up grumbling. He exits violently to what would be the back of the store, and from there he can be heard swearing out loud. Sounds of doors and drawers slamming open and shut. Enter* EMIRO *carrying some suits and shirts. He is still grumbling, in a rage.*

EMIRO. I can't stand this any longer! If she wants the accounts in such perfect, perfect order, she can handle them herself. And she can go find someone else to mess with! That's what you get for being a fool! You work like a mule all night, and what do you get? I have my self-respect, too! If she thinks I'm a crook she can find herself another stooge! She's barking up the wrong tree! That's what you get for living with someone without being married. When you're not legally married, this is what you get, this disrespect! No more, no way! I'm getting out of here.

He exits and enters several times from the back of the store, brings out a leather suitcase and stuffs the clothes in it in a hurry. Every time he exits toward the back he raises his voice a little more and suddenly he shouts: Doris, bring me the magazine I lent you!

He keeps on swearing and goes back several more times for something that he's forgotten.

EMIRO. Five years in this bullshit and what do I have to show for it? [*Imitating* CHELA.] What's up? Have you found the five hundred pesos? I must have had the word "idiot" written all over my face when she met me! That's it, I'm out of here!

He leaves and returns with a handful of magazines. He opens the suitcase and puts them away. He shuts the suitcase. He gets ready to leave. Just as he is leaving, CHELA *talks to him from the place where she has remained since he began to throw his tantrum.*

CHELA. You can get out of here whenever you want, but not with my leather suitcase. You leave it right here.

Sound of drawers and doors, again. He shouts and curses. He enters carrying a plastic bag. He opens the suitcase. He takes out his things and stuffs them in the plastic bag. He hands CHELA *the suitcase.*

EMIRO. There's your suitcase!

Enter DORIS *with the magazine. She hands it to* EMIRO. EMIRO *takes it and puts it in the bag. He turns back, takes out a hat and puts it on. It starts raining.*

OBDULIO *appears from the back, half awake.* EMIRO *walks to the front of the stage but stops because of the rain.* DON BLANCO *walks over to him, looks at the sky, and addresses* EMIRO.

DON BLANCO. Where do you think you're going? No cars ever go by here any more. You know better than anyone else that one can't leave here in this kind of weather!

EMIRO *stops dead in his tracks, and keeps on muttering.*

EMIRO. Sonofabitch! The only thing missing in my life right now is for the devil himself to show up and drag me into the depths of hell!

All of a sudden, opera music is heard at full blast. EMIRO *keeps on muttering but most of what he is saying can't be heard because of the music.*

EMIRO. One fine day all the rain in the world is going to come down at once and flood this goddamned place! Some goddamn life! . . . No, not rain. A ton of shit should fall instead and bury everything! I hope this house of dead men's bones is swamped by rivers of rot! Damn, a thousand times, the day I set eyes on that woman. She's been my ruin! May lightning strike us and turn us all to charcoal, to punish us for living buried up to our necks in the sin of being here!

In the midst of the opera music and while EMIRO *is cursing, a group of* PEOPLE *enter the inn. There are four people, covered with a large sheet of plastic and an umbrella.*

They shake themselves off and clean their clothes. They are: the DRIVER *of an inter-city taxicab, a* YOUNG MAN *with a very elegant* LADY, *and a* PROSTITUTE. *The* TAXI DRIVER *greets everybody and addresses* EMIRO. *He tries to explain what has happened to them.* CHELA *welcomes the couple. She tells* DORIS *to look after the passengers. She calls* OBDULIO. *She takes the plastic bag away from* EMIRO, *who was standing in the middle of the room, not knowing what to do.* DORIS *arranges the tables and chairs. Enter* OBDULIO, *who cleans the tables with a rag. The* COUPLE *walks around the place looking over the seats. The* TAXI DRIVER *explains to* EMIRO *what happened to them.*

About one kilometer from there, the car skidded over to one side; then it wouldn't start. It was the bearings of the rear axle that broke. I'll have to wait for someone to bring him the parts.

EMIRO *asks him why he's telling him this. He doesn't think it's the bearing. From what he's saying, he thinks it's probably the universal. Which is less of a problem. The* TAXI DRIVER *shows him some parts he's got in his hands and assures him it's the bearing.* EMIRO *tells him that he is going to consult his magazine.*

The pair of LOVERS *at last make up their mind, choosing a table at the far end, and they start to clean the seats. The opera music stops.* OBDULIO *appears with a bucket and some cleaning equipment. Very ceremoniously, he puts on a pair of black rubber gloves. He goes into the bathroom. Very carefully, the* LADY *cleans off the chair and the table of the place they have chosen. The* PROSTITUTE, *who has been cleaning a shoe, looks at the* LADY *and starts to laugh. The* LADY *looks at her and the* PROSTITUTE *pretends that she is not laughing. The* LADY *keeps on cleaning off her chair and table, and the* PROSTITUTE *laughs along with* DON BLANCO. *The* LADY *sits down and the* PROSTITUTE *stands up. She moves upstage, looks at the rain and casts a sidelong glance at the* LADY.

PROSTITUTE. This is too much! On top of the car accident, this awful rain!

The LADY *stops looking at her. Laughing discreetly, the* PROSTITUTE *goes back to her original place. She laughs with* DON BLANCO. EMIRO *looks at them without understanding anything and suddenly exclaims:*

EMIRO. The danger of landslides, it's true!

The MAN *and* WOMAN *laugh even harder. When they stop laughing, the* PROSTITUTE *heads for the bathroom but finds that it is occupied by* OBDULIO, *who is cleaning it. She goes back to her seat. A long pause. They all settle down in their respective places and are caught up in their own thoughts.*

CHELA *dictates a letter to* DORIS.

CHELA. . . . Nothing going on here . . . or rather, less than nothing . . . we get news from the outside . . . it's getting worse every day . . . in Torrentes, for example, last week they killed another six men.

OBDULIO *comes out of the bathroom. He takes off the rubber gloves, places them in the bucket and picks up all his cleaning equipment just as he did when he went in. The* LADY *heads hurriedly toward the bathroom. The* PROSTITUTE, *too, tries to go but the* LADY *beats her to the door. The* PROSTITUTE *sits down. Presently, the* WOMAN *comes out of the bathroom. She is covering her nose and mouth with a handkerchief as if to keep from vomiting. She goes over to her* LOVER *and whispers something to him. The* LOVER *goes to the counter and speaks to* CHELA. *Raising her voice a little,* CHELA *tells him:*

CHELA. What do you mean, another bathroom? That's the only one we have!

The LADY, *who is obviously uncomfortable, casts a sidelong look at the* PROSTITUTE, *who has started laughing, and runs out. The* LOVER *rushes after her.*

LOVER. Fernanda! Fernanda!

He grabs the umbrella and goes out to help her. CHELA, *too, runs, upstage. She turns to scold* OBDULIO.

CHELA. Why didn't you clean the bathroom well?

OBDULIO, *obviously annoyed, opens the bathroom door and shows* CHELA *that the bathroom is clean.* CHELA *goes toward him and tells him:*

CHELA. Well, clean it again!

OBDULIO *faces* CHELA *and folds his arms.* EMIRO *gets up from his place, where he was having breakfast, and orders* OBDULIO.

EMIRO. Obey Chela!

OBDULIO *slams the bathroom door and goes to the back of the store.*

CHELA. He's already forgotten where we found him and what we've done for him!

OBDULIO *enters with the cleaning equipment and goes into the bathroom. From the bathroom we hear* OBDULIO *smashing and banging the toilet and the floors. The* YOUNG MAN *emerges from the bathroom.* CHELA *orders* DORIS *to serve breakfast to the musicians. The* COUPLE *return, soaked to the skin. The* LADY *dries herself in a towel handed to her by her* LOVER. DOÑA CHELA *goes over to them to ask them whether they need anything. The* LADY *answers that they don't. The* LOVER *asks for a drink, which* CHELA *brings.* CHELA *goes* back to the counter. DON BLANCO *starts complaining as he approaches the musicians.*

DON BLANCO. Now, she was a woman . . . the woman who understood her man . . . the only one who was able to understand him . . . To serve him as she should . . . the one who always knew what the man wanted . . . what he needed . . . the young girl [*To the musicians.*] Play the song of the young girl . . . Come on . . . come on, that's what you're paid for.

The MUSICIANS *finish their breakfast in a hurry and play the song "Si tú mueres primero"* [*If you die first*]. *During the song, the* LADY *gets up, goes to the counter and asks* CHELA *where she can change.* CHELA *tells her that she can change in the back of the store. She tells* DORIS *to go with her. The* LADY *goes into the back of the store. The* PROSTITUTE *checks her shopping bag and notices that she is missing something. She goes to the counter and asks* CHELA. CHELA *points to* DON BLANCO. *The* PROSTITUTE *approaches* DON BLANCO *and asks him whether he can sell her some tomatoes that she needs.* DON BLANCO *tells her that he will, but later, because right now they have to hear the song of the young girl. He offers her a drink. The* PROSTITUTE *accepts and then returns to her place. The* LADY *enters from the back of the store. She has changed her shirt.*

The sound of an engine can now be heard. It's a car. The people keep on acting as if they didn't hear the noise, which keeps on getting louder.

EMIRO *goes into the back of the store to take out some magazines to show the* DRIVER. *All of a sudden, the noise of the engine stops. Two headlights have been turned on upstage. When the engine noise stops, the* PROSTITUTE *explains that a taxi has arrived. The* LADY *and her* LOVER *pick up their things and run toward the door in the back. The headlights are turned off. The* PROSTITUTE *picks up her shopping bag and she, too, goes toward the back. Everybody is in suspense. The* MUSICIANS *keep on singing.*

From the back, two MEN *appear, dressed almost identically. Blue shirt and white trousers. They are carrying black suitcases. They stop at the door.*

The MUSICIANS *stop playing. After a moment's silence, the* DRIVER *asks them:*

TAXI DRIVER. Are you headed for Denges?

The strangers look at him without replying. They look over everyone who is present and then one of them, the older of the two, fixes his stare on the LOVER. *Afterwards, without taking his eyes off the couple, he crosses the store slowly, to the farthest table. When he's half-way across, the opera music begins to play. They sit down. The* COUPLE *is very nervous. The* LADY *starts to put on a scarf and dark glasses while she talks to her* LOVER. EMIRO *approaches the table where the* STRANGERS *are seated and asks them what they're going to drink. The* STRANGERS *place their order: two glasses of milk.* EMIRO *asks them "Anything else," but they do not answer.* EMIRO *goes to the counter.* OBDULIO *goes over to the newcomers' table and cleans it carefully with a rag. He asks them whether they have already ordered and the* STRANGERS *barely answer him.* EMIRO *has reached the counter and talks with* CHELA. *He lets her know what the* STRANGERS *have ordered.* DORIS *pours two glasses of milk. She goes over to the* MEN'S *table. On the way, she meets* OBDULIO, *who intercepts her and takes the glasses away from her. Upset,* DORIS *returns to the counter.* OBDULIO *reaches the table with the two glasses.*

The LADY *is still speaking with her* LOVER. *She wants to leave, any way she can. These* MEN *look very suspicious; they could be detectives sent by her husband. The discussion grows more heated, until the lover throws one of her suitcases on the floor with unusual violence. The opera music stops.*

Everybody looks at the COUPLE. *The* FIRST STRANGER *gets up slowly and approaches the* LOVER. *The* COUPLE *now seems paralyzed. The* FIRST STRANGER *comes up to the* LOVER. *He stops and looks at him fixedly. The* LOVER *looks at him almost terrified. Suddenly the* STRANGER *asks him:*

FIRST STRANGER. Do you have flowers for the road? [*His voice is barely audible.*]

The LOVER *looks at him, unnerved. The* LADY *says, with a faint voice:*

LADY. What? What was it he said?

LOVER. What?

The STRANGER *looks at them for a moment longer, then, with a vague gesture, he excuses himself.*

FIRST STRANGER. Forget it.

The STRANGER *retreats to his place. The* COUPLE *is left disconcerted.* DON BLANCO *goes over to the* STRANGERS *and greets them, bowing profusely.*

DON BLANCO. Excuse me . . . I am Evaristo Blanco . . . my respects . . . at your service. I am the sole proprietor of the only farm in this area . . . my respects . . . If there's any way I can be of service to you . . . My farm is the only one that has water . . . because around here, although it rains a great deal, there is no water . . . that's life . . . I'm at your service . . . My respects . . .

The STRANGERS *look at him and do not answer. They remain impassive.* DON BLANCO *withdraws, murmuring.* OBDULIO *moves to center stage and places a bucket there, to catch the water that is dripping from the ceiling. After whispering something to the* LADY, *the* LOVER *approaches the* STRANGERS. *He speaks hesitantly.*

LOVER. I think there's been some confusion . . . and the lady, who's a little nervous just now . . . Couldn't help herself . . . It so happens that we . . . I mean she and I . . . she . . . the lady, is an acquaintance of mine . . . We're on our way to Rivalta . . .We had an accident one kilometer from here . . . I mean, the gentleman's car broke down . . . it seems to be the bearing . . . And we . . . she and I have to get to Rivalta . . . so if you could help us to get out of here . . . I don't know how we could pay you back . . . We'll pay whatever we have to . . . If you're headed for Denges . . . it's only a few kilometers back, and then we . . . it seems they have a car there that's in working order.

The STRANGERS *have been looking at him all this time without showing any expression or response, and so the* LOVER *gradually lowers his voice and withdraws to his place.*

During the LOVER'S *monologue, the* SECOND STRANGER *has stood up and gone into the bathroom with his suitcase. Towards the end of the* LOVER'S *speech, he comes out of the bathroom, still holding his suitcase. This is repeated several times. It is still raining heavily. The dog barks outside. The* SECOND STRANGER *stands up, nervously. The* FIRST STRANGER *calms him down and makes him sit down.* DON BLANCO *returns from the back, where the* STRANGERS' *car is supposed to be. He enters laughing and murmuring fragmented sentences.*

DON BLANCO. That's some machine, no kidding! . . . A regular boat. With a car like that . . . it can rain all it wants . . . and every single bridge could collapse . . . Hell, what a ship! A goddamn jumbo! With a car like that I could drive through any rivers and over any roads I wanted to! Damn, *that's* power!

He laughs, directing his laughter toward the STRANGERS *and making all kinds of gestures of approval in their direction. The* STRANGERS *look at him impassively.* EMIRO *approaches the* STRANGERS. *He's carrying an auto mechanics magazine.*

EMIRO. Of course, you have a real car . . . On the other hand, what's wrong with the taxi is . . . look here, in this magazine . . . the problem is made very clear right here . . . you already know that it broke down about one kilometer from here . . . Well, the driver says that the bearing broke . . . but as you can see it's really the universal . . . because . . . forgive me, do you know something about mechanics? You do? Well then, look here, the universal is connected on this side to the transmission axle and when you apply a greater strain than what this type of car can bear . . . then the joint between the main axle and the other one . . . this one here . . . it shifts and then of course the universal is useless and then it seems as if . . . as if the bearing had broken . . . that's what the driver says.

TAXI DRIVER: [*From his seat.*] It's the bearing!

EMIRO. No sir . . . I've got the proof right here, in this article . . . this is a scientific journal . . . it's never wrong . . . it's never failed me . . .

TAXI DRIVER. Well, this time it failed you, because it's the bearing.

EMIRO. When it's the bearing the car makes a very particular kind of noise . . . and according to what you told me . . . the engine is making a noise like this: trc . . . trrrrr . . . tac . . . trrrr . . . tac . . . That is to say, an in-between little noise, you know . . . tac . . . on the other hand, when it's a bearing, it's a continuous noise . . . a rather muffled grrr grrr . . . without any . . . you understand, don't you?

The FIRST STRANGER *has been looking at* EMIRO *all this time without showing any interest in what he is saying. The* SECOND STRANGER *has gone back and forth between his place and the bathroom several times, always carrying his package.* EMIRO *keeps on talking, practically stammering.*

EMIRO. . . . so if you could help us get the car out of the ditch and push it just a few meters . . . slowly, it could get to Torrentes, to a shop where they can change the coupling, which I'm sure it needs to reconnect . . . the drive shaft to . . . the universal joint.

The SECOND STRANGER *comes out of the bathroom without the bag and sits at the table next to his partner.* OBDULIO, *who has noticed the* STRANGER'S *slip, goes into the bathroom and brings out the bag. He takes it to the table. Faced with the* MAN'S *indifference,* EMIRO *withdraws. The opera music plays.*

Surprised, the SECOND STRANGER *snatches the bag from* OBDULIO. *The* FIRST STRANGER *scolds the other one for his unforgivable slip. The group consisting of the* TAXI DRIVER, EMIRO, *and the* PROSTITUTE *look at them with surprise.*

The FIRST STRANGER *calls* OBDULIO *over and walks with him up stage. He speaks to him confidentially. He asks him whether he opened the suitcase or saw anything inside it. To every one of the* STRANGER'S *questions* OBDULIO *answers no. The* STRANGER *slips* OBDULIO *a banknote.* OBDULIO *looks around before accepting it. Then the* STRANGER *shakes his hand, smiling, and thanks him for his cooperation.* OBDULIO *looks at the others with some embarrassment and withdraws toward the back. The* STRANGER *returns to his place. The opera music stops.* EMIRO *and the* TAXI DRIVER *have been arguing about the car problem.*

DRIVER. Why don't we just go and look at it? Then, maybe, you'll finally accept the fact that that magazine of yours has messed up your brain.

EMIRO. You mean that maybe you'll finally accept the fact that science is worth more than your lousy experience.

DRIVER. Watch what you say to me, will you? How long do you think I've been driving that car, huh? Ten whole years!

EMIRO. And how long do you think I've been subscribing to this magazine? Huh?

DRIVER. Cut the crap and let's go see the car!

EMIRO. All right, let's go. Obdulio, come along. And bring the large plastic sheet!

They start to exit. The PROSTITUTE, *the* LADY, *and the* LOVER *walk them to the door and ask them whether they will be able to fix the car.* OBDULIO *follows them with the sheet of plastic, but before exiting he stops for a moment and looks at the* STRANGERS *as if asking for their approval. The* PROSTITUTE *and the* LADY *stand together looking toward the place where the group exited. The* PROSTITUTE *smiles at the* LADY. *The latter, surprised to find herself next to the woman, returns to her place. Pause.* CHELA *continues dictating the letter to* DORIS.

CHELA . . . You say the situation over there is unbearable . . . but I assure you that over here it's worse . . . Ever since they killed my husband . . . and the highway crew left . . .

The LOVER *asks* CHELA *for a drink. She suspends the dictation and takes him his drink.* DORIS *serves* DON BLANCO *a bowl of soup. Then she discreetly approaches the strangers.* DON BLANCO *asks the musicians to play something. The* MUSICIANS *play a happy song. The* PROSTITUTE *goes over to the* STRANGERS *and invites the older one to dance.* DORIS *sits down to talk to the other one. The prostitute dances with the* STRANGER *and tells him all about the groceries she's taking her mother. The* STRANGER *is barely dancing with her and* shows no interest in what the woman is telling him. When the music stops, we can hear what the PROSTITUTE is telling the STRANGER. *She keeps on moving around the floor as if she were dancing with him.*

PROSTITUTE. So there I am, in the taxi with those people, and that car breaks down, and the truth is I'm in a hurry to get to Denges where my mother lives. Once a month I make an effort and take her some groceries, which isn't much, but it's a great help for the poor woman. Besides, now she's a little sick. You know? One has feelings even if one doesn't show it. Because of my trade, you know what I mean. People always assume one doesn't have a heart. But it's not like that. The most important thing in my life is my mom, but above all my little girl. I'd make any sacrifice I had to, for her. Well, I do because you shouldn't think that in this business it's all fun and games . . . there's a certain amount of sacrifice involved. Well, as I was telling you, my little girl fell when she was a year old and hurt her hip. You know? And now she has to walk around with some contraption between her little legs.

Just then, the TAXI DRIVER, OBDULIO, *and* EMIRO *enter, all wet and covered in mud. The* TAXI DRIVER *is swearing at* EMIRO *for being so hard-headed. The* PROSTITUTE *and the* LADY *rush toward them, to ask them whether they were able to fix the taxi.* EMIRO *is the last one to come in, and he stops at the door when he sees* DORIS *talking to the* STRANGER. *When she sees him,* DORIS *stands up and goes over to the counter. The* SECOND MUSICIAN, *who has seemed uncomfortable ever since* DORIS *sat down with the* STRANGER, *addresses her as if to get her attention. Furious,* EMIRO *storms into the back of the store. The* PROSTITUTE *is now telling her story to the* LADY, *since the* STRANGER *has gone back to his place.*

PROSTITUTE. So what am I supposed to do now? How are we going to get out of here? I'm in a hurry to take my mother her groceries and it has to be today, because she's been expecting me for ten days. At the beginning of every month I take her groceries. Because whatever you do with your life, your love and respect for your mother is the one thing you don't lose . . . or your children, of course . . . The older one turned out to be a rascal. But the little one is a darling. She fell, about a year after she was born, you know? . . . They can say whatever they want about me, but they can never say that I failed to love and respect my mother . . .

The TAXI DRIVER, *who is behind her, starts reading her a passage from the Bible.*

DRIVER. Look here, listen to this . . .

He begins reading and the PROSTITUTE *shows him she is bored and sits down in her chair.*

DRIVER. "And Job answered: Man's days upon the earth are limited, and his days are like the days of a hireling. As a servant longeth for the shade."

He interrupts his reading to ask OBDULIO *for a soft drink.*

DRIVER. "My days have passed more swiftly than the web is cut by the weaver, and are consumed without any hope. Remember that my life is but wind, and my eyes shall not return to see good things. Nor shall the sight of man behold me. As a cloud that is consumed, and passeth away, so he that shall go down into the grave shall not come up. Nor shall he return any more to his house, neither shall his place know him any more."

OBDULIO *brings him his soft drink with a glass and pours it. The* PROSTITUTE *raises her handbag abruptly and spills the soft drink on the* TAXI DRIVER's *trousers.*

The TAXI DRIVER *interrupts his reading and throws the book to the floor in a rage. In an attempt to correct the mistake,* OBDULIO *cleans the* TAXI DRIVER'S *trousers with a rag. As he reaches the fly, the man stops* OBDULIO'S *hand with a violent gesture and glares at him. The* MAN *lets go and* OBDULIO *backs off, embarrassed. The* TAXI DRIVER, *as if regaining consciousness from his own violent action, withdraws shyly toward the back.*

The LADY *and the* PROSTITUTE *look at each other and hold back their laughter at the scene they have just witnessed. They conceal their laughter when the* TAXI DRIVER *looks at them reproachfully. All of a sudden, they are all engrossed in their own thoughts.*

There is a long pause. Suddenly, DON BLANCO, *who was drinking his fish broth, starts to wave his arms about like a drowning man. He coughs and tries to breathe. He is choking on a fish bone. Everyone rushes to his aid.* DON BLANCO *falls to the floor and everyone tries to revive him. The only ones who stand aside are the* STRANGERS. DON BLANCO *comes to. A shot rings out in the distance, toward the back. Everybody stops, paralyzed for a moment. The* STRANGERS *stand up. The locals*—EMIRO, CHELA, DORIS *and the* MUSICIANS—*rush toward the back, where the shot came from. The* LADY, *the* PROSTITUTE, *the* LOVER, *and the* TAXI DRIVER *approach the others timidly.* OBDULIO *gets up from where he was kneeling, next to* DON BLANCO, *and takes a few steps back.*

The STRANGERS *call* OBDULIO *over and whisper something to him. They ask him for the check.* OBDULIO *rushes to* DOÑA CHELA'S *side.* DORIS, *who has realized that the* STRANGERS *are planning to leave, rushes up to them and secretly asks them to take her with them. The* STRANGERS *agree, in a vague sort of way.* DORIS *runs out to the back of the store.* OBDULIO *returns to the* STRANGERS *and they pay their bill. The* STRANGERS *pick up their things and prepare to leave.*

Meanwhile, DON BLANCO *has recovered and begins to feel himself all over and to make sure that he's still alive. He has a fit of laughter and heartily embraces everyone in his path, not quite aware of what is happening. Laughter and words rush out of him.*

DON BLANCO. Thank you! Thank you, my friends! You saved my life! My life! Just when I thought I was in the grip of death I came back to life thanks to you! Thanks, thanks, my friends!

He embraces everyone and celebrates his own survival.

DON BLANCO. I was in darkness on the other side, and you saved me. You rescued me and brought me back to life . . . to life! Do you understand? Life! Thank you. I had forgotten that such a thing as friendship existed! I thought

I was alone, but I was wrong! You are here, you who saved my life! Thank you, my friends! Let's have music, music and drinks for everyone!

The STRANGERS *have paid for their drinks and they exit.* OBDULIO *runs behind them as far as the exit in the back. When the* PROSTITUTE, *the* LADY, *and the* LOVER *realize that the* STRANGERS *are leaving, they too run toward the door. The* FIRST STRANGER *turns and gestures to them to stop.*

FIRST STRANGER. Unfortunately we don't have room for anyone.

They turn their back and leave hurriedly. Outside, the sound of the engine starting and the vehicle departing.

The MUSICIANS *play a happy song to please* DON BLANCO. *They all return to their places.* EMIRO *tells* CHELA *something and she burst out laughing. There is a relaxed atmosphere in spite of the frustration that some of the people feel as a result of the* STRANGERS' *departure. The* MUSICIANS *play their song.* DORIS *runs out of the back room putting on lipstick. She is carrying a plastic bag. It is a transparent bag, and one can see that she is carrying her clothes in it. She finds out that the* STRANGERS *have left. She runs toward the back to try to catch up with them.*

When the SECOND MUSICIAN *sees* DORIS *leave, he steps off the platform and continues to play but is obviously worried about the young girl.* DORIS *comes back. The* MUSICIANS *stop playing.* DORIS *crosses the floor, slowly, and sits at the table where the* STRANGERS *had sat. The* SECOND MUSICIAN *looks at her with an anguished sadness. The young woman wipes the lipstick from her lips. Then she reluctantly takes off her high heel shoes. She sits looking outside.* CHELA *moves toward her and stands next to the table. The* SECOND MUSICIAN *goes into the back of the store.* CHELA *taps her head twice, to indicate the hard-headedness of the young woman. She takes her plastic bag and goes into the back of the store. Everyone glances at the young woman and then they all plunge into their respective thoughts. The* SECOND MUSICIAN *enters and approaches* DORIS *shyly. He has a letter in his hand. He stops next to her and offers it to her. She keeps on looking out without paying any attention to him. The* MUSICIAN *places the letter next to her, on the table.* DORIS *picks up the letter and reads it, somewhat surprised. She looks at the* MUSICIAN, *who has gone to stand behind her, awaiting a reply. Suddenly,* DORIS *lets out a huge laugh. Her laughter is sincere and explosive. The* MUSICIAN *is taken aback and starts to walk away.* DORIS *laughs even harder. The* SECOND MUSICIAN, *who is now completely confused, goes back to his place.* DORIS *stops laughing.*

The TAXI DRIVER, *in a fit of rage because the auto parts that he had do not match, furiously throws the parts to the floor. Everyone turns to look at him. He apologizes, somewhat confused by his own violence.*

DRIVER. No, they're no good . . .

OBDULIO *approaches as if he were about to pick up the parts. The* TAXI DRIVER *stops him.*

DRIVER. No, leave them there. You don't have to.

OBDULIO *is going to serve the couple but* CHELA *calls him.*

CHELA. Obdulio.

OBDULIO *approaches the counter.*

CHELA. Here. You have a hundred fifty pesos left over after deductions.
She hands him an envelope with some bills and the money. OBDULIO *looks over the paper and then, restraining his anger, takes the money and puts it in his pocket. He tries to tell* CHELA *something but all of a sudden he slaps his hand down on the counter and moves to the front of the stage. There he stops and looks out in a deep anger.* CHELA, *who followed his actions, orders him:*
CHELA. Obdulio, go clean the dog's bed!
OBDULIO *restrains himself for a few moments, then goes toward the back to obey the order. After a little while we hear heavy banging along with the dog's pitiful whining.* OBDULIO *rushes in to the middle of the room. Everyone looks at him with surprise.* OBDULIO *goes into the bathroom and slams the door.*
EMIRO *murmurs a few words. The* LOVER *asks* CHELA *for a drink. The woman brings him the drink and stands next to him. The* LOVER *takes the* LADY'S *handbag and is about to take out the money to pay. The* LADY *snatches the handbag from him abruptly, looks at him as if to dare him, and pays the bill herself. The disconcerted* LOVER *is about to drink, but he is suddenly overcome with anger, leaves the glass on the table and walks off toward the back. He looks out at the horizon with deep sadness.* EMIRO *approaches* DORIS *as if to speak with her.* DORIS *stands up violently, picks up her shoes and goes into the back of the store.* CHELA *calls her but she doesn't come back.*
EMIRO *remains standing next to the table where* DORIS *had been, looks at the newspaper that the* STRANGERS *left on the table and begins to leaf through it. All of a sudden, he looks at everyone and says, as if to himself:*
EMIRO. Pride will be the death of men and the destruction of women.
He keeps on reading through the news in the paper.
EMIRO. Train crash in Istanbul . . . just look at that, how dangerous . . . Elections postponed . . . they were holding elections . . . Another five unidentified dead . . . they're still hung up on dead people . . . The stock market is in chaos . . . chaos . . . rise in share prices, out of control . . . what do you think of that? A volcano is about to erupt in Mali-Hiuro . . . where could that be . . . cultural news . . . look at this . . . [*To the first musician.*] Say, what was the name of the group you belonged to?
FIRST MUSICIAN. Which one? The Tropical Boys?
EMIRO. Yes, that's the one. Look. Here it says that the Tropical Boys left for New York. That they have a contract to play over there. There's even a picture of them.
The FIRST MUSICIAN *snatches the newspaper from him and starts showing it around to everyone, excitedly.*
FIRST MUSICIAN. Of course, there they are, all of them! The Tropical Boys . . . ! Well, there are two of us missing. Edilberto and I . . . Look. I should be in there. Just like in this picture I've got here.
He rummages nervously through his wallet, pulls out an old newspaper clipping, and shows it to everyone.
FIRST MUSICIAN. See, what I told you is true! The only ones missing are me and Edilberto, who died about five years ago. But all the others are there. A

little older, but they're there. Just the same as they used to be. The famous musical group now in New York! [*Reading aloud.*] "We hope that they harvest the same success as always!" Of course, we were always a great success! We composed the famous song of the Pirulín Pin Pon. You've heard it, Madam. It was a song that made waves in its time . . . ah, the sound of that band was something! Now, that was music, and with special arrangements for trumpet and all . . . I played the guitar . . . but the best part was when the trumpet came in. Those chords made us famous: paparapaparapaparapá . . . but what was really successful, and others tried to imitate but never could, was the beat . . . you understand, it was a syncopated beat, between the trumpet and the drums . . . and I wish my guitar would play up the flats . . . now that was a sound . . . that's how we reached the top . . . no one like us . . . the Tropical Boys . . . no one could sound like that!

OBDULIO *interrupts him.*

OBDULIO. So, if you were so famous, what are you doing here?

The MUSICIAN'S *joy is stopped short. He looks at* OBDULIO *and shouts at him angrily:*

MUSICIAN. Fuck off!

Everyone is silent. Suddenly EMIRO *murmurs.*

EMIRO. People in glass houses shouldn't throw stones.

After a brief silence, DON BLANCO *speaks.*

DON BLANCO. All right, all right, let's forget this and talk about something else. A man can't spend his life paying for a mistake that he's already paid for. He already spent ten years in jail. What else do you want, huh?

The MUSICIANS *return to their places. There is a pause.* CHELA *keeps on dictating her letter to* DORIS.

CHELA. . . . and the highway workers left . . . since then this has never been the same as before . . . a customer stops in every once in a while . . . and it's even worse during the rainy season, like now.

The PROSTITUTE, *who seemed to have started humming the song, suddenly begins to sing it and approaches the musicians.*

PROSTITUTE. Of course, the Pirulín Pin Pon was my favorite record! That's when I fell in love for the first time! When I was fifteen! And that's why they kicked me out of the house. [*She laughs.*] But can you imagine what I would be if I had stayed there? And it's all because of the Pirulín Pin Pon! Aw, why don't you play it? Yes, please play the Pirulín Pin Pon!

DON BLANCO. Of course! Certainly! Play the Pirulín Pin Pon for the lady. With feeling now, boys!

The MUSICIANS *play the song. The* PROSTITUTE *starts dancing gaily and invites* DON BLANCO *to join her.* EMIRO *dances too. The* LADY *smiles and claps to the beat. The* LOVER *slowly approaches the table and drinks the drink that he had left.* EMIRO *makes a sign to* DORIS, *inviting her to dance with him. The young woman ignores him.*

Above the music, we can hear the sound of a car engine coming closer and closer. The sound of the engine drowns out the music. DON BLANCO *and the* PROSTITUTE *are dancing together in the center of the hall.* EMIRO *goes up to*

DORIS *and takes her by the hand to dance with her.* DORIS *refuses, and when* EMIRO *insists she shouts:*

DORIS. Fuck off!

CHELA, *who has realized what's happening, slams her hand down hard on the counter. Suddenly the sound of the engine is turned off. The headlights go off and everyone looks toward the back.*

Someone says, "It's a taxi", and everyone rushes out to the rear entrance.

The MUSICIANS *play on. The* PROSTITUTE, *the* LADY, *the* LOVER, *and the* TAXI DRIVER *stand together next to the door. In the corner the headlights of a car are lit. The headlights are turned off. Soon after, the* TWO STRANGERS *appear at the door. They are wearing black plastic rain capes. The* STRANGERS *stand in the doorway. The* SECOND STRANGER *is carrying a heavy metal box. The* LADY *moves closer to* THE STRANGERS *and asks them:*

LADY. What happened to you?

The FIRST STRANGER *looks at her for a moment, then answers.*

FIRST STRANGER. They blew up the bridge.

The terrified LADY *drops her make-up kit.* EMIRO *turns to the* MUSICIANS *and repeats:*

EMIRO. They dynamited the bridge.

The FIRST STRANGER *steps forward and calls* OBDULIO. *They go to the front of the stage. The* STRANGER *whispers some questions to him. The young man answers; he seems to be complaining to the* STRANGER. *The* STRANGER *asks* OBDULIO *whether they can leave some boxes in the tavern.* OBDULIO *asks* EMIRO *whether they can bring the boxes inside.* EMIRO *goes over to ask for* CHELA'S *permission.* CHELA *shrugs her shoulders, as though giving approval.* EMIRO *goes over to* OBDULIO *and says yes.* OBDULIO *goes over to the* STRANGER *to tell him that they can bring them in. The* STRANGER *goes over to his partner and signals him to bring in the box.* OBDULIO *points the way to the back of the store. The* stranger *asks* EMIRO *to help him. The four men bring in one box after another, from the car to the back of the store. When they have brought in about five boxes,* CHELA *stops them. She seems alarmed.*

CHELA. What's this? You said a few little boxes and look at what you're bringing in here! No, that's enough. You leave those other boxes at the door. What's next?

FIRST STRANGER. Only two more boxes and we're done.

CHELA. No more, I said! There's no room back there for any more boxes!

They place the last boxes near the entrance. All of a sudden the dog howls outside. The SECOND STRANGER *pulls out a revolver from under his rain poncho. Everyone backs off in fright. The* FIRST STRANGER *gestures to reassure his partner and asks* EMIRO *whether he'll let him park a little closer in. His voice is barely perceptible because he is speaking softly and because of the sound of the rain. The same as before,* EMIRO *asks* CHELA *and she agrees reluctantly. The* STRANGERS *exit with* EMIRO *and* OBDULIO. *The car starts. The headlights go on and the car comes closer and closer. The front end of the jeep appears at the back and enters the store. Everyone backs off. The sound of the engine gets louder.* CHELA *screams for the men to stop the car, which has invaded*

the establishment. *The car stops and the headlights and the engine are turned off. The* STRANGERS, OBDULIO, *and* EMIRO *are back in the store.* CHELA *protests, angry because her establishment has been invaded. The* STRANGER *gives* EMIRO *some banknotes.* CHELA *keeps protesting and eyes the money. She refuses the money that* EMIRO *is handing her. The* FIRST STRANGER *offers her two more banknotes, insisting.* CHELA *finally accepts the money, but keeps on complaining about the invasion. The* STRANGERS *enter the tavern and go to the place that they had occupied earlier.* OBDULIO *takes their rain cloaks. The* FIRST STRANGER *opens a small suitcase and takes out a toothbrush, a towel, and toothpaste. He goes to the bathroom, with* OBDULIO *opening the door very obsequiously.*
The PROSTITUTE *has been standing in the middle of the floor as if disoriented. She starts to protest.*
PROSTITUTE. What's going on here? Or should I say, rather, that it's impossible to breathe in here. What we have to do is evacuate the place as soon as possible. [*To the taxi driver.*] Let's get out of here! Come on, let's see if we can find somebody to get us out of this mess! Come on, we'll see if we can get your spare part down the road!
DRIVER. Are you crazy? Over there we won't get anything. We have to wait here . . .
PROSTITUTE. To see whether one of your prophets will bring us the spare part? No, I'm leaving any way I can! Come on, madam. Come walk with me. Up ahead, at the bridge, we'll find someone to help us!
The LADY *begins to gather her things to leave with the woman but her* LOVER *starts to protest. The* PROSTITUTE *puts the shopping bag on her head and stands at the back door.*
PROSTITUTE. If we don't leave right away, do you know who'll get us out of here? The devil, maybe! I'll find my way! If nobody is going with me, I'll go alone!
The PROSTITUTE *leaves by the rear exit. Everyone is left disconcerted. A long pause.* CHELA *keeps on dictating her letter to* DORIS.
CHELA. . . . Go on . . . so give up your plans to come here . . . because regardless of how bad things may be over there, they can't be any worse than they are down here . . . signed . . . your sister . . . Chela Rodriguez (widow of Pérez).
DON BLANCO *starts whispering and laughing and orders the* MUSICIANS *to play something. The* MUSICIANS *play the song "Black flowers"* [*Flores negras*] *. . . The* LADY *starts to argue with her* LOVER. DON BLANCO *secretly signals to her not to give in. The discussion becomes heated. The* LADY *picks up her things and moves to the place where the* PROSTITUTE *had been sitting.* DON BLANCO *gives the* LADY *a drink.*
Visibly upset, the LOVER *hits the chair and walks off toward the back of the store. The* FIRST STRANGER *comes out of the bathroom. He emerges with his toothbrush in his mouth and his towel around his neck. He walks around the room and stops upstage, behaving as if he owned the place. He sits down at his table.*

DON BLANCO, *jealous of the stranger's attitude, calls* OBDULIO. OBDULIO *comes over to the counter.* DON BLANCO *orders two drinks and has* OBDULIO *take them over to the* STRANGERS. OBDULIO *tries to object but* DON BLANCO *insists.* OBDULIO *takes* THE STRANGERS *their drinks. He puts the drinks on the table. The* FIRST STRANGER *refused the drinks and looks over at* DON BLANCO. DON BLANCO *meets the* STRANGER'S *stare and calls* OBDULIO. OBDULIO *goes over to* DON BLANCO. DON BLANCO *orders him to take a bottle to the* STRANGER'S *table.* OBDULIO *refuses to obey.* DON BLANCO *pushes him angrily to force him to take the bottle. Frightened,* OBDULIO *obeys. He brings the bottle and places it on the table. The* STRANGER *looks at* DON BLANCO *and stands up to walk upstage, turning his back on the landowner. The* SECOND STRANGER *stands up slowly and faces* DON BLANCO *with his arms hanging loosely at his side, as if he were about to shoot. The* FIRST STRANGER *turns around, returns to the table, takes the bottle, stares at it and then spills its contents into the bucket a that is in the center of the room.* DON BLANCO *grumbles angrily and moves toward the* STRANGERS.

DON BLANCO. Who's the one who dares to refuse an invitation from Evaristo Blanco? He hasn't yet been born and if he was born he's already dead! Is there anyone on the face of the earth who dares to offend me like this? I'm asking you! Has the he-man been born who can refuse an invitation from me? Never, least of all a pair of fairies like these little punks.

He moves toward the men. The FIRST STRANGER *pointedly turns his back on him to leave the job to his partner, who is getting ready to face* DON BLANCO. *Absolutely drunk, the man stands in the middle of the room and raises a finger. He starts to lower it as if it were a pistol to shoot the* STRANGERS. *Freeze action. The* PROSTITUTE *enters from the back with one shoe in her hand and all covered in mud. She stands behind* DON BLANCO *and starts to speak. Complaining and laughing she tells what has happened.*

PROSTITUTE. This life is a big joke. I slid down a hill and look what happened to me! The shopping bag just kept rolling and rolling and fell into the river. And there went the tomatoes and the onions and all my month's savings! That really is pretty damn lousy! I almost got killed! Besides, I broke my heel. What am I going to do now? I'm going to have to pull the heel off the other shoe! How am I going to look otherwise? . . .

Just then, OBDULIO *lets out a hearty laugh. The laughter is contagious and everyone starts laughing.* EMIRO *takes* DON BLANCO *to the back. The* STRANGERS *sit down again and drink their milk. The* LOVER *tries to take the* LADY's *things back to their place. The* LADY *lunges at him and snatches her belongings from him. They argue. She gets hysterical and starts to weep uncontrollably against the counter.* DON BLANCO *takes her to his table, sits her down and gives her a drink. Once again, everyone lapses into their respective worries. A long pause. The dog barks from the back. The* STRANGERS *stand up, nervously. The* FIRST STRANGER *calls* OBDULIO. OBDULIO *goes over to him. The* STRANGER *orders him to go out and silence the dog.* OBDULIO *goes out. The dog keeps on barking.* OBDULIO *returns. He has not managed to silence the dog. The* SECOND STRANGER *walks out resolutely toward the back.* OBDULIO *follows him. The dog barks. A shot rings out. The dog stops barking. A moment later,* OBDULIO *runs in, visibly upset. Right then, the* SECOND STRANGER *walks in, calmly.* CHELA, EMIRO, *and* DORIS *run out toward the back to see what has happened to the dog. They return and* CHELA *blows up at the* STRANGERS.

CHELA. This is the limit! What do you think of that! You've gone and killed my pet! You get out of my place right now! Scram, and take all your boxes with you! What was the poor dog doing to you, eh? You get out of my place right now! I want you to get your boxes out and leave!

CHELA *takes one of the boxes and throws it violently against the door.* EMIRO, *too, complains angrily but in a lower tone of voice.*

EMIRO. You're savages! Is that how you repay us? You were treated properly here and what do you offer in return? An outrage like this! It's just plain dirty.

EMIRO *keeps protesting and the* FIRST STRANGER *goes over to his partner and scolds him.*

FIRST STRANGER. Can't you see the impression these people have of us because of your lousy temper? You have to learn to control yourself. Get a handle on your nerves! How are we going to patch things up with these people now? You fool!

All of a sudden he starts to repeat EMIRO'S *insults and arguments. He goes over to* EMIRO, *puts his hand in his pocket and pulls out some bills.* EMIRO *is still complaining. He backs off one step and doesn't take the money. The* STRANGER *takes out an additional banknote, as in the previous operation, and stretches them out to* EMIRO.

FIRST STRANGER. If this can in any way make up for the death of the poor animal, please allow me . . . I know its value is only symbolic, but it might help somehow . . . it's been an unfortunate incident. I swear it won't happen again . . .

EMIRO *keeps on complaining, in a voice that can hardly be heard. The* STRANGER *puts the banknotes down on a table in front of* EMIRO.

EMIRO. I don't know when we got mixed up in this. We're a clean living, honest family, and we had never been through anything like this . . . This is unforgivable. . . We've acted blindly.

He moves toward the banknotes very gradually and once he's next to them he is barely whispering his protests. He picks up the bills almost reluctantly and looks at CHELA. *He waits, silently, for what she might say. Suddenly, the woman bursts out:*

CHELA. So do what the hell you want with it!

She goes into the back of the store angrily. The opera music is heard. All the rest, who in the previous scene had been waiting to see what developed, move back to their respective places. The FIRST MUSICIAN *stays near the boxes and leans over to look at something that has attracted his attention. He gets up holding a little box that had fallen out of the larger box that* CHELA *threw near the door. Showing clear signs of concerns, he goes over to* EMIRO, *who is upstage counting the money. The* MUSICIAN *shows* EMIRO *the contents of the box: they are rifle shells.* EMIRO *is startled; he rushes to look for* CHELA. *He goes into the back of the store and re-emerges with* CHELA. *He leads her to where the musician is and shows her the bullets. The three of them go over to* DON BLANCO *and speak to him. They show him the bullets. The* FIRST STRANGER *stands up violently and starts to complain because they opened his boxes. He raises his voice and walks around the room demanding who had had the nerve to open his boxes of merchandise. Everyone shrinks back, obviously frightened by the* STRANGER'S *violent reaction.* DON BLANCO *keeps on insulting them for having come to disturb the peace and quiet of the place. He challenges them to step outside, because this is a respectable place that they have dirtied with their presence. He challenges them as he stands at the rear door. The* STRANGERS *accept and exit with him.* EMIRO, *the* MUSICIANS, *and* OBDULIO *exit behind them. The* LADY, *the* LOVER, *the* PROSTITUTE, *the* TAXI DRIVER, DORIS, *and* CHELA *are left in the room awaiting the outcome. The opera music stops. The* LOVER *walks upstage and picks up his suitcase. Then he approaches the* LADY *and tries to take her out of the saloon. The* LADY *turns around and pulls herself away from his grip.*

LADY. Let go of me! Don't touch me! Don't come any closer! I'm going back to my husband and my daughters! You're not worth my while! I was so stupid! I don't ever want to see you again as long as I live!

The LOVER *backs away, upset, and tries to find a way of sneaking out of the place. The* TAXI DRIVER *goes over to his table and picks up the Bible. He reads aloud a passage from the Book of Revelations.*

TAXI DRIVER. "And he had in his right hand seven stars. And from his mouth came out a sharp two-edged sword: and his face was as the sun shineth in his power. And when I had seen him, I fell at his feet as dead. And he laid his right hand upon me, saying: Fear not. I am the first and the last. And I was alive, and was dead, and behold I am living for ever and ever, and have the keys of death and of hell and the mystery of the seven stars. And behold that I am alive for all eternity. Amen."

The PROSTITUTE *walks over to him and gives him a shove.*

PROSTITUTE. Enough of that bullshit. Come with me to make sure those people don't kill one another!

Right then, two shots ring out outside. Everyone backs off in fright. Moments later, the TWO STRANGERS *come in. The* FIRST STRANGER *walks in ahead of the other one with a revolver in his hand. His partner follows, also with a revolver, but holding one arm, which is bleeding. The* FIRST STRANGER *walks by* DORIS *and tells her:*

FIRST STRANGER. Bring water and bandages for the wounded man!

Then he turns to address the entire group.

FIRST STRANGER. It was in self-defense. There are witnesses out there.

Everyone looks at them in silence. Enter EMIRO *clasping his head. He runs to sit at the table in the middle of the room.* OBDULIO *and the* MUSICIANS *follow.* EMIRO *seems to be on the verge of a heart attack. Everyone helps him except the* STRANGERS. *They try to administer artificial respiration.* EMIRO *is barely whispering.*

EMIRO. They killed him . . . Those savages killed him.

The SECOND STRANGER *is doubled over in pain because of his wound. His partner tries to help him. He turns and shouts to* DORIS.

FIRST STRANGER. I told you to bring water and bandages!

DORIS *stands there as if she had turned to stone and she looks at* CHELA. *The* SECOND MUSICIAN *tries to intervene and he steps resolutely toward the stranger.* EMIRO *signals him to stop. He does. The* FIRST STRANGER *draws a pistol and aims it at the* MUSICIAN. CHELA *signals* DORIS *to obey the* STRANGER. DORIS *goes into the back of the store. The stranger puts away his revolver and turns to aid his partner.*

Just then, in the skies at a distance the sound of an approaching helicopter can be heard. The helicopter flies over the saloon. Everyone looks up, following the sound of the engine. DORIS *comes in from the back of the store with the water and the bandages, and stops in the middle of the room looking up. The engine slows down and it appears that the helicopter has landed next to the roadhouse. Everyone is looking toward the back, anxious to see what happens next. The helicopter rotor can be heard outside.*

Enter a MAN *all dressed in black, who stops at the rear entrance. The* FIRST STRANGER *approaches him and tells him something that is like a password. The* MAN IN BLACK *answers him and they begin to take the boxes out quickly. The wounded* STRANGER *bandages his own arm and exits. They finish taking out the boxes. The* FIRST STRANGER *makes a sign to* OBDULIO. OBDULIO *goes into the back of the store. The* MAN IN BLACK *hands the* FIRST STRANGER *a briefcase full of money. The* MAN IN BLACK *exits and the helicopter can be heard taking off. The wounded* STRANGER *comes in and insists to his partner that they leave.* OBDULIO *enters from the back of the store with a suitcase and the strangers' raincoats . . . He looks at everyone, somewhat ashamed, and exits. The* FIRST STRANGER *approaches* DORIS *and takes her arm, asking her to go with them. The young woman resists and then, in a determined gesture, pulls her arm away from his and takes a step back. The* STRANGER *smiles and looks at the* SECOND MUSICIAN *sarcastically. Then he backs away toward the counter. He pulls out a roll of banknotes and slams them down on the counter. He looks around at the entire group and tells them very slowly:*

FIRST STRANGER. Nothing has happened here. Nothing.

He turns and leaves with his wounded partner. Everyone stares at the spot where they exited. The car motor and the headlights are turned on. The hood of the car, which was inside the saloon, pulls away. The headlights move away until the light finally disappears. The noise of the motor, on the other hand, grows louder and louder and then it stops, abruptly.

—END—

Pilot Project

Introductory Notes

PILOT PROJECT WAS WRITTEN AT A CRITICAL JUNCTURE IN WORLD affairs, along Colombia's road to disaster, and in the author's relationship with his theatre group. It is important to emphasize the flexibility of this script in respect of its original intent, but also to classify its ambiguities and even its contradictions. Although the apocalyptic undertone cannot be ignored, the immediacy of the problems should be foregrounded; hence, the fine line between the normal and the grotesque, the tension between the acceptable and the horrific.

The sinister menace of the rats has none of the comicity of Ionesco's rhinoceros, even though echoes of that metamorphosis will no doubt be recognized. Grigor Samsa's more revolting metamorphosis (the cockroach) in Kafka's story, the rodents in E. T. Hoffmann's "The Nutcracker and the Mouse Prince" (1817) and the images of swarming rats in Nazi propaganda might be closer kin to these ageless furry metaphors. Their metaphoric value, however, is not readily deciphered, and audiences are challenged instead to inform themselves about the ghastly deterioration of a society where drug lords turn peasants into refugees in order to set up cattle ranches (producing beef for export only), where rural priests have been cut to strips with power saws and homeless workers preyed on for body parts sold to a medical school, where university deans and leaders of peace communities have been gunned down, and aboriginal leaders assassinated for opposing the dam that is flooding their ancestral lands.

Some readers see the "Shooting Clubs" as transparent references to the small circles of people who seek ways of protecting their own definition of a superior humanity against the destructive elements of society. As the socioeconomic gap grows, this attitude of the elites finds an outlet in "social cleansing". The gun club members might thus be upstanding members of Colombian society who in the 1980s and 1990s formed death squads with the sole purpose of cleansing their environment of what they perceived to be subhuman and disruptive elements (prostitutes, thieves, homeless persons, street children, homosexuals, in addition, of course, to left-leaning reformers and organizers).

María Mercedes Jaramillo describes the choice of the grotesque in *Pilot Project* as a moral metaphor of spiritual degradation, and sees echoes of the didactic–moralist genres like the *auto sacramental* and the Dance of Death with its "democratic levelling of human beings." According to this reading, the Four Deaths are supernatural figures, operating from across the invisible barrier, unseen by the humans they watch and affect. Jaramillo also sees the play as a critique of the Colombian power elites, the institutions that back them, and the people who become their accomplices through passivity and cowardice. She goes on to observe that, because "rata" in Colombia also means *thief*, the meaning becomes a more straightforward critique of the pervasiveness of dishonesty and corruption, as club members turn into rats and turn on others less privileged than themselves, killing them off like rats. The club members, "despite having the same animal qualities, still maintain their freedom and social status . . . : in a society of thieves only the weakest and most defenceless are punished."

For another scholar, who has studied the ideological shifts of the past two decades quite closely, *Pilot Project* is Buenaventura's bewildered response to the apparent collapse of a worldwide social project rooted in history and the utopian project for radical social change (Pianca 1992). After the fall of the Berlin Wall and the loss of a counterbalance to the U.S.-NATO power, those who were committed to that vision of history became, in the words of Uruguayan journalist and novelist Eduardo Galeano, like "children lost in the storm."[1]

The "funeral of social revolutions"[2] coincided with the bicentenary of the French Revolution: in Pianca's words, a time when many felt themselves overtaken by these "deaths" and stopped believing in themselves as possible agents of change. Pianca goes so far as to suggest that this loss of belief *is* the "enratecimiento", the "ratefaction", described in *Pilot Project*, and what replaces this belief is "the promise of a consumerist nirvana, which Buenaventura might name *Opulent Death*, another path toward ratefaction."

Between the semiologic lines of Pianca's and Jaramillo's studies lies an intertextual reference to another grotesque, repulsive emblem of the extreme loss of humanity, also an offspring, so to speak, of Kafka and Ionesco. From Osvaldo Dragún's paired allegories of thirty-five years earlier we recognize the degradation of workers in "The man who turned into a dog" and the slaughter of rats in "The story of how Panchito González felt responsible for the bubonic plague in southern Africa."[3] These two short plays from Dragún's *Historias para ser contadas* (1957) ring true more than ever now, for most societies affected by neoliberal globalization.

Pianca appropriately categorizes *Pilot Project* as a chronicle of "Darwinian involution . . . toward a world of diminished expectations" (Pianca 8). Society in this play becomes a microcosm of inverted values, spinning out of control, with social groups obsessively purging themselves of parts of themselves that are turning into rats, by killing their own members.

Enrique Buenaventura always had a razor-sharp sense of humor and the ability to satirize and to harness the grotesque. His plays about Haitian history, about the *Violencia*, about social greed, drew variously on Jean Genet, Eugene O'Neill, historical anecdote, folk tales, and religious ritual, and effectively integrated speech–act violence and comedy. Yet *Pilot Project* does not fit neatly into the continuum of Buenaventura's works, because it was spawned in a triply dark period for the author, when the personal, the ideological, and the sociopolitical certainties began to crumble almost simultaneously.[4] This intense confluence of desperate dead-ends might explain why the author's emotional and intellectual distance seems to be diminished.

Some readers, citing the grim outcome of several of his plays, may be inclined to see this play as a step in the natural continuum of Buenaventura's work. The difference between *Pilot Project* and those plays, however, lies in the object of the destruction. In *The Orgy* or *Historia de una bala de plata* [*Tale of a Silver Bullet*], the protagonist-victims can be isolated as individuals who are examples to be transcended or avoided, or at most are symbols of a doomed class. *Pilot Project*'s "ratefaction", on the other hand, is identified with the failure of our species, a failure that, in Pianca's words, "invades the very centre of the existential project of human beings," an "existential failure imposed by fostering the basest instincts" (Pianca 11). Recognition of this abysmal juncture left many writers of this period dumb. Buenaventura, however, according to Pianca,

> writes *Proyecto Piloto* with the courage of one who leaps into the abyss in the belief that only by touching rock bottom—by facing death head on—can one remain alive. In *Proyecto Piloto* Buenaventura faces both the historical and the existential Furies, to be reborn as a creator and as an emerging voice of the crisis. A voice transformed in a cry of profound echoes, the cry of a fighter who faces the dystopia of "nothingness", of a world that seems bereft of *spaces of ethical participation*. . . . For Buenaventura, the great funeral of our time may well be all about the apparent death of our aspiration to greatness, of that drive toward perfectibility which defines us as the most evolved of the animal species.

As an afterword to all these end-time scenarios, it should be added that Buenaventura wrote other plays in a different key after *Pilot Project* including successful plays based on documentation about the adventures of Spanish explorers who "went native," and on female pirates.

Notes

1. Eduardo Galeano, "El niño perdido en la intemperie," *Página 12* (Buenos Aires), 18 March 1990, 22–23.
2. Daniel Singer, quoted in Pianca, p. 5.
3. Panchito has the rat kills ostensibly to clean the cities, but really to win a tender for the company to supply canned meat to non-white populations.
4. An additional element of ambiguity is injected by the immediate context of the author's circumstance: his leadership of the TEC (Teatro Experimental de Cali) faced a legal challenge from some of the veteran members of the group and bankruptcy brought on by a manager's mishandling of funds. This problem, rooted in the financial uncertainty of the TEC and with the group's morale, was partly a consequence of the sea change in Colombian cultural life, where theatre of critical engagement had been largely sidelined by a more successful commercial theatre, by experimental performance art, and especially by television. Buenaventura won his battle over control of the group, but this period was all the more difficult because it coincided with the failure of the Unión Patriótica's third-party project and the assassination of thousands of its members, in the context of a general demoralization of Colombian society and the capitalist triumphalism discussed by Pianca.

Pilot Project
[Proyecto Piloto]
by Enrique Buenaventura (1925–2003)
Translated by Judith A. Weiss (c) 1998

The main set pieces are cages, located at various points around the stage area. There could be a group of cages, or a single large cage, at the director's discretion. A screen or scrim upstage, backlighted.

Set includes, on one side, locker or wardrobe, and on the other, a table, set for an intimate but elegant dinner, and two chairs. At least two benches.

The naturalistic characters cannot hear or see the symbolic Death figures, whose function is like that of a Greek chorus.

Cast of Characters

The Symbolic Figures:
Opulent Death
White Coat Death.*
Rat Death
Death Death

The naturalistic characters
The Club President
His Wife
Marta, a Club member
Alfredo, her husband
Miguel, a trainer
Rosa, an employee

The rats may be played by actors or represented by puppets or shadow puppets.

I
1

[*The previous performance is over and another one is beginning.*† White COAT

---

*The class connotation of "white collar" is double, allowing for either of two possible readings of the metaphor: "cuello blanco" can refer to the office worker, bureaucrat or technocrat, as it does in English, or it can refer to the white coat of doctors in clinics or hospitals. Either way, it is an institutional Death. Translating it as "White Collar" rather than "White Coat" biases the reading, of course, but the substitution here remains optional for the reader.
†This stage direction highlights the metatheatrical character of the play, while suggesting that the performances are ritual re-enactments.

DEATH *picks up a newspaper from the floor. Looks at it. Others clear the space and bring on the various components of the set.*]

OPULENT DEATH. You now see this empty world.
WHITE COAT DEATH. That we alone now occupy.
RAT DEATH. Because we have won a battle.
DEATH DEATH. And we have lost the war.
OPULENT DEATH. I can assure you that I took it seriously, in spite of my infinite experience.
WHITE COAT DEATH. It promised in every way to become something quite extraordinary.
RAT DEATH. But in this world nothing is guaranteed.
DEATH DEATH. Not even death. [*They make the* DEAD *from the previous performance appear and disappear. Some of them even levitate, as in a magic show at the circus.*]
OPULENT DEATH. We operate all the way from birth to the very end.
DEATH DEATH. And after the end, when the last sigh is covered with dirt . . . We start all over again.
WHITE COAT DEATH. Our life is one long struggle.
DEATH DEATH. And . . . you can't see it, you can't tell . . .
OPULENT DEATH. On and on it goes, ticking by like seconds and minutes, unnoticed.
DEATH DEATH. But we, today.
OPULENT DEATH. Here.
WHITE COAT DEATH. Are going to show it all.
RAT DEATH. It's already a legend.
DEATH DEATH. A lost legend.
RAT DEATH. A wasted opportunity . . .
DEATH DEATH. That brought us together, somehow.
OPULENT DEATH. And . . . this might be hard to believe . . .
RAT DEATH. Excited us.
DEATH DEATH. Clap your dry hands, sister, that we may begin.

[*They have left only two of all the dead* PERSONS, *one at either end of the stage. They are a little disoriented. One, then the other, moves to center stage and they look at themselves in an invisible mirror. They "recognize" themselves, then return to the places where they had been left.*]

2

PRESIDENT. Let us begin!
WIFE. I'm afraid.
PRESIDENT. Come on! Have you lost your confidence in me? Answer me! Don't you have faith in me any more?

[*The* PRESIDENT *goes to the wardrobe and puts on his training uniform, while*

OPULENT DEATH *and* WHITE COAT DEATH *give each other a gentle tap, like a pair of elegant old ladies, and go over to his* WIFE.]

OPULENT DEATH. You must understand that it's definitely not improvised.

WHITE COAT DEATH. And that he's earned world-wide recognition for his unrelenting war on rats.

OPULENT DEATH. And that if he's reached a conclusion it must be taken seriously.

WIFE. Yes, I think so . . . But it frightens me. [*She disappears. The* PRESIDENT *returns and addresses the cages.*]

PRESIDENT. And how are my dear, dear enemies this morning? How have my hateful and disgusting dearest friends slept? [*His* WIFE *appears.*]

WHITE COAT DEATH. Without you, he can't achieve his goal.

OPULENT DEATH. He is the man he is thanks to your help.

WHITE COAT DEATH. And, of course, because of his own exceptional intelligence.

[*They put on their ear protectors, and the* PRESIDENT *shoots at the cages. Some rats fall, while others shriek. The* WIFE *shudders and covers her face with her hands. The* DEATHS *have left her side.*]

PRESIDENT. Aren't you going to change your clothes?

WIFE. I need a little time . . .

PRESIDENT. [*Taking off his ear protectors.*] What did you say?

WIFE. I said that I haven't made up my mind yet.

PRESIDENT. [*To the rats.*] Do you understand her? Do you understand what she's saying? I can hardly ever understand her.

WIFE. You should keep at your poisons. Stick with your experiments, to control those animals; they're out of control.

PRESIDENT. [*Goes to the opposite side of the wardrobe, where the shelves are. Opens a drawer and takes out a flask.*] Do you remember this one? Look at it, look at it closely. [*She does not look.*] You have such poor taste. It's lovely. [*To the audience.*] I began to use it about . . .

RAT DEATH. Exactly twenty-five years ago.

PRESIDENT. [*He does not see or hear the Rat.*] Yes, yes . . . February 1945 . . . During the first invasion. [*He raises the flask, shakes it, and shows it to the audience.*] It liquefies the blood, it spreads it throughout the organism, it makes it gush out through the pores . . .

RAT DEATH. In the hovels, in the slums, outside the city limits, inside the sewers, where I am on duty day and night, the pools of blood appeared. It was a revolting massacre.

WHITE COAT DEATH. The city had a difficult clean-up job.

DEATH DEATH. And a hell of a time picking up the thousands upon thousands of dried skins, bristling with fur, claws, and sharp teeth.

PRESIDENT. Five years later I had developed an antidote. Remember? [*His* WIFE *has disappeared.*] Where are you? No one can dodge this! Least of all you! You are the Club President's wife! [*He goes over to the shelf and takes out another flask.*] I beat them with this one!

RAT DEATH. It turns the blood into a solid mass. The body swells up. A hairy ball that the boys in the slums used to play soccer with . . . He was the exterminating archangel and they were the demons that lived on.

PRESIDENT. Come back here, sweetheart! [*The* WIFE *reappears.*] Come, sit here, calm down. We have to train.

WIFE. You should keep at it. . . .

PRESIDENT. [*Goes to the shelf, opens another drawer, takes out a little box.*] Do you remember this one?

WIFE. You have to keep on inventing more and more and more! You can! Don't give up!

PRESIDENT. [*To the audience.*] It's an antimetabolic agent. It stops the body from converting food into energy.

DEATH DEATH. It practically starves them to death.

RAT DEATH. They lose weight, they dry up like raisins and end up on their backs with their feet in the air, looking like skeletons.

PRESIDENT. I'm not giving up, darling. I know I've received a fair warning, that's all. [*Lowering his voice.*] They have declared war on us. [*Whispering in secret.*] They have a plan . . . They are going to turn us into rats, little by little . . . Our snout will grow longer. We'll start growing hair all over and we'll grow a tail . . . [*The* PRESIDENT *and his* WIFE *disappear.*]

OPULENT DEATH. It was the third invasion.

WHITE COAT DEATH. There were already three rats per inhabitant.

RAT DEATH. And some were as big as dogs.

OPULENT DEATH. Their specialty was devouring cats.

WHITE COAT DEATH. They would slink around in couples or in families toward the avenues. They hung about near the offices of large corporations, where I hold sway.

OPULENT DEATH. Once in a while, one of them would climb over the walls, in spite of the alarms and the security guards. Their curiosity would lead them inside my realm and their trembling snouts would peer out once in a while from among the crystal and the jewelry.

[*The Deaths disappear. Fade to half light. A screen lights up, slowly. A number of beings in various stages of becoming rats appear behind the screen.*]

FIRST RAT. The first thing that happens, as you start to grow fur, is that you gradually lose interest in most things. Fur protects the body and, with fur on their body, those who used to be naked and, sometimes, bald, not to mention those who had little body hair or even facial hair, feel secure. [*Disappears.*]

SECOND RAT. When you stop feeling a sense of duty, your ears grow larger and, the more pious the advice you hear . . . [*Voices off.*] Don't run away! Don't run! Don't hide! the more pink your ears become, and when they're the right size and the right color, you say: I think I'll turn a deaf ear to that crap.

THIRD RAT. When you start feeling the pleasure of turning into a rat, your snout grows and, instead of climbing, instead of moving upward, you feel pleasure in going down. [*He sinks just a little.*] Lower and lower. [*Sinks lower.*] Until you're at rest. [*Lower still.*] To the very lowest level. [*By now, every part of him is out of sight, except his head.*] Of the animal order. [*Disappears. The screen fades gradually. The* PRESIDENT *and his* WIFE *appear.*]

PRESIDENT. [*Takes a dead rat out of the cage.*] With my latest invention there are no remains. Not even a trace. [*Drops the rat in a kind of horn that digests it with a mix of human and mechanical noises.*] No one has yet devised a means for bringing them back to life, but the method has been devised to effect a rebirth, or, if we can use that exotic term, of being reincarnated in others who have turned into rats.

WIFE. Aren't you going to stop?

PRESIDENT. On the contrary. I'm going to move faster, before it's too late. Before too many people turn into rats, wiping out the veneer of civilization we have right now. [*He takes her to center stage, hands her a pistol and puts protectors over her ears.*] No, don't shut your eyes. You have to do this with your eyes wide open. Legs apart, and stand up straight. Balance is a straight line, a plumb line, all the way from the top of your head down to your ass and from your ass to the ground. Stretch your arm. [*She stretches her arm and aims at the audience.*] Look here. [*Shows her the gunsight.*] Brace that hand with the other one. Now turn. [*She turns and fires and rats fall. The two embrace.*]

WIFE. I did it! I did it!

PRESIDENT. You did it! And very well, too! [*Rats shriek and the* DEATHS *make rapid motions indicating their enthusiasm. The* PRESIDENT *and his* WIFE *disappear.*]

3

Enter MIGUEL. *He is a young man who, when he changes out of his elegant clothes into his training outfit, takes on the appearance of a Superman or a Rambo. He walks over to center stage and preens in front of the invisible mirror that stands between him and the audience. He shoots at his own "image" with his fingers held like a pistol and making conventional onomatopeic sounds.*

MIGUEL. Bang! Bang! Kaboom!

MIGUEL *drops as if he had been shot dead. The* DEATHS *appear, one by one, and approach him slowly.*

DEATH DEATH. Very funny!

OPULENT DEATH. I love these deluded people bursting with conceit.

WHITE COAT DEATH. They return to their childhood in a time machine as tiny as their brains.

OPULENT DEATH. They squander life.
RAT DEATH. In a city surrounded by death.

[MIGUEL *gets up and starts into high-energy aerobics. The* DEATHS *comment on it with a song.*]

DEATH DEATH. It's a pleasure.
OPULENT DEATH. It thrills me.
WHITE COAT DEATH. To see life stretch.
DEATH DEATH. And twist.
RAT DEATH. And jump.
OPULENT DEATH. Trying to run away.
WHITE COAT DEATH. To escape from gravity.
DEATH DEATH. [*In a low, hoarse voice.*] From gravity.
OPULENT DEATH. From serious things.
RAT DEATH. That are frightfully boring. [MIGUEL *stands still. Silence. He walks slowly toward the cages.*]
MIGUEL. [*Very softly.*] I'm from down there, from the hole, from the same place you're from.
RAT DEATH. His father was a pathetic little drunk. He'd turned into a rat, to the core.
MIGUEL. My mother was a saint. That I'm sure of . . . although I never knew her . . . But I don't resemble you at all . . . [*Goes to the "mirror".*] No snout . . . A proper mustache, ears in perfect harmony with the rest of me . . . In harmony? Are they really in harmony with anything? It's a shame that human beings have these flags . . . or pieces of cartilage, or whatever . . . Nature should have invented something less elementary for us . . . Beautiful, dreamy eyes, all women agree . . . Not too much hair on my chest . . . [*He yells and turns on his heels, pulls out his pistol and points at the cages. The rats squeal. They disappear, and only one is left.*] What's the matter? Can you tell me what you plan to do? You. You're the only one left. Walk around. Walk a little . . . I like it like that. You look like a beauty queen. Walk like them. I'll spare your life if you don't change the way you walk . . . If you keep the rhythm.
OPULENT DEATH. You want her to dance, to swing her hips. There! [*The rat is dancing.*] She's putting on a show for you.
DEATH DEATH. Do you find it entertaining?
OPULENT DEATH. Do you find it exciting? [*The* DEATHS *guffaw, concealing their laughter.*]
MIGUEL. [*To the audience.*] It's like killing a showgirl . . . A famous actress. It would have all the makings of a murder.
[*The* DEATHS *have sat down with their backs to the audience, as if they were an extension of the audience on stage.*]
WHITE COAT DEATH. It's not a garden variety war.
MIGUEL. [*Does not see the* DEATHS. *Addresses the audience.*] Of course not.
OPULENT DEATH. It's not just any old conflict.
MIGUEL. It certainly is not.

DEATH DEATH. It's not just a simple mutual extermination.
MIGUEL. If only it were just that.
OPULENT DEATH. Nor a matter of efficacy.
MIGUEL. There's something more to it...
RAT DEATH. We hadn't come across anything quite so attractive in a long time.
MIGUEL. I understand... [*Acknowledges the audience with a slight gesture of greeting.*] And I'm glad you came.
OPULENT DEATH. A duel like this is not very common.
MIGUEL. I don't doubt it.
WHITE COAT DEATH. Perhaps it's not the end of the world.
RAT DEATH. Perhaps.
DEATH DEATH. Everything hangs by a thread.
MIGUEL: [*Runs toward the cages.*] Hey you... Aren't you going to sing? I can't hear you.
OPULENT DEATH. She's not singing for this world.
RAT DEATH. She sings only for the rat world.
DEATH DEATH. A very ancient rattesque opera.
WHITE COAT DEATH. Based on a very ancient text: the Rat's Progress.
MIGUEL. How strange! [*To the audience.*] We're so ignorant... One learns something new every day. [*To the rat.*] What shall I do with you? [MARTA *appears.*]
MARTA. Miguel! [MIGUEL *turns abruptly and aims his gun at her. She drops to the floor.*] Careful! [*The* DEATHS *scatter.*]
OPULENT DEATH. Crawl. Crawl a little. That's what he likes.
WHITE COAT DEATH. Slither, slide toward him like the serpent in the Garden of Eden.
MARTA. Stop pointing that gun at me.
MIGUEL. Don't come any closer.
MARTA. That's not a toy.
MIGUEL. I'm not kidding.
MARTA. The Club has rules and regulations.
MIGUEL. I don't give a damn about the rules. What rules do you observe?
MARTA. All of them.
MIGUEL. Is flirting with the old man a regulation or a rule?
MARTA. Don't call him the old man. He's the distinguished President of this Club. A scientist... And I have my own way of expressing my admiration.
MIGUEL. A very original way.
MARTA. Don't you spy on me.
MIGUEL. Do you think you're irresistible?
MARTA. The other one might be irresistible. I'm unbearable.
MIGUEL. You're a rat. [*The rat squeals.* MIGUEL *turns to her.*] You're right! She's worse than a rat! A rat in heat wouldn't behave like her! [MARTA *takes advantage of the distraction and jumps on him. The pistol goes off. They both roll on the floor.*]

MARTA. Are you hurt?

MIGUEL. No. [*The rat squeals.* MIGUEL *turns to her.*] And what about you? Are you hurt? No. You're still the queen.

MARTA. [*Handing back the pistol.*] That's how I am and you have to accept me the way I am. [*They sit with their backs to each other. Pause. Silence.*]

RAT DEATH. You'd like to kill her.

OPULENT DEATH. There's a more or less innocent one waiting for you in the cage.

WHITE COAT DEATH. And another one who's perverse and whom you find attractive and who challenges you.

MIGUEL. [*Stands up and points the gun at* MARTA. *Turns slowly and points the gun at the rat.*] Look closely. See how I get someone out of my way.

MARTA. [*Without turning around.*] What is your way?

MIGUEL. Up. Step by step.

MARTA. As a ladder for promotion, I'm far too brittle.

MIGUEL. To the top leadership.

MARTA. My husband's there.

MIGUEL. He's no good. He'll ruin you.

MARTA. Shoot.

MIGUEL. I don't need you to tell me when to shoot.

MARTA. Your grip is shaky. [*She aims calmly.*] Observe carefully. You haven't practised enough. I'm an expert.

MIGUEL. I don't have the slightest doubt.

MARTA. My aim . . .

MIGUEL. Your ass.

MARTA. [*Slapping him.*] Right on, you son of a bitch!

MIGUEL. Don't you ever try that again. [*He holds her tight. He shakes her.*]

MARTA. That's it! Like that! Come with me!

MIGUEL. No! He could show up any minute now! [MIGUEL *takes off the Club uniform to put on his clothes.* MARTA *chases him. They appear and disappear. The rats squeal.*]

RAT DEATH. And the rats are getting all excited. Goodness! They're all bristly! What pretty animals humans are! [*The* DEATHS *guffaw, concealing their laughter.*]

OPULENT DEATH. And the husband leaves the house.

WHITE COAT DEATH. Gets in his car, crosses the avenues, fearlessly.

RAT DEATH. He stops at a low-down tavern.

DEATH DEATH. His stomach's on fire.

RAT DEATH. A fire that can only be quenched with another fire.

DEATH DEATH. Because it is written: The hair of the dog that bit you.

MIGUEL. He's a born loser. He hasn't caught anything. None of these creatures has nuzzled or licked or even touched him. But he's turned into a rat.

MARTA. Jealousy, resentment, envy . . . They'll kill you. Come.

MIGUEL. He'll be here any minute and I must be at my post.

MARTA. As if you were a slave.

MIGUEL. I am a slave, but one day I'll be boss. [*He disappears.* MARTA *looks around for him. Looks at the audience.*]

MARTA. What kind of animals are they? [*Goes toward the cages.*] I resemble you so much that killing you is a sort of suicide. [*She laughs. The* DEATHS *laugh. The rats laugh. They are different musical sounds that mix into an infernal harmony. Suddenly she breaks it up shooting wildly and killing lots of rats. Silence. Pause. She stumbles toward one of the benches. She collapses onto the bench.*] This game will be the end of me! It wipes me out and brings me back to life, every day. [*Goes to the "mirror".*] Sometimes I see big pink ears, round protruding eyes, a trembling snout, and a smile with large pointed teeth. [*She covers her face, bends down, then looks at herself in the "mirror" again.*] Then my mask appears. My everyday mask. I go over the wrinkles carefully . . . They've become more prominent . . . Good God! We accept ourselves with so little shame! We should reach the point when we reject our own selves so decisively that there's nothing visible left of us. Nothing at all. [*She passes through the "mirror" and approaches the audience.*] Nothing! [*She turns. Walks slowly and collapses on a bench.*]

[*Alfredo appears singing the Club's anthem, with different words. He's pretty soused, but handles it very well.*]

ALFREDO.

> We are few and that's o.k.,
> and it's all a stupid fray . . .
> Onward, onward, my brave men,
> we're soon going to lose the day . . . !

[*He approaches Marta and looks at her with a drawn-out stare.*]
Marta! Do you hear me? Marta! What happened to you?

MARTA. I don't need protection.
ALFREDO. Just look at your clothes!
MARTA. I haven't been raped or anything like that. [*She smiles.*] I was so keen that I didn't change my clothes.
ALFREDO. I've always [*touching the fabric*] loved this dress.
MARTA. Let's go and train! [*Goes toward the wardrobes.*] We've got to change our clothes!
ALFREDO. [*Goes toward the cages.*] Do you know something? I like you more than I like people . . . If you were really planning to take over from us I'd say it would be an excellent idea. [*Shouting.*] Hurrah for ratefaction! I can't wait to turn into a rat! [*Stumbles and falls into* MARTA'S *arms just as she appears, wearing her uniform.*]
MARTA. Be quiet! Don't say those horrible things!
ALFREDO. I only want to be with you. Come on, let's go home . . . I hate this and I don't have the slightest desire to go back to the office.
MARTA. Let go! Go, get dressed for practice.
ALFREDO. I'm not training today.
MARTA. Then, go to sleep . . .
ALFREDO. All by myself?
MARTA. Or with whoever you feel like.
ALFREDO. I came for you. I need you.

MARTA. I'm going to train, do you understand? [*She puts on her ear protectors.*]

ALFREDO. [*Takes off her protectors.*] Listen. You're my wife. I need to talk to you.

MARTA. But I don't. [*She puts on her protectors. Aims. He moves over, to stand between her and the cages.*] What are you doing? You're not going to accomplish anything . . . [*The* DEATHS *become visible. They approach.*]

OPULENT DEATH. Perhaps he is . . .

DEATH DEATH. Of course not. It's a game.

RAT DEATH. But there's always a chance . . .

WHITE COAT DEATH. They'll take it to the limit . . .

ALFREDO. Aim, don't be afraid. Just aim.

MARTA. Please, I need to meet my quota for the week.

ALFREDO. Use me to meet your quota.

MARTA. Enough of your clowning.

ALFREDO. Look at the profile of my snout. It's growing . . . and my incisors too. Just a little, a thousandth of a millimeter . . . but my bite is really dangerous now . . . A little while ago I sank them into a lily-white neck.

MARTA. It must have been the boss-lady's buttock.

ALFREDO. You know that my love for the illustrious wife of the Club President is strictly platonic.

MARTA. Don't insult her. The poor woman deserves better.

ALFREDO. Well . . . one has to be gallant once in a while.

MARTA. Of course.

ALFREDO. Just gallant, not like you.

MARTA. Get off my case.

OPULENT DEATH. She's cocked the gun.

DEATH DEATH. And she's going to shoot.

RAT DEATH. But this good soul isn't about to die just yet.

WHITE COAT DEATH. Are you sure?

RAT DEATH. Quite sure.

ALFREDO. You're a real expert.

MARTA. Yes, I am.

ALFREDO. You can hit the target with your eyes shut . . . You are going to kill a rat through me.

MARTA. I don't understand.

ALFREDO. You have to kill one of the ones that are right behind me . . . without touching me.

MARTA. Don't dare me.

WHITE COAT DEATH. The end might be close . . .

RAT DEATH [*Shakes its head, with a little laugh that the rats take up in a chorus.*]

ALFREDO. I belong to a vanishing species . . . Decent people, people from good families. A luxury that has outlived its usefulness . . . If you kill me, nothing will be lost . . . If you kill one of the rats in there, behind me, without touching me, you'll chalk up one more triumph, another medal for your collection.

OPULENT DEATH. Give him the pleasure.
DEATH DEATH. You don't ever please him any more.
WHITE COAT DEATH. He enjoys being at your mercy
RAT DEATH. And so do you.
MARTA. Be quiet.
ALFREDO. I am being quiet.
MARTA. You're asking for it. Don't.
OPULENT DEATH. Because you'll find what you're looking for.
WHITE COAT DEATH. We're always ready.
DEATH DEATH. And we are so obliging . . .
MARTA. I'm going to pull the trigger. [*She shoots.* ALFREDO *collapses while the rats howl brutally.*] Alfredo! Oh God, Alfredo!
ALFREDO. [*Sits up. Shows her a hole in his jacket.*] I heard it, I felt it . . . I thought it had entered my ribs and I assumed I'd been killed.
MARTA. You clown!
ALFREDO. It's true. I chose the wrong career. [MARTA *pulls out a dead rat.*] It's my soul, Marta! You've killed my soul!
MARTA. You'd have been better off in the circus.
ALFREDO. Your act, on the other hand, was truly marvellous. Tonight I'll pin a medal on you.
MARTA: (*Throws the rat down the horn and it makes its guttural noises.*] I'm busy tonight.
ALFREDO. If you keep that up I'll fire him. The affair is becoming pretty public.
MARTA. I will not be blackmailed.
ALFREDO. You must understand!
MARTA. What.
ALFREDO. These matters have to be handled some other way.
OPULENT DEATH. The Club has its moral code.
WHITE COAT DEATH. And protects its image
MARTA. You handle your business any way you want to. I'll handle mine my own way.
ALFREDO. What, exactly, is my business?
MARTA. I don't know and I don't care. [ALFREDO *disappears and she goes to the "mirror".*] You can die like a rat . . . or rule like a queen [*To the rats.*] You put up with sacrifices knowing that your day will come . . . Not me! I'm going to fight them and you! I won't accept the fate that you have in store for me or the one they are imposing on me!

5

MARTA. [*Seeing* ROSA'S *reflection in the "mirror."*] Good morning.
ROSA. Good morning, ma'am.
MARTA. So you're the new girl.
ROSA. Yes.
MARTA. Miguel brought you.

ROSA. Yes.
MARTA. Where do you work?
ROSA. For his business, ma'am.
MARTA. No. I believe the business belongs to the lady President of this Club.
ROSA. Isn't it the same thing?
MARTA. Yes and no.
ROSA. Well, I work in that yes and no. Liaison work. That's what I do.
MARTA. You're in love with Miguel . . .
ROSA. Yes, I am.
MARTA. It's not the first time you come in here, is it?
ROSA. No.
MARTA. Have you trained here with him several times . . . Sit down . . .

[*Rosa sits.*]

MARTA. You're very young. [*She strokes her head, her neck, her shoulders.* ROSA *removes her hands gently.*] What's the matter?
ROSA. I don't know . . .
MARTA. Do I scare you?
ROSA. Yes. [*She gets up.*] What are your intentions?
MARTA. [*She sits down. Speaks coldly, taking* ROSA'S *hands in hers.*] To kill rats, to eliminate those who've turned into rats, to put an end to this plague of people turning into rats, and to live every moment of my life as if it were my last.
ROSA. [*Wanders around the enclosed area as if in ecstasy.*] Miguel's been here!
MARTA. [*Shouting.*] Yes! [ROSA *disappears.*] Come over here! Come back! [ROSA *appears.*] Sit down! You're here because of Miguel and that's not right. You should be here for your own sake. You must assume it as something personal. [ROSA *starts to move away from her.*]
ROSA. If I were turning into a rat . . . Would you shoot me?
MARTA. I wouldn't think twice about it. [ROSA *half disappears.*] Come back! There's nothing ratty about you.
ROSA. It's just that I can't accept it!
MARTA. We have to defend ourselves.
ROSA. Yes, yes . . . but it's not the same . . . Rats and people aren't the same thing!
MARTA. Of course not! We have to kill rats and whoever's turned into a rat in order to save people!
ROSA. Where are the people?
MARTA. We know where the people are. A superior mind is directing all this and we share its conclusions and put them into practice . . . Come on, now! Cheer up! Go and get changed!
ROSA. No.
MARTA. What do you mean by that?
ROSA. First I have to clear my head.

MARTA. It's not up here. [*She taps her head.*] It's in the body. [*She aims, fires, turns, and fires again.*]

ROSA. No, I don't want to!

MARTA. It's not about what you want. It's all about doing. It's war! [*She turns around* ROSA, *she fires.*] Win or lose! Die or survive!

ROSA. No more! No more! [*She runs from* MARTA. *Sits on a bench. The* DEATHS *approach her.*]

WHITE COAT DEATH. She doesn't have much to gain.

OPULENT DEATH. Nor much to lose.

DEATH DEATH. She's not fearful enough.

RAT DEATH. Or contemptuous enough.

MARTA. Rosa! [*The* DEATHS *disappear.*] Get up! Stand right here! Hold the gun! Fire!

[ROSA *obeys like a robot. Fires again and again, and shouts like a savage. The rats squeal, the* DEATHS *laugh. The two women disappear. For a few moments, the space is empty.*]

II

1

The DEATHS *bring out the cages, change the benches, and reorganize the stage as an "open" place, in relation to the audience, like a place where a lecture is taking place with actors and audience in attendance. While they do this,* RAT DEATH *will speak, sing, and recite a scanned text.*

RAT DEATH. I've been enjoying my stay here for quite a while now. Here, where we city deaths ended up one fine—or not so fine—day. I'm doing fine, for sure. And they don't like me.

[*The* DEATHS *suspend their work. They look at her.* RAT DEATH *approaches the audience.*]

Because I eat meat and taste cake even though I'm a mud rat.

WHITE COAT DEATH. Damned rat. Sewer death. Aren't you coming to work?

RAT DEATH. I've worked all my life while they would just flit around from funeral to funeral.

OPULENT DEATH. Say, you dirty death, what the heck do you think you are?

[*They disappear. On the stage we see the benches that "prolong" the audience. A table. A seat, a pitcher of water, a glass. The makings of a lecture. Seated on the benches,* ALFREDO, MARTA, ROSA, MIGUEL, *and the* WIFE. *From the outset,* ALFREDO, *who's a little wobbly, gives his back to the lecturer and looks at the audience. The* WIFE *and* MARTA *struggle discreetly but in vain to seat him properly.* MIGUEL *glares at him.* ROSA *soothes* MIGUEL. *The* PRESIDENT *enters ceremoniously and goes to the table.*]

PRESIDENT. Distinguished authorities, honorable professionals, outstanding academic specialists, dear colleagues, ladies and gentlemen . . . It is not our intention to alarm you. [*He pours himself some water, parsimoniously.*]
ALFREDO. Just to worry you. [*The* PRESIDENT *fills the glass.*]
MARTA. In the best sense of the word.
MIGUEL. The situation in the city is reaching its breaking point.
MARTA. You know that very well.
ALFREDO. Most people know it even better than we do.
PRESIDENT:[*Who has just finished downing his endless glass of water.*] It's a matter of being warned and being prepared . . . A stitch in time . . .
ALFREDO. Saves all nine of us in this room. [MARTA *and* MIGUEL *look daggers at him, while the* PRESIDENT, *unaware of the comment, takes another drink, raises his hand and shows two fingers.*]
PRESIDENT. I'm going to start at the beginning.
ALFREDO. That's the most logical place to begin.
MARTA [*Leans over to get close to him.*] Shut up!
MIGUEL [*Taking* MARTA *away discreetly.*] Doctor, please . . . [*To the audience.*] It's really not just a lecture . . . This is a club, not a sect . . . We accept debate . . . A little democracy is absolutely necessary.
PRESIDENT. Well, ladies and gentlemen, let us look at something . . . [*Stage lights dim and screen lights up. On the screen, a mastodon and a rat.*] We have here a small, modest animal, but one that has been around for a truly respectable long time. Look at it walking around between the woolly mammoth's legs.
THE RAT. When you're no longer in this world, I'll still be here. When all memory of you is lost and no one knows how or why or at what moment you vanished from the face of the earth, I will remain.
O hairy millenary mass! I shall gnaw your bones patiently and I will do the same with other species, especially with the special species,the so-called intelligent species that's at this demonstration here today.
ALFREDO. And don't trust that proverb, that forewarned is forearmed.
MARTA. They know when and how they'll finish us off.
WIFE. Please go on, Mr. President.
PRESIDENT. Men or, rather, hominids, have kept company with rats from those remote times.
ALFREDO. Man had terrible taste even before he had any taste at all.
MARTA. Ssshhh!
PRESIDENT. Even in the huts they built up in trees, humans were surrounded by rats known as tree rats.
ALFREDO [*Looking at* MIGUEL.] Which we call climbers or mountaineers.
PRESIDENT. Afterwards, they follow him into the deepest caverns . . .
ALFREDO [*Looking at* MARTA.] How very faithful!

PRESIDENT. And when man adapts to the cold, to ice, there is the snow rat adapting right along with him ... Then the tropical rat, the amphibian rat, the marsh rat.

ALFREDO. The rat joined to us by the sacrament: until death do us part.

RAT DEATH. Yours, of course. [*A huge rat jaw and a human head appear.*]

THE HEAD. Behold one of the most destructive and devastating forces on earth. The crushing power of those jaws is comparable to twelve tons per inch. [*It is swallowed, and continues talking from inside.*] Proportionately equivalent to the shark's bite. [*It disappears and we see the sectioned brain of a rat.*]

PRESIDENT. And, what's most important, one of the most developed brains, which holds a privileged position next to the dolphin's, the ape's, and the human being's.

ALFREDO. Certain human beings ... [*The* PRESIDENT *breaks the glass.* MARTA, *the* WIFE *and* ROSA *run to pick up the shards of glass and to clean up the water, while* MIGUEL *and* ALFREDO *square off without coming to blows.*]

PRESIDENT. Rats that are exposed, in the first ten days after their birth, to intense sunlight, to electric shocks, to fright, or to freezing-cold water, are not only able to put up with hunger and isolation, but they also develop a voracious appetite for understanding ... for controlling their circumstances.

ALFREDO. Which is not the case with us ...

WIFE. Go on, Mr. President.

MARTA. We'll spit you out of the Club.

MIGUEL. And out of life.

ALFREDO. Rat threats! A typical sign that they're turning into rats.

WIFE. The audience is following what you are saying ...

PRESIDENT. [*Coughs. Takes a drink of water. On the screen, the images are, in their own way, a comment on the text.*] Experiments have shown that, if they are hounded and crowded together, their aggressiveness is unleashed. They don't only attack one another, but they also practice a form of birth control: they devour their young. At present none of this is happening, even though they are being subjected to extreme overcrowding. The rat population is growing and no one seems to know how, why, or how far.

ALFREDO. Which means that they are able to think.

MARTA. Of course! We consider ourselves to be the only thinking creatures on the planet, and, while we are blindfolded by pride, they are carrying out a plan.

ALFREDO. Since when?!

MARTA. Now! They're taking over the city!

ALFREDO. Why this city in particular?

MARTA. Because we're being blocked by red tape! The bureaucracy has been taken over by rats! The institutions have been taken over by rats! We have to do away with privileged people who have turned into rats and with people who have turned into rats even though they don't enjoy any privileges! [*The screen goes dark and the shadows and figures disappear in a stampede. The* PRESIDENT *spills the remaining water and hastily assembles his papers. Everyone seems to be talking at the same time.*]

PRESIDENT. [*To* MARTA.] It's an absurd exaggeration! [*To* ALFREDO.] And all you can offer is that miserable sabotage! What do you all hope to achieve? To destroy the Club?

WIFE. It was all said with the best of intentions.

PRESIDENT. But it's been said and it is utterly stupid.

WIFE. We have the utmost respect for the authorities.

PRESIDENT. We love the institutions.

MIGUEL. What we would like to do is increase the number of Clubs.

MARTA. Put an end to this problem of people turning into rats.

WIFE. Yes, yes, but how? Not everything is legal!

MARTA. [*Shouting.*] Everything is legal if we cleanse the city!

PRESIDENT. And who's to decide that? Damn it! There is such a thing as order here.

MIGUEL. We must do away with the rats! [*Facing* ALFREDO.] All the rats!

ALFREDO. Starting with those in your own family, the tree rats or climbers . . . [*What follows is unintelligible.*]

PRESIDENT. Silence! [*They obey him. The light dims. Everyone gathers together and submissively sing the Club's anthem.*]

Club Anthem

We are few,
It is true,
And some have what others lack,
But it's war,
And in a war,
We can't turn back.

Forward, forward my brave comrades
increase in every way
for the cause that joins us
will spread, day after day.

No room for doubt, no room for thought,
No room to hesitate,
If we go on and on and on
And neither stop nor stop to wait
Our role as men who forge ahead
Will gradually grow and spread
And in this persevering fight
Will grow and grow with all our might.
Forward, forward, my brave comrades,
Increasing every day.

2

Set change. We are back in the closed world of the polygon, with the furious squealing of the rats. While the DEATHS *change the set, with the lighting increasing gradually, they intone the Ode to Logic.*

Ode to Logic

OPULENT DEATH. Don't lose your minds.
WHITE COLLAR DEATH. Don't go mad.
DEATH DEATH. Don't give up logic.
RAT DEATH. Or your methods of organizing.
OPULENT DEATH. Or good manners.
WHITE COLLAR DEATH. Or regulations.
OPULENT DEATH. Or measures.
DEATH DEATH. Or limits.
RAT DEATH. Nor that feeling that you're doing the right thing, Regardless.
WHITE COLLAR DEATH.
>If you do something,
>however terrible it may be,
>do it well.
>Plan it
>and execute it
>with a cool head.

OPULENT DEATH.
>Don't allow any hesitation
>or doubts
>and above all
>banish anarchy
>and chaos.
>Expel that pair
>for being dissolute,
>cast them out of the circle
>like the scapegoat.

3

Once the work is completed, the DEATHS *exit. The polygon is empty, in a half light, and, gradually,* MIGUEL *appears with* ALFREDO'S *lifeless body over his shoulder.*

MIGUEL. Your buddies bit him. [*Squeals and agitation among the rats.*] I found him lying on the sidewalk outside some two-bit tavern . . . He'd been bitten. I had to finish him off. [*The* PRESIDENT *and his* WIFE *appear.* MIGUEL *lowers* ALFREDO'S *body, which falls into the* PRESIDENT'S *arms.*]
PRESIDENT. Oh my God!
MIGUEL. Mr. President, you knew the symptoms . . . This patient had them all. Now you can check the bite marks. It's a perfect example of a man turning into a rat.
PRESIDENT. You fool! You don't have the authority or the right to make decisions about a Club member! [*The* PRESIDENT *passes the corpse to his* WIFE.]

WIFE. About a very good man. A saintly soul! [*She caresses him.*] Weak and frail, like every superior spirit, but a rat—never. [*She hands the corpse to the* PRESIDENT *and confronts* MIGUEL.] He wasn't just anybody. He had a name, a surname, a distinguished lineage . . . You have committed a serious crime!

PRESIDENT. Which spells the end of the Club. [*Lets go of the dead man, who remains upright for a moment until* OPULENT DEATH *receives him and disappears with him.*]

4

MARTA *appears with another corpse on her back. It's an effigy of the* PRESIDENT. *She places him on the floor and* MIGUEL *holds him.*

MARTA. Here you are.
PRESIDENT. But . . .
MARTA. It's you . . .
PRESIDENT. Yes . . . it's me.
MARTA. No. It's the President of a great institution and a club, at the height of his career.
WIFE. So, what was he guilty of?
MARTA. He became increasingly involved in killing rats and only rats.
PRESIDENT. Well, rats are the cause . . .
MARTA. And the result is people who turn into rats. We have to do away with both. Especially with the consequences!
PRESIDENT. The rats have won! [*Squeals, howl of joy.*] Quiet! They have succeeded in winning you over to their side. [MIGUEL *slips away.* WHITE COAT DEATH *appears and takes away the puppet effigy of the* PRESIDENT.]
MARTA. Me? With the rats?
PRESIDENT. Yes, you . . . There's no way out! They have pitted us against one another! It was a far more subtle plan than we had thought possible. [*They disappear.*]

5

ROSA. [*Appearing.*] Miguel! Miguel! [*She disappears and reappears.*] There's no one here.
OPULENT DEATH. No, there's no one.
WHITE COAT DEATH. Just us . . .
DEATH DEATH. Who are always around.
ROSA. [*Letting out a scream.*] Miguel! [*She disappears. An enormous rat starts to force the wires of the cage apart.*]
RAT DEATH. Someone's waiting for you.
DEATH DEATH. Someone's challenging you.
OPULENT DEATH. Come . . . go and face her.

[ROSA *appears, sees the rat who is half out of the cage, and steps back. The* DEATHS *surround her.*]

RAT DEATH. You're not going to get away.
ROSA. I'm going to face you . . . I swore I'd face you . . . [*She picks up a pistol, but she is still trying to get away.*] Miguel!
OPULENT DEATH. It's useless.
WHITE COAT DEATH. Don't call him.
DEATH DEATH. He's not exactly coming to save you.
RAT DEATH. He'll come to bury you.
OPULENT DEATH. Miguel knows what he wants.
WHITE COAT DEATH. Aim.
DEATH DEATH. You were never fully committed to the Club. You were never fully committed to death.
RAT DEATH. And it is going to avenge us. It's not just any rat. It's your executioner.

[*The weapon won't fire.* ROSA *runs around in a circle, chased by the rat, which soon catches up with her and bites her. As* ROSA *cries out,* MIGUEL *enters and kills the rat.*]

6

WHITE COAT DEATH. Behold the Archangel Michael.
OPULENT DEATH. He's come to save you.
DEATH DEATH. He'll send you to heaven.
ROSA. Now, me. Do it fast! I want all this to be over. [*In a very soft voice.*] I'm doomed. Turning into a rat . . . and you've done it so many times already . . . Or else I'll do it. [*She raises the pistol to her temple. Cocks the trigger. Naturally, the pistol doesn't fire. She hands it to* MIGUEL. *He examines it.*]
MIGUEL. Nothing doing, when they jam like this.
ROSA. Hand me one that works. [MIGUEL *obeys. She repeats the gesture, which seems to last an eternity. She returns the pistol and goes over to the "mirror".*] I look horrible . . . I want to be beautiful and not wait for my snout to get longer or my eyes to start protruding . . .
MIGUEL. Let's make a pact.
ROSA. We'll die together!
MIGUEL. Yes.
ROSA. Because I love you and you love me.
MIGUEL. Yes.
ROSA. No. [*She returns to where* MIGUEL *is standing.*) It's not true. You don't love me . . . But if you don't keep your part of the bargain I'll hound you for the rest of life in the form of a rat. [*They raise their weapons. She shoots, gets up, twirls in a fantastic dance and fall into the arms of the* DEATHS. MIGUEL *lowers his gun and, crestfallen, approaches the cages.*]
MIGUEL. I had to help her and it seemed to be the most humane way. [*The

DEATHS *dress* ROSA *in a wedding gown. They stand her up and* MIGUEL *stands next to her. The* WHITE COAT DEATH *pantomimes a priest.*] It could have been different if we had been other people . . . and in that case we could have been happy . . . or frightfully unhappy . . . or a little of both. We could have had many children or been completely sterile, or . . . [MARTA *appears and takes him away. The* DEATHS *make* ROSA *disappear.*]

7

While they clear the set, as they did earlier, for the PRESIDENT'S *"lecture", the* DEATHS *intone the elegy to a lost opportunity.*

Elegy to a lost opportunity

OPULENT DEATH. And here, where something extraordinary was being readied.

WHITE COAT DEATH. Emptiness is left.

DEATH DEATH. Here, where the opportunity existed, where we, the four Deaths from the city came, full of enthusiasm . . .

RAT DEATH. Only oblivion is left.

OPULENT DEATH. We were wrong, in spite of our infinite experience.

DEATH DEATH. Something truly wonderful could have taken place, a real holocaust . . .

WHITE COAT DEATH. And all that's left is a bitter taste in our mouth.

RAT DEATH. [*To the rats.*] You will continue to threaten people. And people will keep on looking more and more like you.

DEATH DEATH. But an opportunity like this one doesn't arise every day.

8

The DEATHS *place the table and two chairs in the center of the stage, very ceremoniously. They cover the table with a table cloth. Then, they bring out the flasks of poison and place them on the table. They put flowers on the table, as if it were all for a very high-class banquet. They disappear and a moment later the* PRESIDENT *and his* WIFE *appear. They walk slowly, stealthily, toward the table, and they sit down.*

PRESIDENT. [*Raising two of the flasks.*] Which one do you prefer?
WIFE. I don't care.
PRESIDENT. Do you think we should each take one of them?
WIFE. I don't care.
PRESIDENT. Or perhaps the same one, as if to say: Together until death.
WIFE. You decide.
PRESIDENT. Do you remember this one? When I invented it, I thought it would be the final one.

WIFE. It will be now.

PRESIDENT. It certainly will be. What about this one? Do you remember this one?

WIFE. I'm not going to open my eyes.

PRESIDENT. You never have opened them.

WIFE. Now less than ever.

PRESIDENT. We are giant rats.

WIFE. The largest of the species.

PRESIDENT. And the most highly evolved. [*He pours a few drops from the flasks and then a little wine.*]

WIFE. But we didn't survive.

PRESIDENT. [*Tasting.*] An excellent wine. Taste a little. [*She shakes her head.*] Cheers! [*They drink. After a few moments, they stand and walk about. The* DEATHS *appear and the couple fall into their arms. They disappear and then* WHITE COAT DEATH *appears, holding a newspaper.*]

WHITE COAT DEATH. What's left as a remembrance is this note that appeared in the local paper: "Doctor Venenum and his worthy wife are the latest casualties in the war being waged against rats. The city is preparing a tribute to them." [*It drops the newspaper. Fade to black.*]

—END—

Femina Ludens

INTRODUCTORY NOTES

Foreword
JUDITH WEISS

The title of this play appropriates Huizinga's concept of *homo ludens* (man the player, the counterpart of *homo faber,* man the worker) and adapts it to signify "woman the player" or "woman at play": in contrast to male agency, women here express the freedom of the pleasurable as well as of the performative functions, witnessing, catharsis, analysis, in collective agency. Through play and humour, and through the constant shift between levels of representation (actors, actors playing named characters, and actors playing unnamed characters in support of the named characters), the play enters the spectator's consciousness "under the radar," hence its unique effectiveness.

As a very timely performance piece, it combines the rational, objective elements of the social and the political with their subjective spheres of influence and the emotional lives of women. There is a continuous weaving of stories through a fluid (but not predictable or lulling) alternation of sound and silence, voice and gestus, music and speech, and song and sounds and noise.

The unusual script, in which the narrative and the stage directions meld with dialogue and song and at certain moments take on a lyrical personality of their own, is not an easy one to read or to stage. The process of re-enacting it (Windsor Theatre, Mount Allison University, February 2000) involved much second-guessing of these lyrical directions and indirections. It also involved an unusual effort to recreate emotions in circumstances far-removed from the original emotional context of the characters.

The five lives are woven together, also, by the solidarity played out in each instance by the other four actors in support of the named character. The political background may seem less prominent here than in other plays, but, in a radical challenge to authoritarian male society, the collective equates the personal politics of abuse and loss of autonomy with the politically-motivated massacres and with the political implications of the drug-connected economy. *Femina Ludens* is one of very few Latin American plays/performance works of this scope. Play as it is presented here is Circe's spell, it is the laughter of a children's circle game, it is the dream state of love or of a drug, it is the rite of revenge, it is the repetition of gestures to fix memories or to exorcise them, and it is, in the end, the familiarization of the sacred, of the most beautiful or of the most horrible.

Notes from an Essay
M. M. JARAMILLO

The five female characters are brought close to one another because of the day-to-day similarity of their otherwise different life stories. One of the central themes of the play is the relationship of couples. Men are visibly absent from the stage but their presence is guessed and felt at every turn; their actions and their speech are present through the female counterpart, while their absence is emphasized by the gestus of the women who evoke them and point to them.

The home with its routine that revolves around the *other* (husband or children) loads the woman with a series of repetitive and mechanical tasks that enslave her and could turn her into a moldy, neurotic, or obsessive being, but her survival instinct is recreated in the play with ludic scenes in which women overcome the daily hardships through gallows humor, parody, play, and gossip. The domestic sphere is filled with images and sounds that, on the one hand, unmask the conflicts created by routine and, on the other, reveal cultural attitudes, convictions and marks of identity. For example, the scene that evokes the kitchen and each one's favorite recipe reaffirms this particular domestic space and permeates it with recipes that connote the rich culinary world found in Colombia; there is also a playful insinuation of the possibility of making love potions to captivate the object of one's affection. The laboratory/kitchen is transformed into a creative space where woman regains control and the enjoyment of everyday lfe.

Public space, on the other hand, is designed by men and for men, and it is inhospitable to women who move through it and are subjected to sexual harassment, mockery, and violence. With the street scene, there is a recreation of the difficulties encountered by women as they negotiate external space, which is filled with aggressive phrases of flattery, provocative stares, and obscene gestures and words; some of the women defend themselves and answer back

("Don't you touch my ass!" "Stop that, you pig!" "You dirty old man!") Others dodge the aggression or try to ignore it. In this scene, the presence of children is also hinted at, victims of their own mothers' abuse and of the violence present in the streets, a space that does not accept or evan envisage the presence of women, children, old people and the handicapped. The noise of horns and cars and the street is the sound that accompanies this scene and reinforces the image of urban violence, signalling the presence of the others through the women's reaction and in the defensive attitudes that the women assume.

The play dramatizes moments when women enjoy their own space, their lives, their own bodies (salsa, clothes, makeup, chit-chat, children, their relationship with the *other*), moments that enrich the domestic space and the world of women. The scene in the beauty parlor recreates feminine coquettishness and the need to possess and dominate the body and its appearance; the dis/approval of makeup hints at different aspects of men's conduct and their insecurities; women are objects to be controlled and possessed (as they are allowed or forbidden to beautify themselves). But there is also a questioning of the importance that physical appearance takes on when the body becomes an object and women become slaves of other people's stares. With the parade of beauty queens, the play parodies the important role these events play on the national scene and the objective they fulfill in the alienation of women, who learn to see themselves and define themselves through masculine desire and the male gaze. Luz Estrella, the drug trafficker's girlfriend, screams when she finally realizes that her beauty has been a trap that enslaves her as an object-woman and limits her potential for emotional and intellectual growth.

The myths of love, motherhood, fidelity, and domestic bliss are deconstructed, along with the havoc they wreak in everyday life. The happiness promised in songs and ads is undermined by the gestus that reveals the boredom and the desire for freedom. The songs that each of the characters sings throughout the play and the radio ads they hum enrich the theme of the play by unveiling cultural attitudes reinforced daily in the mass media which are generally hostile to women. We see a universe of unbridled sentiments that imprison women and eliminate other existential possibilities, since women belong to the *other* and those who manage to break through this sentimental fence are represented as perverse, with death, suffering or prostitution as their only way out. Most singers and authors of songs in Spanish are men and the musical discourse reveals a patriarchal ideology, as Florence Thomas demonstrates in her study of media.[1]

The music that accompanies the mechanical movements of the chores, the gallows humor, and the parody help to assimilate and recognize the conflicts and vices that plague our existential obligations. For example, Nury hums a *ranchera* that reveals her motivation, including the motivation that led her into marriage: "With burning devotion you promised me songbirds and castles, and you even spoke of wedding rings to win over my love." Her gestus (continually counting the money she hides in her cleavage) reflects her urge to consume and to get more money in order to be able to live in a space more in keeping with her dreams. Rosaura's song unveils her loneliness and her limited world as a housemaid, where her only companion is Michigo the cat: "Pa' qué más vivir, que me llegue el fin. Cebolla, tomate, ají, yo me voy de aquí" [I don't want to go on living, I want an end to all this fear. I'm going to get out of here"]. Amalia, at the opposite extreme, evokes the happy moments she shared with her partner and obsessively describes the details of the disappearance and the clothes he wore, while she holds up the photograph; her gestuality evokes the uncertainty in which she lives and the fears that assail her all the time.

The commercials that harass us all day, every day, in the media, have a connotative function that helps place each of the characters in her sphere of activity and to point out her needs and her limitations; hence, the fabulous cleaner that eliminates every type of impurity cannot wipe away the bloodstains of a massacre. Rosaura, the domestic, the sole survivor of the deadly attack, remains obsessed with the bloodstains left by the assassins who arrived in the five black Isuzu Troopers with no license plates; her constant activity cannot erase the traces of the crime and, like a Lady Macbeth, she obsessively rubs the invisible stains that cannot be forgotten. Luz Estrella sings jingles for beauty products that point to her role as an object, a victim of her own beauty and her ambition to be better dressed. She tries to erase from her body the marks of physical abuse. Her addiction, first to alcohol and finally to drugs, which she finds in her partner's coat pocket, signals her double dependency: on her man and on drugs. The play successfully shows the limited horizons of the girlfriends of minor drug dealers, held down by violence, addicted to drugs and to superfluous luxuries, and bound by fear. Ironically, Rosa advertises the qualities of a tape that seals everything, even the mouths of victims or witnesses, who see, hear, and are silent, reproducing an attitude that is common in a society controlled by fear and violence. Nury, the housewife, hums an ad for stockings that remind us of her husband's infidelity and of her desire to lead a more glamorous life. The ads, therefore, fulfill a double function in the play: they situate the character and her environment and denounce the fallacies of the commercial world, which offers happiness, beauty, or domestic peace in the form of a consumer product.

The interrogation recreates the political and social violence that reigns in the country. The witness and survivor of the massacre says only that all the guilty men wore the same type of boots. This phrase denounces the violence of the right and the left: military, paramilitary, or guerrilla violence that wipes out the citizenry, destroys homes, creates orphans and widows, and generates even more violence and social and economic instability. The waiting scenes (women looking, peering through windows) show the women as witnesses of one another's work; they show the seclusion of the home, as the woman waits for her *other*, and her impotence before the violence that has invaded every corner of Colombian reality.

The relationship with death is recreated in the funeral scene, with jokes and nervous laughter that are designed to control fear and accept the inevitability of death. Without resorting to any euphemisms to hide reality, the play negotiates with death through laughter and the erotic joke that recalls life and its pleasures.

Note

1. Los estragos del amor: el discurso amoroso en los medios de comunicación (Bogotá, Editorial Universitaria,1994), 112.

Femina Ludens

Original concept: Nohora Ayala
Developed collectively by: Fanny Baena, Liliana Ruiz, Gabrielle Quin, Patricia Ariza, Adriana Cantor
Director and author of final texts: Nohora Ayala
First performed in May 1995. Translated by Judith Weiss (c) 1999.

Cast of Characters

NURY, *Housewife, 35 years old*
LUZ ESTRELLA, *Gangster's lover, 24 years old*
ROSAURA, *Housemaid. Survivor of a massacre. 38 years old*
ROSA, *Hit man's wife. 48 years old*
AMALIA, *Wife of a disappeared person. 28 years old*

The action takes place in different spaces suggested by five metal frames that are handled by each of the characters. The frames vary slightly according to the height and/or the physical makeup of the actors. Another element that serves as a frame of reference is a window, also handled by the actors. Backdrop: Pink drapes in a semi-circle. The floor is bull's-blood red.

INTRODUCTION.
On the empty stage, a low-intensity blue backlight goes on, progressively illuminating the actors as they make up and dress. And, above the strong light that is shining on them, they look at the audience and take a few small steps downstage.

They each assume their position on stage, with each character in a sort of photographic pose, and, one by one, they introduce themselves through a gesture that signifies a character trait that will be developed throughout the play.

HOUSEWIFE (NURY).
She emerges energetically out of her calmness, looks one way and the other to make sure that no one can see her, then she takes out a wad of money from between her breasts. She counts it over and over again, slamming the money in her hands with a gesture of dissatisfaction as if some of it had been stolen. She returns to her place and goes back to her photographic pose.

WIFE OF THE DISAPPEARED MAN (AMALIA).
She breaks up the figure, steps forward, stretches out her arm, shows the palm of her hand in different movements and directions. She finally stamps a photograph on her forehead. It is a synthesis of her daily wanderings, asking people whether they know the man in the picture, her disappeared husband, or whether they have seen him.

GANGSTER'S LOVER (LUZ ESTRELLA).
She mimes a large wall and manages to break it. She walks through it, falls, picks herself up, and signals her most outstanding physical traits: breasts and hips. She sings:

> Looking up.
> I want to rise up.

HOUSEMAID (ROSAURA).
She walks out of her self-absorbed state, sees a stain on the floor, wipes it and wipes her own hands over and over, disheartened (a stain she hasn't been able to erase). She returns to her place.

HIT MAN'S WIFE (ROSA).
She moves down gaily singing Rosa's stanza. She is suddenly attacked by an imaginary assailant, raises her hands, moves back, as the song chokes in her throat.

> Rosa, you're so pretty.
> Oh Rosa, how pretty you are.

They all break up their photographic compositions and sing in a chorus:

> Rosa, you're so pretty.
> Oh Rosa, how pretty you are.

They line up on one side of the stage, expectantly.
The HOUSEMAID *on one side takes out a small radio. She turns it on. A romantic song about women plays. She puts on a pair of rubber gloves and takes a bucket and a mop from another character.*
She steps down stage and begins to mop the floor from one side to the other. She squeezes the mop. She is cleaning, cleaning, cleaning in an odd way.
She has finished. She looks at the floor, obsessively.
She moves to one side of the stage. She takes out a frame. She places it in a corner. She leaves a box next to the frame.
JAZZ ROCK MUSIC.
The music breaks up the line.
The women move hurriedly in different directions.
As if they were arriving at a street corner.
They stare in surprise as if something were about to happen . . .
What's the matter?
They go back to their places.
AMALIA *stays inside her frame, which the* HOUSEMAID *has placed in front of her. She picks up the box, which has a photograph of her missing husband stuck to one side.*
She traces the outline of the frame
In mime. She walks through it,
Moves forward,
Marks the space showing the picture.
She drops it accidentally,

Notices it,
Picks it up, distanced from her movement.
She picks up the picture.
Something draws her attention.
The picture falls again.
She repeats the movement, once and twice.
She moves forward circling,
The picture in her hands, her hands raised.
She shows it toward the sides, toward the front,
Like a trophy recovered after a defeat . . .
But the picture falls back down on the frame.
The other women move in at either side of her.
Each one takes out her frame,
Stands in it, forming a semicircle,
Mimes the shape of a glass,
Suggestive of her imprisonment.
AMALIA *breaks the glass.*
She sings a fragment of her song.
AMALIA [*sings*]

    You're looking for a story you don't know,
    And find a feeling.

She taps her forehead with the palm of her hand.
She returns to her place.
Music.
The woman in the third frame (ROSA) *walks through the frame.*
She moves downstage.
She sings happily.

ROSA
Rosa how pretty you are.
Oh Rosa you're so pretty.
They interrupt her.
She raises her arms, disarmed, and repeats the song with a diluted voice.

ROSA
Rosa how pretty you are.
Oh Rosa you're so pretty.
She returns to her place.
The women grab the frames.
They repeat Rosa's chorus euphorically.

CHORUS
Rosa how pretty you are.
Oh Rosa you're so pretty.
They sing while they assemble the set for NURY (*Housewife*).
They place two frames behind.
In one of them, a jacket that belongs to the "fat man" (NURY'S *husband*).

They hand her a pair of men's shoes.
They leave a chair to one side.
In front there's a frame that looks like a door.

NURY'S SCENE
NURY [*Pushing the door*]*
I love my husband
The woman has to look
After the children
La mujer ama a sus niños.
Los cuida, los consiente,
Yo amo a mi esposo.

She holds up the piece of clothing:
A large, fat man's clothes.
Downstage, she constructs a male figure with the clothes.
She cleans the fat man's shoes.
She places the shoes
Under the fat man's trousers,
looks at him, admires him,
Decides to take some money out of her cleavage,
and, after setting aside several bills, she says, emphatically, almost screaming

NURY
And let this be the very last time!

She puts the money in one of the pockets. Suddenly she discovers a woman's nylon stocking.

Red light.
Music (accelerated pianos).
NURY *executes a dance with the nylon stocking*
As a replacement for her rage and anguish.
She is holding a switchblade in her hand
And is trying to cut the stocking.

Music stops.
The other women, from the opposite side,
Look through the window, and now they rush in,
Toward NURY, *and dissolve the scene.*
ROSAURA *(the Housemaid) the cleaning woman. The survivor. The woman alone. Takes the knife away from* NURY.

NURY [*Like a sleepwalker.*]
My name is Nury.

---

*In the original, Nury sings part of her song in English, inexplicably. In this edition we chose to invert the order of the original text. For readers who prefer a monolingual version: "The woman loves her children. She looks after them, she spoils them, I love my husband."

CHORUS
My name is Nury.

The women set up a different space.
It's a beauty parlour.

Music (drums predominate)

Choreography:
They comb one another's hair
They put makeup on one another
They wax one another's legs and faces
The dry one another's hair
They paint one another's nails

Soft music

ROSAURA *(the Housemaid)*
rushes madly onto the stage.
She runs and runs and runs
Defends, defends . . . defends?
She tries to defend.

ROSAURA
If I had been there
I would not have allowed them to kill him.

She returns to her place.

The music gets louder.

The choreography is repeated at different rhythms and levels of intensity.
  They all freeze in the same gesture.

City sounds (car horns, etc.)

The women pretend to be walking through car horns, cars, streetcorners, one
  way, the other.
Until the space for Amalia's song is set up.

AMALIA'S SONG.
The other women have remained to one side
Stuck to their frames in an expectant stance.
To the right, AMALIA'S *frame.*
They hand her the yellow wooden box
With the picture of the disappeared man (her husband).
She walks through the frame,
Plays with the box,
Sits on it,
Takes off her shoes.

Music: The man's distorted voice can be heard with distorted background
  music (African drumming)

AMALIA *gets up and sits down*
Gets up and sits down
Hugs herself and breaks free
It's the destruction of everything that could have been a dream
Always interrupted, startled,
Someone who at any given movement
Could come back or "never, ever, perhaps."

AMALIA [*sings*]
You're looking for a story you don't know.
You find a feeling.
You're asking, in your own way,
How to find the the way out.

Music ends.
CHORUS
Getting up and sitting down
Getting up and sitting down

AMALIA
To walk and walk
finding the lonely memory
of love in your shoes

CHORUS
Getting up and sitting down
Getting up and sitting down

There is no separation between the woman and the box
The missing man's picture is a lighted, burning presence
That doesn't let her breathe.
She returns to the initial image
Always stuck to the box.

Light change.

ROSAURA *the woman alone*
Looks out at the audience.
A strong light interrogates her.
She is wearing black boots and scarf, an apple-green apron.
She answers what supposedly are questions . . .
Questions, questions?
Over ROSAURA'S *text, there are texts spoken simultaneously by the other*
 women, while they repeat gestures and postures of hugs and farewells.

ROSAURA	THE WOMEN
What?	Don't be long
No, no sir	Take care
Yes sir, they all wore the same boots	I love you
Noooo!	Come here
I don't know which branch they might	Kisses kisses all over

have belonged to.
Many, about fifty
All tied up
Yes, to the courtyard out back
They took the rest
Around the river bend.
No one ever heard from them again.
No, no sir,
I only heard the cries
And the thundering shots.
Stains, stains
Stains, everywhere.
Us women?
Alone,
Yes, with the children.

Be careful

The flashlight

Don't forget me
Call me

Don't be long

Take care
I love you

I already told you that I know nothing more.

Music: A march, with piano and bass.
The women suddenly
Grab their frames wildly.
They advance as a block toward the audience.
They place the frames inside each other, at both sides of the stage.
They extend their ritual of frenzied commotion.
They mime carrying a child.
Over the music that accompanies this mad race
Loose phrases and words can be heard but not made out.

ROSAURA
Stop crying.

LUZ ESTRELLA
Run, run.

NURY
There, there baby.

AMALIA
Take your finger out of your mouth, goddamn it.

ROSAURA
Hurry up, child.

ROSA
Dumb brat.

Music ends.

They all look at ROSA. *She doesn't know how to answer.*
They take the baby and stretch their arms out as if they were passing it on,
  handing it over for safekeeping.

They freeze their gesture.
They break up in circles around the stage
While each one repeats her recipe
Some of these texts stand out above the rest.*

ROSAURA.
    To make a good stew, I need a fat chicken, but one that's been killed with love, or else it's no good. One pound of green plantain, one pound of lightning bolts and sparks, three leaves of wild coriander. Onion, tomato, green

---

*Suggested "score" for this scene:

ROSAURA 1   To make a good stew, I need a fat chicken,
NURY 1   Mix on a very hot stove: powders of bitter night,
AMALIA 1   Ingredients: One rainbow moon
LUZ E. 1   Two pounds of angel hair

ROSAURA 2   but one that's been killed with love, or else it's no good.
NURY 2   cracked lips in lascivious portions,
AMALIA 2   One dash of city
LUZ E. 2   Two clown's noses

ROSAURA 3   One pound of green plantain, one pound of lightning bolts and sparks,
NURY 3   3 drops of whisky,
AMALIA 3   One lightning bolt along the road
LUZ E. 3   One tablespoon of Pierrot's tears

ROSAURA 4   three leaves of cimarrón. Onion, tomato, green pepper.
NURY 4   a dash of salt,
AMALIA 4   All mixed with wine
LUZ E. 4   Three scraps of Peter Pan's cape

ROSAURA 5   Wash the yucca and cut up the plantain with your fingers,
NURY 5   promises to taste,
AMALIA 5   2 dozen photographs in syrup
LUZ E. 5   A jar of whole memory

ROSAURA 6   otherwise it goes bad.
NURY 6   hip bumps with raving moans and
AMALIA 6   7 heads of garlic
LUZ E. 6   Two tablespoons of rhythm

ROSAURA 7   Throw it all into a pot of boiling water
NURY 7   a tablespoon of pepper,
AMALIA 7   Powders of black hen
LUZ E. 7   Dissolve it all in seawater

ROSAURA 8   that's hotter than hell.
NURY 8   then cook it all for the exact length of time.
AMALIA 8   One large onion and
LUZ E. 8   And cook over a low, low flame, until it is dilated.

AMALIA 9   Mountain lilies to taste.
LUZ E. 9   Serve in a precarious balance

LUZ E. 10   And, after it is served, add a dash of disobeying the director.

pepper. Wash the yucca and cut up the plantain with your fingers, otherwise it goes bad. Throw it all into a pot of boiling water that's hotter than hell.

NURY.
    Mix on a very hot stove: powders of bitter night, cracked lips in lascivious portions, 3 drops of whisky, a dash of salt, promises to taste, hip bumps with raving moans and a tablespoon of pepper, then cook it all for the exact length of time.

AMALIA
Ingredients:
One rainbow moon
A dash of city
One lightning bolt along the road
All mixed with wine
2 dozen photographs in syrup
7 heads of garlic
Powders of black hen
One large onion and
Mountain lilies to taste.

LUZ ESTRELLA
Two pounds of angel hair
Two clown's noses
One tablespoon of Pierrot's tears
Three scraps of Peter Pan's cape
A jar of whole memory
Two tablespoons of rhythm
Dissolve it all in seawater
And cook over a low, low flame,
Until it is dilated.
Serve in a precarious balance
And, after it is served, add a dash
Of disobeying the director.

They freeze.
LUZ ESTRELLA *(the lover)*
The decked-out woman
Moves to the front
On a bench with the heel of her shoe
She smashes a potato
Puts it on her black eye
Sings a piece of her song

LUZ ESTRELLA [*sings*]
Looking up
I want to rise up
with pearls and stars
and a thousand dresses

ROSA
After marinating it for a week
place the fish with all its bones
on a shiny silver tray
decorate it with laurel as one does heroes
5 drops of Chanel no. 5
one carmine red lipstick
one whole jar of hot peppers
and, just in case, just in case,
a spike-heel shoe
and serve it to him in bed.

CHORUS
In bed?

The women break up this chorus,
Set up another space imitating stairs
ROSA is on the last stair
With a suitcase,
She paints her lips in a grotesque manner
The other women are in suspense
Next to the window

ROSA
He couldn't stand it when I wore make-up.

Enter Music: Six pianos.

ROSA bursts out front and center
Zips up fly
Pretends to aim a revolver

ROSA
Stop right there motherfucker!

The scene fades
Each one returns to her frame, expectantly.

MUSIC: *Heartbeats accompanied by a clock's ticking that marks the waiting period . . . Suspense . . .*

The women (characters) stress a variety of postures

Minor choreography of pregnant quiet . . .

In the end they all bless one another.

Music: classical. Storms, funerals, bells, papayera birdsong. All mixed up.

The characters (the women) drop their frames on the floor imitating a burial ceremony.

Music: papayera birdsong mixed with sound effects of bells and storms.

The women (characters) shift around.

Disconcerted, they hold their hands to their heads.

They weep, they pray.

They don't know what to do. It's the end.

They embrace.

They stand in a group.

They comment among themselves, but the comments can't be heard.

The situation changes from drama to comedy.

The following text is left up in the air when the music starts.

ROSA
A toast: To cunts everywhere!

CHORUS
To cunts?

They raise the frames and burst out laughing

Music: Clock, heartbeat

The choreography of waiting is repeated
With an increasingly anxious rhythm
Despair
AMALIA *walks in front of the frame*
And does her gesture.
NURY *does the same*
The space changes
The women set up a fan with the frames
On one side only
Leaving one frame in the centre
Enter percussion music
The women, in a group, flee toward one corner
Then the other
Then a third
The woman with the attributes (LUZ ESTRELLA)
Stands with her back turned
She turns toward the audience

LUZ ESTRELLA [*Pulling the petals off a flower, she sings*]
He loves me, he loves me not . . .

LUZ ESTRELLA'S SONG

LUZ ESTRELLA
Looking up

I want to rise up
with pearls and stars
and a thousand dresses

To dress in red
to dress in grey
to dance what I want to dance
to feel happy all day

CHORUS
Heart of stone
heart of silver
heart of gold
poor, poor heart

LUZ ESTRELLA
To dress in red
to dress in grey
to dance what I want to dance
to feel happy all day

I want to feel
the wind in my face
to fly through the streets
and be next to you

CHORUS
Heart of stone
heart of silver
heart of gold
poor, poor heart

LUZ ESTRELLA *turns the flower round and round*

LUZ ESTRELLA
He loves me, he loves me not

A telephone rings.
She answers.

LUZ ESTRELLA
No, I already said no.
All right, it's all right,
just this once.
What about the money for my mom?
Oh, sweetie pie!
I'm your queen.
I'm your little queen.

CHORUS
Heart of stone
heart of silver

heart of gold
poor, poor heart

She hurls herself against the wall
She hits herself
She hurts herself
She tries again
It doesn't matter if you strangle yourself
She crowns him
She smiles
She poses as a queen
But each time she's struck
A smile that turns into a grimace
A caress into a threat
Trampled
Cut, wounded, beaten
Until she falls
Once
Twice
Three times
The women repeat in a chorus the song of ROSA *(the hit man's wife)*
ROSA *mimes a confrontation with the imaginary man*
Who is attacking LUZ ESTRELLA *the woman of the handrail*
The others look on
They burst out laughing at the impotence to which they can be subjected in a split second
They all gather near one of the frames
Transforming it into a mirror
They wash their hands
They wash their face
And while they put on makeup, they comment

NURY
Eighty pounds of dynamite

ROSAURA
The water flowed on, tinted, tinted

ROSA
There were loads of people watching

AMALIA
The tarot assures us he's alive

LUZ ESTRELLA
Five black Isuzu Troopers, with no licence plates.

ROSA
38 caliber, sawed off

ROSAURA
Oh, Holy Mary Mother of God!

AMALIA
The day he shows up, we'll party all night

ROSA
Anyway, they say it's men's business

ROSAURA
But they didn't leave a stone standing

ROSA
They say it could be heard clear across the city

LUZ ESTRELLA
Total indifference

AMALIA
In the airport?

They move back. Freeze. They start singing, very softly, as they show themselves to the audience as if in front of a mirror.

CHORUS
Pretty budding gillyflower
if you only knew how sad I feel
you'd love me too
and end my suffering
Because you know that
life means nothing to me
without you
you know that very well
gillyflower bud
tara ra

One by one they address the audience, saying:
AMALIA
Madam! Does your heart beat faster because of the news of the day?
Is it about to burst?
You, ma'am:
does anxiety give you an irregular heartbeat?
Don't think twice!
A heart so fragile
wasn't made for you!
Rip it out!
Wrap it in the new imported
Glad Plastic Wrap
Glad Wrap makes it stronger!
Glad Wrap
For a safe heartbeat!

NURY
Madam! When you looked in the mirror did you find scars on your body?
Did you look more closely and find them in your soul?
Did you find him staring at your neighbour's legs?
Madam! sheer stockings are the answer!
Use only sheer nylons
and he'll be faithful to you!

ROSA
Madam, are you having difficulty speaking, answering or contradicting?
Are they asking you to be quiet at dinner time?
No need to worry any more, ma'am
Duct tape across your face is the answer
Scotch Black Tape

ROSAURA
Stains, stains, stains,
On the floor, in the past, on your conscience?
Has your whole life turned into
one huge, out-of-control stain?
No need to worry any more,
Blanquita stain remover kills the roaches
in your kitchen
and in your head,
removes guilt
and regrets. It leaves your environment
as clean as if nothing had happened.
"Blanquita"
Whiter than white!

LUZ ESTRELLA
Madam!
Do you feel that you don't exist for your husband?
Or for your neighbor,
or for him,
or for them?
Do you have freckles, wrinkles,
moles, spots on your skin?
Cellulite on your legs?
Do you feel ugly, very ugly,
uglier and uglier?
The new "Magic illusion" cream is perfect
It wipes out wrinkles,
it wipes out moles,
it wipes out your skin!
Buy it now!!

In the background, the women keep murmuring "gillyflower bud"

They gather center stage facing the audience
With blank faces they stifle a cry
They shut their eyes tight
They cover their ears
In a crescendo they sketch out the same action over and over again.
I say nothing
I see nothing
I hear nothing
They merge again with the gillyflower bud stanza
They back away
They stand aside, pointing at a spot on the floor.

ROSAURA'S SCENE

ROSAURA *enters stage right*
Walks toward a specific spot on stage and discovers a stain on the floor
She collapses
She points at the stain
And begins a desperate scrubbing action.
The despair becomes obsessive. Rosaura loses herself in a dance
Where her grand partner
Is the mop

Red light
Distorted music with ROSAURA'S *theme song*
Which will be heard at the end of the play
Until she crowns herself with the mop.
She spins. She spins
She spins with a big smile on her face

Lighting: general wash.

She returns to the stain
She cleans and cleans and cleans
Then stops at last
Exits stage left or right
Then immediately joins a sort of collective dance of
embraces
It's a love complaint
To faint
Shoulder upon shoulder
To lean
To be carried in an embrace
To want to be
To find oneself
To slip away
To approach
It's a dance of fear

Of startled states, of absence
At the end of the dance
ROSA *(the hit man's wife) is left standing centre stage in front of the frame*
she's been playing with all along
In the center
The other women set up the scene

ROSA'S SONG

ROSA [*Looking at herself in a mirror.*]
I didn't realize
I had you
Until the very day
I lost you
And it became so clear
to me how much I loved you
when there was no longer
anything I could do.

She takes out a pencil and draws a mustache on her own face
Take me along
streets of bile and bitterness
tie me up
and beat me, even
Throw a fistful of sand
in my eyes
kill me with sorrow
but do love me.
There's nothing
in this world for me
but you
Let my eyes
be struck blind
if I am lying . . .

Minimalist music. Red light

ROSA *opens a suitcase*
Takes out a man's suit
With which she performs a dance of rejection
Against her husband, "her enemy"
As if the man wanted to subjugate her by force
At last the woman, ROSA, *pulls out a gun*
As if the man (the hit-man, her husband)
Wanted to wipe her out
She tries to get away, she lets herself go lets him go
Light up.

Music.

ROSA *continues.*
For you, I'd count the sand in the sea
for you, I could kill
with my very own hands.
On the Bible I swear this to you.

She shuts the suitcase with quick, dry movements, marking the end of the scene. The women all move away in different directions, to specific places. They look, they stop. And continue the action.

NURY [*in a gossipy tone*]
He's worked her over again.

ROSA
If he ever did anything like that to me I'd kill him.

NURY
I wonder how many times he's done it to her.

They cross the frames diagonally
From one end of the stage to the other.

AMALIA'S SCENE

AMALIA (*the wife of the disappeared man*)
Enters from the side.
She slides among the frames
Showing her man's photograph again.
AMALIA, *as if she were answering questions:*
He was wearing jeans and a striped shirt
yes, he's 28
he likes to bring me mountain lilies every Sunday
he likes to bring me mountain lilies every Sunday
he's 28
he was wearing jeans and a striped shirt
he left work and headed home
he's 28
he likes to bring me mountain lilies every Sunday
he doesn't like onions, if he even looks at one . . .
She laughs.
Music: Richie Rey.
She dances to this music
Shows her taste for this type of dancing.
She's interrupted again and again by the possibility of finding him
Unexpectedly
She joins the group of women behind
She stamps the picture of the missing man upon her forehead.
The music merges with the following:
The women who have formed a group behind

Slide, lose themselves among the frames
Time and again
they show the stalking in the city
the discomfort of the street
make room for others
save themselves.

ROSA
Hey, don't you grab my ass!

NURY
You rude old man!

LUZ ESTRELLA
You want some of this? Here!
You wanna suck on these? Go ahead!

ROSAURA
Put that thing away, you pig!

This sort of dance is repeated over and over,
With each woman taking a specific route
They come and go and run,
They're surprised, go back
Walk
Break the ice
The sea of the street
The cold that hovers inside and between them
It's the marketplace of the street
They fall down
They get up
They whistle NURY'S *song*
While they arrange the frames like in NURY'S *first scene*
They place the fat man's shoes and suit
They stand behind the window
NURY *enters with a suitcase*
She observes, she looks
She admires him

NURY
Good evening ladies and gentlemen
my name is Nury
welcome to my home
sweet home

As she puts the fat man's clothes away, she sings a ranchera tune (country and western might do)

NURY
The things you promised me

the night that we made love
are locked away inside me
inside my heart.
Your kisses aroused my passion.
I've been on the road to ruin
ever since the day we met
CHORUS
You promised me
songbirds and castles.
You even spoke of wedding rings
to win over my love.

NURY
But I want you to love me
and to soften my pain
oh my love, please don't die
because of me
—I've forgiven you again.

CHORUS
You promised me
songbirds and castles
and you even spoke of wedding rings
to win over my love.

She stops
She bangs on the suitcase furiously
She closes the suitcase
She tries to throw it through the window
And Mexican music starts playing

MUSIC: Negrita de mis pesares . . .
NURY *goes crazy with joy*
It's the fat man, serenading her
She's happy, pleased,
Full of life.
The others contribute to this bliss
Dancing around with their frames
They form a semicircle, where they execute a choreography of chores.
Each one's character performs a musical score of chores.
They clean,
They scrub,
They wash,
They iron,
They sweep, etc. They end with a chorus.

CHORUS
I can't understand
how such a tiny little bum

can shit so much
and make such a mess.

Music

LUZ ESTRELLA'S SCENE

LUZ ESTRELLA *in front of the frame*
Looks at herself in the mirror
Puts on a man's jacket
Puts her hand in her pocket
Finds a small envelope with cocaine
In a hallucinatory gesture
Sprinkles it over her face
Red light
She dances
She totters
She comes back with another swing
She puts on lipstick
She freezes in a runway pose
Which the other women join
They turn the frame around
Background music

To end the scene
They parade, one by one. In the distance, a voice announcing:
"everything for a dollar"
As if at a fair
Beauty queen poses
Repeated mechanically
Until they stand still like store dummies
Stuck and sewn to a display window
All except LUZ ESTRELLA *who goes on meaninglessly*
On and on endlessly
They interrupt her
She reacts
She looks at herself
She spots a pimple and screams in horror
The action changes
The women call a kitten
"Here, kitty kitty kitty"
while they assemble the frames
for ROSAURA'S *song*

ROSAURA'S SONG
Enter ROSAURA *(the survivor of the massacre) crossing the stage. The group of women are all visible.*
They stand lined up in perspective toward backstage

In one of the frames
One woman combing the other one's hair
The other one, the next one's hair
And so on, in succession
Rosaura arrives home
She takes out a little bag of crumbs
She calls her little pet, but it doesn't appear
She sits down, she seems tired, exhausted
She rubs her legs
A scream is heard, outside
She pulls out a weapon (a knife)
She heads toward the door
It's nothing. She bursts into song.

ROSAURA
The trees in the bush
the heat of the sun
the blackbird, the mockingbird
the seeds of soursop
I shut the door
I haul out my mattress
I leave for another land
And leave my heart behind.

CHORUS
Why go on living
I'm leaving, I'm leaving this place
Tomorrow, if not today
Tomorrow, if not today.

ROSAURA
The streets are cold
I have no reason to go on living
Little broom of mine
take the pain away
sweep away my sadness
sweep away my shame.

CHORUS
Why go on living
I'm leaving, I'm leaving this place
Tomorrow, if not today
Tomorrow, if not today.

ROSAURA *joins the others*
At that moment a dull thud is heard
They all rush in, wildly,
Choreography in which they mingle,

*interrupt, argue, distrust and
conspire in a caravan of fragmentary gestures:*

NURY
Oh, my God,
the milk!

ROSAURA
If I'd been there I wouldn't have let them kill him!

AMALIA
Getting up and sitting down

LUZ ESTRELLA
That's enough you son of a bitch
They freeze on the last gesture
AMALIA *enters new spaces*
Each one different from the previous one
Spaces that others follow
And drive her to wit's end
Note: the following should be tried in different ways. Choral or simply movement, with no words.
You have very little, very
Little time to party
Time's at the door
There's no time to rest
What will you find?
What will you take with you?
How do you react when something
Marks your life?
A fluctuating second
A new space
Phrases that die suddenly
Complain to the void
Earn a living
Try it all again

ROSA
A sawed-off 38
Dancing Embraces Music

LUZ ESTRELLA
Five black Isuzu Troopers with no license plates
Dancing Embraces Music

ROSAURA
They didn't leave a single stone standing
Dancing Embraces Music

ROSA
They say it's men's business
Dancing Embraces Music

NURY
It could be heard all over the city!
They dance
They dance they fill the stage
The music gets louder
There's an explosion
The music stops
They run run
In terror
They peek out
What's going on?
The women. The characters:
AMALIA *the wife of the missing man*
ROSA *the hit man's wife*
ROSAURA *the survivor*
NURY *the housewife*
LUZ ESTRELLA *the lover*
... They're there again throbbing
The light dissolves ... slowly.

—END—

The Orgy

INTRODUCTORY NOTES

Notes
GERARDO LUZURIAGA AND ROBERT RUDDER

The Orgy at one time formed part of the series of one-act plays titled *Los papeles del infierno*. One critic has compared this piece to the baroque work of Glauber Rocha and Luis Buñuel in the cinema (the references to the central scene of "Viridiana" are evident); he has also noted the grotesque and nightmarish character of the beggars in the play, and pointed out the vigor and even frenzy of the acting by the TEC (*Le Figaro*, Paris, 31 June 1971). On the stage, in fact, Buenaventura and the TEC do not rely on spectacular effects of a technical nature, but on forceful acting. The use of stage sets is minimized or ignored altogether. Lighting effects are used very little. Sound effects are limited to the physical resourcefulness of the actors, which at times is astounding. In a production of *The Orgy* directed by Buenaventura for an international festival held in San Francisco in 1972, a male actor played the role of the female dwarf in the following way: dressed in a hoop skirt, he was made to squat at all times, while moving about freely, and even to leap and bounce in that position, as if he were in reality a three foot tall pigmy; in addition he held two large marbles in his mouth, so that he squealed out his utterly distorted speeches. The overall effect was one of a "menina" created, not by Velázquez but by a mad Goya.

Foreword
JUDITH A. WEISS

The Orgy presents a challenge to directors and other readers who desire to transfer it, to "translate" it into a more familiar setting. In one such production (Sanctuary Theater, Washington, DC, April 1986), the Old Woman spoke in a heavy southern accent, coming across like a slightly anachronistic Blanche Dubois or Scarlett O'Hara. Thus, even though the production was pleasing and powerful, its characters seemed more suited to an antebellum U.S. setting, or to a south that was still dealing with its phantoms yet made no reference to race. However, the effectiveness of staging the play in a performance space that shared a church building with a soup kitchen and a food bank, where a multi-ethnic array of poor people lined up during the day, and where immigrants and refugees came for English lessons and free clothing, could not be lost on any of the evening's audience members who were familiar with the Adams-Morgan community of the nation's capital. The very staging of the play in that particular space was sufficient to highlight the relevance and poignancy of the problems that Buenaventura wrote about in the Latin American context.

Readers and spectators familiar with the work of Jean Genêt will find some very obvious traces of the French playwright in *The Orgy*. It should be said that intertextuality is an unavoidable feature of most of Enrique Buenaventura's work (as it is with Brecht's). The concern can be framed most constructively by determining whether this intertextuality serves to foreground the Latin American problematic, and whether the author, in adapting the original texts to this purpose, has struck a balance between the universality of the "human condition" and the particular paradigm of Latin America.

For readers interested in authors' models and in biographical sources, this playwright's sources of inspiration can undeniably be traced to his own family. María Cristina's journey to Patagonia and her encounter with the Prince of Wales was modelled on the adventure of Buenaventura's maternal grandmother, Ernestina Rosas de Alder, who on the death of her husband spent a good part of her inheritance on the journey of a lifetime (where she apparently did meet the Prince of Wales on the train). But, far from running a dramatic soup kitchen and being murdered by beggars, Mrs. Alder lived out her life as a schoolteacher and mother, and died of natural causes at a ripe old age. The figure of the Mute was inspired by Mrs. Alder's son, Guillermo, who according to the family was left deaf and dumb by meningitis, and who did die tragically, hit by a moving vehicle he could not hear approaching.

The peculiar choice of the Dwarf to play the Bishop has both a satirical dimension and a touch of the biographical, mutually reinforcing rather than exclusive. The emblematic value of the Bishop as a dwarf—an eternal child, a personage tied to the power of his senior—is suggestive of the paintings of Fernando Botero, the internationally acclaimed artist, who has portrayed the ruling elite of Colombia as a grotesque family of rounded figures. The casting choice that feminizes the authority figure undercuts further the established patriarchal dominance; it could also intimate the Old Woman's flip attitude toward religion, and it is also suggestive of the buffoonery of the Church's leaders in the country's mix of politics and power. The character is further problematized by the shifting politics of the Roman Catholic Church: *The Orgy* appeared shortly after the watershed conference of Latin American bishops held at Medellín (Colombia) in 1968, where Liberation Theology (with its "preferential option for the poor") first established itself as a major current in the Church and in society, inspired by the late Pope John XXIII and his Vatican Council. Few bishops in Colombia, where most of the hierarchy was close to the most powerful socioeconomic classes, espoused this radical new theology. It is on all counts a touching bit of irony that it should be the clownish Dwarf in the role of Bishop who knocks down the woman.

A third approach, made plausible by the child-like quality of the Dwarf, recalls the playwright's childhood games in which he would dress up as a priest and play at saying Mass—or rather, performing it: Buenaventura, in characteristically jocular conversations, has told this author that his parodic play-acting was what first engaged him in acting and directing. Raised for part of his childhood by a very devout paternal grandmother, strict and puritanical, and by a loving maiden aunt, it is conceivable that the miming of the mass would be one of the few ways he had of entertaining himself—and of impressing them, since such games are sometimes seen by adults as an early indication of a religious vocation.

This archaeological reading of the text is particularly seductive because it makes the Bishop of *The Orgy* more than a simple echo or derivation of the character in Genêt's *The Balcony,* or a *menina,* or a Botero figure brought to life: the ritual games of the child mimicking the religious rituals that lie at the source of western drama elevate the value of Buenaventura's character type into a polysemic archetype. This process is humanized by the author's symbolic sacrifice of fragments of ambiguous personal memory on the altar of tragicomedy: the serpent of ritual drama biting its own tale.[1]

Note

1. This spelling is deliberately intended to draw attention to the diachronic and the synchronic in both religion and drama: their sacred timelessness and their semantic evolution.

The Orgy*
[La orgía]
by Enrique Buenaventura (1925–2003)
© 1970 Translated by Gerardo Luzuriaga and Robert Rudder (1974)

Cast of Characters

THE OLD WOMAN
THE MUTE
FIRST BEGGAR
SECOND BEGGAR
THIRD BEGGAR
THE DWARF

Sitting in a very old easy chair in front of a mirror, the OLD WOMAN *primps. On both sides of the chair are two piles of clothing that had once been lovely and elegant.*

OLD WOMAN. How could I possibly know where you hid it! You always hide it in the strangest places, and then you accuse me of stealing it. It's always the same thing! God, our heavenly Father, who is on high and can see everything we do, knows I don't steal your money! Who knows where you stuck it, you greedy little pig! Your greed is eating you up. [*A pause. She starts to primp again. Her son, a mute, grunts furiously. He looks everywhere. Then he turns to the audience and makes motions, accusing his mother of stealing the money he earns from shining shoes.*]
  Besides, even if I spend a few cents, I'm not stealing them. I have the right to spend them, because I gave birth to you, and I raised and supported every inch of you. I'm your mother. [*The* MUTE *turns to her and asks again for the money.*]
  What's wrong with you is that you're jealous. You're jealous! Jealous . . . jealous; jealousy is going to eat you up. How long has it been? Oh, forget about that money! Listen to me! Oh, how could he hear, anyway? He's as deaf as a post! This is my punishment from God! How long has it been? Thirty . . . forty years. Forty-five? Forty-seven, maybe . . . You looked exactly the same then as you do now; you were born that way. [*The* MUTE *makes indications that she has stolen thirty-five dollars from him.*]

"Translated by Robert S. Rudder and Gerardo Luzuriaga." In addition, it is to be clearly stated in Professor Weiss's book that any performance of this English translation must have the prior approval of the principal translator, Robert S. Rudder, and specifying the means by which I may be contacted, giving both my e-mail address (RSRUDDER@aol.com) and my home address: 1556 Lafayette Road, Claremont, CA 91711 (U.S.A.)

Thirty-five! That's not true. I took twenty miserable dollars for the Orgy of the Thirtieth. Twenty miserable dollars. You liar! Now he's going to say that he's the one who supports me! If it wasn't for the generosity of those people, that's right, of those people you hate, those people who make you so jealous, I would die all alone in this hovel. [*A pause. She begins to primp again. The* MUTE *grunts in an impotent rage. He makes signs that he would like to kill her, that he would like to wring her neck.*]

You would, too. You would. [*A pause. She continues to primp; she ostentatiously combs her gray hair.*]

How long has it been? Fifty years? Has it been fifty already? I didn't steal thirty-five dollars from you. I took twenty for the Orgy of the Thirtieth. Today is orgy day. And don't you say one word to me. You talk too much. [*A pause.*] How could he talk? He's as dumb as a doorknob. [*A pause.*] Look at your father there. [*The* MUTE *smiles beatifically. He feels a great veneration for his father. He looks at the picture. His rage melts away.*] He was the gabbiest man in the world. How his moustache used to move . . . In fact, I sometimes get the feeling it's still moving. [*The* MUTE *grunts.*] You're even jealous of him. How long has it been? Let's say it was exactly forty years ago. [*She starts to do an actual striptease as she talks. She takes off clothes that are so old they're about to fall apart.*] The prince who was to be king kissed my hand on the train in Argentina. Come on, come on, help me. Do it for your father! He loved this story! My!

[*She caresses him. That calms him down, and he begins to help her.*] You're there. We're on the train. [*The* MUTE *smiles. He likes the train. He imitates it.*] We can see the Pampa through the window. The whole Pampa! This is the prince's first trip to South America. He's in my compartment. Straighten up! The prince looks like he's swallowed an umbrella! Come to attention! The prince looks like he has a pea stuck up his ass. [*She pulls back her hand that the* MUTE *is clumsily trying to kiss. The* MUTE *clutches desperately at the hand, struggling to kiss it.*]

Stop it! Stop it, you imbecile! Now you're just trying to flatter me! You greedy thing! [*The* MUTE *becomes furious. He grabs hold of a pot that's on the table, backstage.*]

Our food. Leave the food for the orgy there: I bought it with my money. With my money. Mine! Oh, my God! God, why did you give me this punishment? I'm paying for my sins with him, Lord! Mea culpa! Mea culpa! Mea fucking culpa! [*The* MUTE *lets go of the pot and goes to her. He kneels down beside her. He crosses himself amid tender grunts. He lays his head in her lap. He pushes against her, as though wanting to return to the womb. She caresses him. She smiles.*]

You'd like to get back in there, wouldn't you? You'd like to curl back up inside here again. [*She touches her stomach.*] And when you were there, you used to kick, trying to get out. That's just like a man! They spend nine months struggling to get out, and all their lives fighting to get back in. [*She laughs so hard that tears come to her eyes.*] All right, all right, calm down. Don't hug me so tight that you wake up the devil in me. Instead of being so loving you should be more generous. Get up. Don't grunt. You have to go to Jacob's and to Peter's and . . . Stop your growling and grunting. Let's have no jealousy here. There's nothing here any longer, my dear. I don't get aroused now. My poor flame has burned itself out. It doesn't even smolder any more. And their flames have all gone cold too. Peter's, John's, Jacob's, Anthony's, and the ones who are dead too, may they rest in peace. What you used to watch through the cracks doesn't exist anymore. Oh, you little rascal. You used to like to look at your mother. You liked to see these things, didn't you? I know that you hate these men, but you have to go to them and pry money out of them. Since you're such a greedy fellow, I have to beg them to help. I'm a beggar too! Like my own beggars! Like my beggars from the Orgy of the Thirtieth. The ones you hate. [*The* MUTE *makes signs that she's wasting money on these disgusting people. He spits on them, actually spitting toward the audience.*]

It's my money; I earned it. I earned it when I was myself, and I still earn it for old times' sake. [*He makes signs, indicating that that is not true, that she steals it all from him. He turns his pockets inside out to indicate what she does to him.*]

You're a greedy pig, a goddamn greedy little pig. Yes, I spend money on those beggars—I have fun with the beggars. I have a right to enjoy myself. Go on, get out and make some money. Go shine the shoes of the whole world. You despicable thing, get out! [*She threatens him with a broom. The* MUTE *runs off, laughing and playing with her. The* OLD WOMAN *sits down on her decrepit old chair, exhausted. A pause.*]

Jacob, is that you? The prince who was to be King of England took his first trip to South America back at the time of the first war. And his last trip too. How could you want him to come to this horrible South America we have now? We were on the same train. I had a whole compartment all to myself . . . You could see the Pampa through the windows . . . the train . . . Little money, not much money, little money, not much money. [*She goes faster and faster until she ends in convulsions.*] But that cost . . . [*She begins quickly, and gradually slows down to a complete stop.*] Lots of money, loads of money, lots of money, loads of money . . . Shshshshshshshshsh . . . [*As though the engine were letting off steam.*]

FIRST BEGGAR. Lord be praised.

OLD WOMAN. Did you get here all right? Where were you, you scabby son of a bitch?

FIRST BEGGAR. I don't feel so good . . . my chest . . . [*He coughs. He spits into a bloody rag.*]

OLD WOMAN. Don't act so pompous. You don't have any right to get such a delicate illness. In my time that was a very distinguished illness. Now everybody's uncle has it.

FIRST BEGGAR. If I could get something to eat at these Orgies of the Thirtieth, I'd feel a lot better. At least once a month!

OLD WOMAN. Well, this is a spiritual observance. A memorial. I won't allow it to be dirtied by the materialism of these days.

FIRST BEGGAR. Today I'm charging a dollar thirty.
OLD WOMAN. Why?
FIRST BEGGAR. I live further away. I have to take a bus.
OLD WOMAN. Jacob used to ride in a carriage. A big horse-drawn carriage.
FIRST BEGGAR. Who?
OLD WOMAN. Get dressed. [*The beggar, who is nearly skin and bones, takes off his clothes. He shivers. He pulls an old, fancilly decorated shirt from one of the piles of clothes, and puts it on. He coughs.*]
Don't you go and get Jacob's clothes dirty. [*The beggar puts on a moth-eaten jacket. Pants. Everything is too big for him. He puts on the top hat, but he can't get the gloves on. His fingers are all bent and twisted from arthritis.*]
Jacob, you've grown smaller . . . Oh, my dear, bring me a chair. Pull that curtain open; I can't see very well. Hand me the binoculars. My God, you old scab! Stick your gloves up your ass, but don't keep twisting them around, trying to put them on . . . You're going to make me dizzy!
FIRST BEGGAR. They don't fit.
OLD WOMAN. Don't talk.
FIRST BEGGAR [*Enraged.*] But I can't get them on.
OLD WOMAN. Shut up.
FIRST BEGGAR. Don't shout at me. [*He throws down the gloves.*]
OLD WOMAN. Do you want to leave here without the orgy? Do you want to lose your alms? [*She shouts.*]
FIRST BEGGAR [*Humiliated.*] No. No, Ma'am.
OLD WOMAN. Pick up your gloves! [*The* BEGGAR *picks up his gloves, and goes into a fit of coughing.*] Don't cough! [*The* BEGGAR *struggles to stop coughing.*]
FIRST BEGGAR. What . . . [*He starts coughing again; he holds it back.*] I've got to cough!
OLD WOMAN. Hold it back.
FIRST BEGGAR [*With a great effort*]. I've got tu-ber-cu-lo-sis.
OLD WOMAN. Don't talk about that. [*A short pause.*] Start in. I'm anxious to get started. [*A pause.*] While we wait for the others to get here.
FIRST BEGGAR. You want me to start?
OLD WOMAN. Go ahead.
FIRST BEGGAR [*He takes a deep bow*]. How beautiful you are, Maria Cristina. [*He has a coughing fit in order to cover up his laughter.*]
OLD WOMAN. Don't cough.
FIRST BEGGAR. Listen to the way my chest sounds. [*His chest rumbles.*]
OLD WOMAN. Dear Jacob, pull up that chair for me. And draw back that curtain; I can't see very well. Hand me the binoculars. [*She looks at the audience through the pair of rickety binoculars that the* BEGGAR *hands her.*] Look. There they are. And every one of them with his little private life all under lock and key . . . They've come here *not* to see. They don't want to see. That's why they come. If they could see they'd be frightened. Do you think they're dead? No. That one over there just moved. Old what's-his-name. What's-her-name supports him and she's so and so's mistress. Look at that

one. [*She whispers animatedly in his ear. They both laugh.*] Look at her, over there. [*She hands him the binoculars. He looks. He gives the binoculars back to her and whispers at great length into her ear. He talks so long that he chokes and starts coughing.*] You goddamn pig, turn your head away when you cough! [*She looks through the binoculars.*] And that one, that one there! Oh, that one over there! [*She whispers in the* BEGGAR'S *ear. The two start laughing louder and louder. The* BEGGAR *points to someone in the audience, and they burst into shrieks of laughter. Suddenly the* OLD WOMAN'S *laughter breaks off, and she pulls the* BEGGAR'S *arm down.*]

Don't point. They're starting to notice. [*She motions the* BEGGAR *to stoop down so she can tell him a secret. He bends over. She whispers the secret to him. He nods his head. He looks through the binoculars and whispers into her ear. The game begins to move faster. They pass the binoculars back and forth very quickly and say things in a jumble.* SECOND BEGGAR *comes in.*]

SECOND BEGGAR. 'Evening.

OLD WOMAN. Don't interrupt. We're at the theater. [SECOND BEGGAR *pretends to become interested. He looks at the audience.*]

SECOND BEGGAR. What are they performing?

OLD WOMAN. Their own lives. [*She points at the audience.*]

SECOND BEGGAR. How is it?

OLD WOMAN. Boring. Get dressed. It's your turn to play Peter today.

SECOND BEGGAR. From now on I'm going to charge a dollar fifty for the Orgies of the Thirtieth.

OLD WOMAN [*To* FIRST BEGGAR.] What an interesting play. The best one I've seen. Look. [*They start the game again, but more slowly this time.*] Oh, Jacob, gossip excites me so. [FIRST BEGGAR *whispers at length into her ear. In the meantime the* SECOND BEGGAR *undresses. Under his ragged clothing he has on an old prisoner's uniform. He puts on a large silk coat over it, and a ragged top hat. The* FIRST BEGGAR *is still whispering in the* OLD WOMAN'S *ear.*] That one? [*She points. The* BEGGAR *moves her hand.*] Oh, that one? [*He moves her hand. The* OLD WOMAN *gets up.*] Oh, oh, that one, that one. [*He moves her hand. They both move forward, toward the audience.*] Oh, that one? [*He moves her hand. They move even closer.*] This one then? [*He moves her hand. They reach the edge of the stage.*] This one. [*The* OLD WOMAN *pulls back her hand, as though her finger had been burned.*] We're pointing. Do you think they've noticed? No? [*She looks out tenderly at the audience.*] They haven't noticed. They're so innocent ...

SECOND BEGGAR. I said that from now on I'm going to charge a dollar fifty for each Orgy of the Thirtieth.

OLD WOMAN [*To* FIRST BEGGAR.] Wash out your mouth once in a while, you scabby old thing. It's nothing but a sewer. [*To* SECOND BEGGAR.] The others aren't here yet.

SECOND BEGGAR. If you aren't going to pay, then I'm going to take off these clothes. [*He makes a motion as though he's going to undress.*]

FIRST BEGGAR. That's a lot of money, Ma'am. He's taking advantage of you.

SECOND BEGGAR. You suck-ass!

OLD WOMAN. That lazy bunch of good-for-nothings. Those scabby old bums. I always have to wait for them.

SECOND BEGGAR. Then I'll be getting out of these clothes. [*He takes off his coat.*]

OLD WOMAN. You goddamn ungrateful bastard. Who got you out of jail? Who do you owe your freedom to? How much is your freedom worth?

SECOND BEGGAR. I live a long way from here. I get here all out of breath ... and then ...

OLD WOMAN. Then what?

SECOND BEGGAR. Then the food gets worse at every orgy ...

OLD WOMAN. Can't you people think about anything besides eating? Is food the only thing you live for? Don't spiritual things mean anything to you? That's why this country is in the shape it's in. Because the only thing anybody thinks about is eating.

FIRST BEGGAR. That's true, Ma'am. [*To* SECOND BEGGAR.] All you think about is eating.

SECOND BEGGAR. It's because my stomach always hurts.

FIRST BEGGAR. He's so materialistic, Ma'am. [*To* SECOND BEGGAR.] I'm asking for a dollar thirty, and I have to take the bus.

SECOND BEGGAR [*Going up to him.*] You poor thing. Do you want me to tell some other things about you?

FIRST BEGGAR. Ma'am, we're at the theater. [*He looks at the audience through the binoculars.*]

SECOND BEGGAR. You Jesuit.

OLD WOMAN. All right, let's cut the squabbling. I'll raise the alms of the Orgy of the Thirtieth to a dollar twenty, but not one cent more.

FIRST BEGGAR. The bus costs thirty cents, and it's going to go up to forty.

OLD WOMAN. A dollar twenty, and no more.

SECOND BEGGAR. That's exploitation.

FIRST BEGGAR [*To* SECOND BEGGAR.] You lost it all. I already had my dollar thirty.

OLD WOMAN. If you don't like it, I'll get some other beggars. They're like this. [*She opens and closes the fingers of her right hand to indicate how many there are.*] We're swarming with them.

SECOND BEGGAR. Pure exploitation.

OLD WOMAN. And the others still aren't here.

SECOND BEGGAR. If we can all agree on this ...

OLD WOMAN. Everyone knows that it's on the thirtieth of every month. The thirtieth. Every month has thirty ...

FIRST BEGGAR. We should have agreed on it before. The only one that doesn't have thirty is August, and it has thirty-one.

SECOND BEGGAR. And every time she gives us less food. What does she do with the leftovers? Why doesn't she put out all the food?

OLD WOMAN. Nobody can forget the thirtieth.

FIRST BEGGAR. She gets crazier every time we get together.

OLD WOMAN. Thirty miserable beggars.
SECOND BEGGAR. Thirty thirsty thieves . . .
FIRST BEGGAR. Thrashing through the thorny thicket. [*They laugh.*]
OLD WOMAN. On the thirtieth of every month.
FIRST BEGGAR [*Keeping up the joke.*] Today is the 29th. There's only twenty-nine days in a month.
OLD WOMAN. And what happens to the thirtieth? [*The* BEGGARS *shrug.*] In other countries I've been to—even Argentina—all the months have thirty days. But since this country is full of thieves, they steal the thirtieth from some months.
SECOND BEGGAR. They stole the thirtieth today.
FIRST BEGGAR. And this is the twenty-ninth.
OLD WOMAN. Then not everybody will come.
SECOND BEGGAR. All the better. There'll be more for us to eat.
FIRST BEGGAR. We could take the lid off the pot.
OLD WOMAN. Jacob, remember that you have a very small appetite.
FIRST BEGGAR. Who?
OLD WOMAN. You.
FIRST BEGGAR. Me?
OLD WOMAN. Yes.
FIRST BEGGAR. I didn't know that.
OLD WOMAN. You're Jacob today, and Jacob never ate very much. He was a gentleman.
FIRST BEGGAR. A gentleman with no appetite . . . What a goddamn waste.
OLD WOMAN. Set the table. [*The* BEGGARS *jump to get the pot.*] I said the table; I didn't say to bring the pot. Put it back.
FIRST BEGGAR. But, Ma'am . . .
SECOND BEGGAR. I haven't had a bite to eat since yesterday.
OLD WOMAN. I said the table.
FIRST BEGGAR. Please.
SECOND BEGGAR. Come down to earth, damn it.
FIRST BEGGAR. A crumb for a poor, starving old man. [*He takes the lid off the pot.*]
OLD WOMAN. Put the lid back on the pot.
[SECOND BEGGAR *puts in his hand and pulls something out, quickly putting it in his mouth.*]
OLD WOMAN. You goddamn pig.
SECOND BEGGAR [*With his mouth full.*] Mmm. Mmm . . . mmmmm. [*He indicates that he is hungry.*]
OLD WOMAN. You thief. You thief. [*She runs after him with a stick. Meanwhile the* FIRST BEGGAR *puts his hand into the pot and starts stuffing his mouth. The* OLD WOMAN *throws down the stick and goes over to the table. She picks up a knife and stands next to the pot.*] If either one of you comes one step closer I'll send his soul packing.
FIRST BEGGAR. My soul is very weak, Ma'am.
SECOND BEGGAR. I ate mine quite a while back.

FIRST BEGGAR. Don't make such a big thing out of it, Ma'am. Remember, I'm Jacob. [*He straightens his clothing.*]

SECOND BEGGAR. And I'm Peter. [*He does the same.*] How were Peter's grinders, Ma'am'?

OLD WOMAN [*Going along with the game.*] He was toothless.

SECOND BEGGAR. Like me. But I have gums as hard as a rock.

OLD WOMAN [*With the knife in her belt.*] Put the flowers on the table. [*They bring out a jug with old, decrepit artificial flowers. The* OLD WOMAN *starts playing the game again.*] Colonel Gray sent them to me this morning. Aren't they beautiful? Smell them.

SECOND BEGGAR [*Going along with the joke.*] What an aroma.

OLD WOMAN [*To the* SECOND BEGGAR.] You smell them, sir.

SECOND BEGGAR. They're roses.

OLD WOMAN. They're fuchsias.

SECOND BEGGAR. I mean fuchsias.

OLD WOMAN [*Remembering, caught up.*] Colonel Gray always used to send me fuchsias. [THIRD BEGGAR *enters.*] Colonel! [*Her hand is trembling. The* BEGGAR *hesitates for a second. The other two* BEGGARS *are dying of laughter. The* THIRD BEGGAR *kisses her hand. She turns away in disgust.*] What made you so late? You goddamn pig. Hurry up and get dressed. Put on the uniform. Today you're Colonel Gray. The full-dress uniform. [*The* THIRD BEGGAR *begins to rummage through the pile of clothes.*] Law and order are here. If you don't keep order and discipline, you'll lose your alms and the orgies of the thirtieth each month.

FIRST BEGGAR. But every time we meet we get less to eat.

SECOND BEGGAR. Last month there was a lot left over.

OLD WOMAN. There always have to be leftovers.

FIRST BEGGAR. Why?

OLD WOMAN. Because there's a lot of food.

SECOND BEGGAR. And what do you do with the leftovers?

OLD WOMAN. I throw them away, I fling them away, I pitch them out . . . like this.

FIRST BEGGAR. Where do you throw them?

OLD WOMAN. Jacob!

FIRST BEGGAR. Damn Jacob to Hell! I want the leftovers!

OLD WOMAN. Shut up, you mangy old animal. If you start in again, it's all over for you, and you'll never get back in here again. Colonel, I have a lot of complaints for you about these two.

THIRD BEGGAR. You ought to throw him out, Ma'am. He's nothing but a lousy bastard.

SECOND BEGGAR. Or not let him into the orgies of the thirtieth. The members of the orgies ought to be chosen very carefully.

FIRST BEGGAR. You sons of bitches! [*He throws down his gloves.*]

OLD WOMAN. Shut up. Pick up your gloves, Jacob. Are you ready, Colonel?

THIRD BEGGAR. Yes, Ma'am, but I wanted to tell you . . .

OLD WOMAN. No, no, no. Don't tell us again.

THIRD BEGGAR. . . . that the orgies . . .

OLD WOMAN. Don't tell us again.

THIRD BEGGAR. . . . are really cheap. I mean, Ma'am . . . I mean, a dollar isn't much for an orgy . . . I was thinking . . .

OLD WOMAN. We don't want to know how you lost your leg in the Thousand Day War . . . There are so many versions. But it's the ten thousandth time you've told it, Colonel . . . How did it happen?

THIRD BEGGAR. I don't want to make out that I'm a big shot, but I've got something that's really good for orgies, Ma'am. I'm missing a leg. That's something not everybody can say.

OLD WOMAN. Your leg. Your precious leg that's on the country's altar. Lying there. Along with the other ideals. [*A brief pause.*] Rotten, stinking, full of worms. It's disgusting.

THIRD BEGGAR. [*Shouting.*] No, Ma'am. It's something . . . something special. If you won't pay me two dollars for the orgy, my leg won't work. [*A pause. An awkward silence.*]

FIRST BEGGAR. It went up to one twenty. She won't give a penny more.

SECOND BEGGAR. Either we all get more money, or none of us gets any.

THIRD BEGGAR. You two have both your legs.

OLD WOMAN. All right, it's over. You can all get out of here. This is an orgy of art and memories, it's not something commercial. Do whatever you want to. I can get other beggars. I have a lot of them who want to join. Right out there. [*She repeats the gesture with her fingers.*] They're just swarming all over the place. [*The* BEGGARS *huddle into a conference. A pause.*]

THIRD BEGGAR. [*Coming to attention.*] Ma'am! I'm ready.

OLD WOMAN. Your leg, your tired old leg . . . How did it get up and start to walk away all by itself?

THIRD BEGGAR. I was marching along at the head of the liberal forces. I was carrying the red flag, and it was waving and waving in the breeze.

OLD WOMAN. Fluttering, you say fluttering.

THIRD BEGGAR. Fluttering. And there, up in front of us, were the damn conservatives.

SECOND BEGGAR. Don't you start saying bad things about the conservatives. I won't allow it, Ma'am. He's always using the orgies of the thirtieth for political purposes.

THIRD BEGGAR. The fuckin' conservatives, those goddamn, almighty conservatives . . .

SECOND BEGGAR. I won't allow it, Ma'am. I won't put up with it! Do you want to lose another leg? [*The* FIRST BEGGAR *is shaking with laughter.*] Do you want to lose another leg? [*He pulls out a knife, presses the button, and the blade flies open.*] Do you want another wooden stick full of termites on the other side? [*The* THIRD BEGGAR *pulls a dagger from his crutches.*]

OLD WOMAN. I just adore political battles. [*To the* FIRST BEGGAR.] Jacob, what are you?

FIRST BEGGAR [*Breaking off his laughter, and crossing himself.*] A Christian.

THE ORGY

[*The female Dwarf enters.*]

DWARF. Ooh hoo hooo: Here I am! [*A pause. Silence. The* DWARF *looks at everyone.*] Has the orgy begun yet? [*The two* BEGGARS *slowly put away their weapons. The* DWARF *turns to the* OLD WOMAN.] I got here late because today's not the thirtieth; it's the twenty-ninth. But I asked this morning at church, and they told me it was the end of the month. But it's not the thirtieth, I said. It's leap year, they told me. Then I came.

OLD WOMAN. And now, my story.

SECOND BEGGAR. It's already been told ten zillion times.

FIRST BEGGAR. You were on the train.

OLD WOMAN [*Carried away.*] Yes.

SECOND BEGGAR. You could see the Pampas out the window.

OLD WOMAN. Yes. [*A pause.*] There it is.

FIRST BEGGAR. Out there in the Pampa [*He points to the audience.*] the sun hasn't come up yet. It's still dark.

DWARF. Should I get dressed'?

OLD WOMAN. Yes.

DWARF. What should I dress as?

OLD WOMAN. Anything. The Bishop, if you want.

DWARF. Oh, yes! The Bishop! [*She begins to dress up.*]

THIRD BEGGAR. The prince who was to be King of England . . .

FIRST BEGGAR. . . . was taking his first and last trip through South America.

SECOND BEGGAR. He was on the train . . .

OLD WOMAN. Little money, not much money, little money, not much money . . .

THIRD BEGGAR. You had an entire compartment all to yourself.

OLD WOMAN [*Speeding up.*] Little money, not much money, little money, not much money . . .

FIRST BEGGAR [*Raising his voice.*] And then the prince who was to be king. . . .

OLD WOMAN [*Like background music.*] Little money, not much money, little money, not much money, little money, not much money . . .

SECOND BEGGAR. He came to your compartment and . . .

THIRD BEGGAR. He kissed your hand! [*He kisses her hand.*]

OLD WOMAN. Ohhh. [*This cry is the signal for the orgy to begin. The* FIRST BEGGAR *grabs an untuned guitar and begins to play. They all dance. The* OLD WOMAN *passes around the bottle and everyone takes a drink. The* DWARF *puts the pot on the table and everyone rushes over to eat.*] Just a minute. Another drink and another dance. [*They pass around the bottle. They take enormous swigs, and they dance. The* DWARF *and the* OLD WOMAN *raise their skirts and the* BEGGARS *fondle them. The women affect prudishness. The* OLD WOMAN *pushes away the* SECOND BEGGAR *as he puts his hand around her waist.*]

SECOND BEGGAR. That's enough: let's eat.

FIRST BEGGAR. Let's eat.

THIRD BEGGAR. It's time to eat.

DWARF. I'll serve. [*She says the blessing.*] In nomine Patris, et Filium . . .

OLD WOMAN. All right, that's enough. Pass the bottle, you filthy little midget. Let's drink freely and eat moderately, like ladies and gentlemen. This is a decent orgy.

FIRST BEGGAR. It's getting harder and harder to eat at these friggin' orgies.

OLD WOMAN. Come here, Jacob. You're the Governor. You here, Mr. Mayor. You tell me how the Government is doing. [*The* FIRST BEGGAR *gives a very complicated pantomime of how the Government is doing.*] I don't understand a bit of it, and I'm laughing. [*She laughs very dramatically.*]

DWARF. I'm on the Government's side. Dominus, Dominus . . .

OLD WOMAN. Jacob, give your speech.

DWARF. Dominus, Dominus, Dominus. [*She goes on as background music.*]

OLD WOMAN. Speak, Mr. Governor, we're waiting.

FIRST BEGGAR [*Standing on the chair, with the pathetic tone and gestures of a very serious political leader.*] I would like something to eat.

BEGGARS. Hooray!

OLD WOMAN. He's always such a demagogue! [*The other* BEGGARS *applaud.*]

FIRST BEGGAR. We ought to be able to eat all we want at these damn orgies of the thirtieth. I ask you, ladies and gentlemen: Why can't we eat? Why do we have to go hungry when the meal is sitting right here? What is the answer to this riddle, ladies and gentlemen? Who can solve it? My stomach is stuck against my spine, we're starving like dogs, the meal is sitting here, and we can't even move our little fingers! Let's have something to eat at these orgies of the thirtieth! [*He has a coughing fit.*]

OLD WOMAN. One of the best speeches from one of the best governors at one of the best orgies.

SECOND BEGGAR. It's not right for there to be leftovers.

THIRD BEGGAR AND DWARF. No! It's not right!

OLD WOMAN. Even the masses are getting stirred up!

DWARF. Christ gave out the loaves of bread and the fish and the beans and the tortillas.

FIRST BEGGAR. We want the leftovers.

SECOND BEGGAR. We want the leftovers.

DWARF. We want the leftovers.

THIRD BEGGAR. We want the leftovers.

ALL THE BEGGARS. We want the leftovers! We want it all!

FIRST BEGGAR [*Taking the lid off the pot.*] All!

OLD WOMAN. Let's stop this right now! I'll give out the food when I get good and ready! [*She grabs hold of the pot.*]

SECOND BEGGAR. Let go of that pot!

THIRD BEGGAR. You stingy old bitch!

OLD WOMAN [*Struggling.*] You animals! You filthy drunks! You're all full of shit. Get back. [*For a second the* BEGGARS *move back. The* DWARF, *still standing behind her, tries to reach the pot with her cane. The* OLD WOMAN *picks up a knife. The* DWARF *moves back.*] You're nothing but a pile of crap. You aren't my gentlemen. You just take advantage of a helpless old lady who has only a mute son.

SECOND BEGGAR [*Advancing toward her.*] The play is over! The play is over!

THIRD BEGGAR. You crazy old lady! You crazy old lady!

OLD WOMAN [*Throwing the knife.*] Get back, you stinking pile of shit.

FIRST BEGGAR. You old murderer. You stabbed me. You stabbed me.

SECOND BEGGAR. You murderer.

DWARF. Ooh hoo hee! Let's have the orgy. [*She hits the* OLD WOMAN *over the head with her cane. The* OLD WOMAN *falls back onto the table. The* BEGGARS *fall on her, beat and stab her. She lies sprawled out on the table. Her head hangs down and her grey hair touches the floor. Silently, the* BEGGARS *devour the meal. The* FIRST BEGGAR *starts to leave.*]

SECOND BEGGAR. Where are you going?

FIRST BEGGAR. To take a leak.

SECOND BEGGAR. You're lying.

THIRD BEGGAR. You're going out to look for the MUTE's money.

DWARF [*To the corpse of the* OLD WOMAN.] Ego te absolvo in nomine Patris, et Filium, et Spiritu Sancti . . .

SECOND BEGGAR. Let's get out of these clothes and we'll all go looking for it. [*They take off their costumes and put on their ragged old clothes again.*]

FIRST BEGGAR. She was crazy as a loon.

SECOND BEGGAR. They say the Mute has a lot of money hidden somewhere. He's been hoarding it for thirty years.

THIRD BEGGAR. That's not true. She stole it all from him.

FIRST BEGGAR. Someone stand guard while we look for the money.

DWARF. Requiet canti in pace. Amen.

SECOND BEGGAR. Let the Dwarf stand guard. [*They lift her up to the table and she pretends to be looking through a window.*]

DWARF. Here comes the Mute. [*The* BEGGARS *run out, following the* DWARF. *The* MUTE *enters, counting his money. He sees the* OLD WOMAN, *runs over to her and lifts up her head. Then he goes to the front of the stage and asks the audience why, why did all this happen . . . Why?*]

BLACKOUT

Bibliography

Primary Sources

Plays

Ayala, Nohora. "Femina Ludens," in *6 Obras del Teatro La Candelaria*. Bogotá: Ediciones Teatro La Candelaria, 1998 177–218.

Buenaventura, Enrique. "La orgía," in Enrique Buenaventura, *Teatro*. Bogotá: Instituto Colombiano de Cultura, 1977 135–59.

———. "Proyecto piloto," in Enrique Buenaventura, *Teatro inédito*. Bogotá: Presidencia de la República, Biblioteca Familiar, 1997 515–50.

———. "Soldados," in Enrique Buenaventura, *Teatro*. Bogotá: Instituto Colombiano de Cultura, 1977 161–94.

Niño, Jairo Aníbal. "El Monte Calvo." *Antología colombiana de teatro de vanguardia*. Bogotá: Instituto Colombiano de Cultura, 1975.

Samudio Cepeda, Álvaro. *La Casa Grande*. (The Texas Pan American Series.) Translated by Gabriel García Márquez and Seymour Menton. Austin: University of Texas Press, 1991.

Teatro La Candelaria. "Golpe de suerte," in Teatro La Candelaria, *5 obras. Creación colectiva*. Bogotá: Editorial Colombia Nueva, Grupo de Teatro La Candelaria, 1986 321–414.

———. "El paso," in Teatro La Candelaria, *Tres obras de teatro*. Bogotá: Ediciones La Candelaria, 1991.

Essays

Jaramillo, María Mercedes. "Una visión apocalíptica," in *Antología crítica del teatro breve hispanoamericano, 1948–1993*, edited by María Mercedes Jaramillo and Mario Yepes. Medellín: Editorial Universitaria de Antioquia, 1997 278–83.

Pianca, Marina. "De la utopía a la distopía en el teatro latinoamericano: *Proyecto Piloto* de Enrique Buenaventura." Manuscript, 1992, 14 pp

Secondary Sources

Selected Materials on Collective Creation and on Colombian Theatre

Arcila, Gonzalo. *Nuevo Teatro en Colombia: actividad creadora y política cultural*. Bogotá: Ediciones CEIS, 1983.

Bernard Beycroft. "Brecht in Colombia the Rise of the New Theatre." Ph.D. Thesis, Stanford: Stanford University, 1986.

Boudet, Rosa Ileana. *Teatro Nuevo: una respuesta.* Havana: Editorial Letras Cubanas, 1983.

Garavito, Lucía. "'Aquí no ha pasado nada': Narcotráfico, corrupción y violencia en *Golpe de suerte* y *El paso* de La Candelaria." *Latin American Theatre Review* 30: 2 (Spring 1997): 73–88.

———. "Estrategias de descolonización en el teatro histórico de Luis Alberto García." *Gestos* 10 (Nov. 1989): 101–11.

———. "*Guadalupe años sin cuenta*: El lenguaje oral como instrumento de resistencia ideológica." *Latin American Theatre Review*, 20:2 (Spring 1987): 5–16.

Garzón Céspedes, Francisco, ed. *Recopilación de textos sobre el teatro latinoamericano de creación colectiva.* Havana: Casa de las Américas, 1978.

García, Santiago. "Estoy aquí y sigo haciendo teatro porque estoy convencido que vamos a salir de la barbarie" [Interview by Guillermo González Uribe]. *Colombia Hoy Informa*, X: 65 (1989): 30–33.

González, Patricia. "El Nuevo Teatro en Colombia." Ph.D. Thesis, Austin: University of Texas, 1981.

Jaramillo, María Mercedes. "La creación colectiva y la colonización cultural en América Latina." *Gestos* 7 (April 1989): 75–91.

———. *Nuevo teatro colombiano: arte y política.* Medellín: Editorial Universidad de Antioquia, 1992.

———. Betty Osorio deNegret, and Angela Inés Robledo, eds. *Literatura y diferencia: Escritoras colombianas del siglo XX.* Santa Fe de Bogota and Medellín: Uniandes—Editorial Universidad de Antioquia, 1995.

Luzuriaga, Gerardo. "El proceso de creación teatral segun La Candelaria." *Gestos* 2 (Nov. 1986): 2, 75–85.

———. ed. *Popular Theater for Social Change in Latin America: Essays in Spanish and English.* Los Angeles: UCLA Latin American Center Publications, University of California, 1978.

Márceles Daconte, Eduardo. "La identidad del teatro latinoamericano." *Conjunto* 63 (Jan.–Mar. 1985): 13–23.

Reyes, Carlos José, and Maida Watson Espener, eds. *Materiales para una historia del teatro en Colombia.* Bogotá: Instituto Colombiano de Cultura, 1978.

Rizk, Beatriz. "La Asociacón de Colombianistas y el teatro en Colombia," *Latin American Theatre Review* 29: 2 (Spring 1996):165–72.

———. *Buenaventura: la dramaturgia de Creación Colectiva.* México: Grupo Editorial Gaceta, 1991.

———. "The Colombian new theatre and Bertolt Brecht: a dialectical approach," *Theatre Research International* vol. 14 (Summer 1989): 131–41.

———. "El Nuevo Teatro colombiano, una ruptura que se afianza en la tradición," *Alba de América: Revista Literaria* (Westminster, CA) 7 (July 1989):12–13.

———. *El nuevo teatro latinoamericano: Una lectura historica.* Minneapolis, MN: Prisma Institute, 1987.

Taylor, Diana. *Theatre of Crisis: Drama and Politics in Latin America.* Lexington: The University Press of Kentucky, 1991.

Velasco, María Mercedes de. *See* Jaramillo, María Mercedes.

Versényi, Adam. *Theatre in Latin America: Religion, politics and culture from Cortés to the 1980's.* New York: Cambridge University Press, 1993.

Watson Espener, Maida. "Enrique Buenaventura's Theory of the Committed Theatre." *Latin American Theatre Review* (Spring 1976): 43–47.

Weiss, Judith A., Leslie Damasceno, Donald Frischmann, Claudia Kaiser-Lenoir, Marina Pianca, and Beatriz Rizk. *Latin American Popular Theatre: The First Five Centuries.* Albuquerque: University of New Mexico Press, 1993.

Selected Materials on Colombia—History, Politics, etc.

Alape, Arturo. *La paz, la violencia: Testigos de excepción. Documento.* Bogotá: Planeta, 1985.

Bergquist, Charles, Ricardo Penaranda, and Gonzalo Sánchez, eds. *Violence in Colombia: The Continuing Crisis in Historical Perspective.* Wilmington, DE: SR Books, 1992.

Braun, Herbert. *Our guerrillas, our sidewalks.* Niwot: University Press of Colorado, 1994.

Caicedo, Edgar. *Historia de las luchas sindicales en Colombia.* Bogotá: Ediciones Suramérica, 1974.

Caldwell, Jim. "Korea—50 years ago this week, March 20–26, 1953." *Army Link News.* Available at http://www.dtic.mil/army link/news/Mar2003/a20030317 mar20–26.htm.

Castrillón, Alberto. *120 días bajo el terror militar.* Bogotá: Tercer Mundo, 1973.

Cortés Vargas, Carlos. *Los sucesos de las bananeras.* Bogotá: Imprenta La Luz, 1929.

Dix, Robert H. *Colombia: The Political Dimensions of Change.* New Haven: Yale University Press, 1967.

Duzán, María Jimena. *Death Beat: A Colombian Journalist's Life Inside the Cocaine Wars.* Translated and edited by Peter Eisner. New York: Harper Collins, 1994.

Fluharty, Vernon Lee. *Dance of the Millions: Military Rule and Social Revolution in Colombia, 1930–1956.* Pittsburgh, PA: University of Pittsburgh Press, 1957.

Gilhodes, Pierre. *Las luchas agrarias en Colombia.* Bogotá: La Carreta, 1972.

Kalmanovitz, Salomón. "Sobre algunas teorías del imperialismo en Colombia." *Ideología y Sociedad* 8 (December 1973): 27–47.

Kohut, Karl, ed. *Literatura colombiana hoy: imaginación y barbarie.* (Proceedings of the November 1991 conference on Colombian Literature today, Catholic University of Eichstatt) Frankfurt: Vervuert, 1994.

LeGrand, Catherine C. "The Colombian crisis in historical perspective." *Canadian Journal of Latin American and Caribbean Studies*, 28/55 (2003): 165–209.

López Restrepo, Andrés, and Álvaro Camacho Guizado. "From Smugglers to Warlords: Twentieth century Colombian Drug Traffickers." *Canadian Journal of Latin American and Caribbean Studies*, 28/55 (2003): 249–75.

McGreevey, William Paul. *An Economic History of Colombia.* Cambridge: Cambridge University Press, 1971.

Oquist, Paul. *Violence, Conflict and Politics in Colombia.* New York: Academic Press, 1980.

Payne, James L. *Patterns of Conflict in Colombia.* New Haven: Yale University Press, 1968.

Pearce, Jenny. *Colombia: Inside the Labyrinth.* London: Latin America Bureau and New York, Monthly Review Press, 1990.
Ramsey, Russell. *La revolución campesina 1950–1954.* Bogotá: Ediciones libros de Colombia, 1973.
Rippy, J. Fred. *The Capitalists and Colombia.* New York: Vanguard Press, 1931.
Ruiz Novoa, Alberto. *El Batallón Colombia en Korea, 1951–1954.* Bogotá: Empresa Nacional de Publicaciones, 1956.
Tirado Mejía, Alvaro. *Introducción a la historia económica de Colombia.* Bogotá: Universidad Nacional, 1971.
Tittler, Jonathan, ed. *Violencia y literatura en Colombia.* Madrid: Orígenes, 1989.
Valencia Tovar, Álvaro. *Inseguridad y violencia en Colombia.* Bogotá: Fondo de Publicaciones, Universidad Sergio Arboleda, 1997.

Selected Materials on Translation

Bassnett-McGuire, Susan. "Ways through the Labyrinth: Strategies and Methods for Translating Theatre Texts." In *The Manipulation of Literature: Studies in Literary Translation.* Edited by Théo Hermans. London: Croom Helm, 1985, 87–102.
Bharucha, Rustom. *The Politics of Cultural Practice. Thinking Through Theatre in an Age of Globalization.* Hanover and London: Wesleyan University Press, 2000.
Brisset, Annie. *A Sociocritique of Translation: Theatre and Alterity in Quebec, 1968–1988.* Translated by Rosalind Gill and Roger Gannon. Toronto: University of Toronto Press, 1996.
Palimpsestes, Traduire le dialogue. Traduire les textes de théâtre. Paris: Université de la Sorbonne Nouvelle, 1987.